Transforming Enterprise?

"In the face of the formidable challenges of post-secularism and vicious consumerism against authentic Christian life within the market system, we need to listen to Andrew Yancey's judicious and astute exhortation about how to practice Christlike and selfless love through the cultivation of the values of *gelassenheit*. This is a must-read for all people who are struggling with the question of how to transform the dominant cultural ethos with the radical message of the Christian gospel."

—**Sung Wook Chung**, Professor of Christian Theology, Denver Seminary

"*Transforming Enterprise?* is a brilliant and engaging book in which the author challenges the silos of practical theology and stakeholder theory in a discerning and intelligent manner. By drawing on theological and religious aspects rooted in Christian traditions and on ethical principles embedded in the field of business ethics, the author demonstrates how an open and enriching dialogue between stakeholder theory and practical theology can be transformative and beneficial to enterprise and the practice of religion."

—**Emanuel Gomes**, Associate Professor in International Business and Strategy, Nova School of Business and Economics

"There are millions of people who both confess Christ and go to work each day. They are longing to connect belief and practice, ideas and meaningful action. Though they often don't articulate it, they're longing for *practical theology*. Yet for many American Christians, their faith has been shaped by capitalism far more than they often think. We need to pause and think through whether Christians are transforming capitalism, or whether capitalism is transforming us. Yancey has done us all a favor by critically looking at American evangelicalism and modern business, but also pointing a way forward for those of us who long to live a life of love in both church and business."

—**Jeff Haanen**, CEO and Founder, Denver Institute for Faith & Work

"The scope and details of the argument developed in this book impressed me. Readers will be challenged by—and will learn from—its interdisciplinary engagement with the fields of theology, philosophy, and business. It is insightful and well-informed in its analysis of the current context of evangelicalism and business, and their interrelation. Andrew Yancey presents theological reflection as an antidote to conformity to patterns of consumption and management in contemporary culture."

—**Kent D. Miller**, Professor of Management, Michigan State University

"By combining practical theology with stakeholder theory and ethics, Yancey offers us an important foundation for building transformative linkages between spiritual values, practices, and ethics. This remarkable book gives fresh thought to living out our faith in a relevant and relational way in a postsecular society. Yancey puts a fundamental dagger in the artificial sacred/secular divide and lays the groundwork for meaningful human flourishing."

—**Lowell Busenitz**, Michael F. Price Chair in Entrepreneurship Emeritus, Price College of Business, University of Oklahoma

Transforming Enterprise?
American Evangelicalism, Capitalism, and the Challenge of Practical Theology

Andrew Yancey

FOREWORD BY
Stephen Pattison

◆PICKWICK *Publications* • Eugene, Oregon

TRANSFORMING ENTERPRISE?
American Evangelicalism, Capitalism, and the Challenge of Practical Theology

Copyright © 2020 Andrew Yancey. All rights reserved. Except for brief quotations in critical publications or reviews, no part of this book may be reproduced in any manner without prior written permission from the publisher. Write: Permissions, Wipf and Stock Publishers, 199 W. 8th Ave., Suite 3, Eugene, OR 97401.

Pickwick Publications
An Imprint of Wipf and Stock Publishers
199 W. 8th Ave., Suite 3
Eugene, OR 97401

www.wipfandstock.com

PAPERBACK ISBN: 978-1-7252-5602-6
HARDCOVER ISBN: 978-1-7252-5603-3
EBOOK ISBN: 978-1-7252-5604-0

Cataloguing-in-Publication data:

Names: Yancey, Andrew, author. | Pattison, Stephen, foreword.

Title: Transforming enterprise? : American evangelicalism, capitalism, and the challenge of practical theology / by Andrew Yancey ; foreword by Stephen Pattison.

Description: Eugene, OR : Pickwick Publications, 2020 | Includes bibliographical references and index.

Identifiers: ISBN 978-1-7252-5602-6 (paperback) | ISBN 978-1-7252-5603-3 (hardcover) | ISBN 978-1-7252-5604-0 (ebook)

Subjects: LCSH: Capitalism—Religious aspects—Christianity. | Evangelicalism. | Business ethics. | Anabaptists—Doctrines.

Classification: BR115.C3 Y33 2020 (print) | BR115.C3 Y33 (ebook)

Scripture quotations are from the ESV® Bible (The Holy Bible, English Standard Version®), copyright © 2001 by Crossway, a publishing ministry of Good News Publishers. Used by permission. All rights reserved.

Manufactured in the U.S.A.   03/18/20

To my wife—you show me every day a practical theology.

To my kids—may you seek, for the journey and not just the destination.

Thank you for your many sacrifices.

And we all, with unveiled face, beholding the glory of the Lord, are being transformed into the same image from one degree of glory to another. For this comes from the Lord who is the Spirit.

—2 Cor 3:18

Contents

Foreword by Stephen Pattison | xi
Acknowledgments | xv

Introduction | 1
    Shape of the Argument and Research Methodology   6
    The Intended Audience and Need for the Research   9
    Conclusion   12

Introduction to Part One | 13

1 What Practical Theological Method Is Being Utilized? | 15
    Overview of the Discipline   18
        Key Historical Developments   19
        Contemporary Trajectories in Practical Theology   25
    My Position within Contemporary Practical Theological Methodology   28
        Capitalism's Diffusion   29
        Practical Theological Assessments   33
        The Role of Reflexivity   37
    Conclusion   41

2 What Are Potential Roadblocks to Contemporary American Evangelical Reflexivity? | 43
    Foundationalism   43
    Scriptural Authority   50
    Conclusion   53

3   What Is the Current State of Transformationalist Thinking in Contemporary American Evangelical Theology? | 54
    What Is the Theme of Transformation?   55
        Hard Transformation   56
        Soft Transformation   57
        Hard and Soft Transformation Contrasted: The Example of BAM   59
    Where Does the Theme of Transformation Come From?   61
        Key Pre-Twentieth Century Figures   61
        Key Twentieth Century Figures   65
    Why Is the Theme of Transformation Significant?   68
    Conclusion   69

4   What Is Postsecular Consumerist Spirituality and How Does It Impact the Theme of Transformation? | 70
    What Is Postsecularism?   72
    The Nature of Postsecular Consumerist Spirituality   78
    What Are the Implications of Postsecularism for Contemporary American Evangelical Theological Perceptions of Enterprise?   82
    Conclusion   88

Introduction to Part Two | 89

5   What Is Stakeholder Theory? | 91
    The Stakeholder Framework   91
    The Relational Individualism of the Stakeholder Framework   96
    Conclusion   103

6   How Can a Critical Engagement with Stakeholder Theory Help Contemporary American Evangelical Theology? | 104
    The Postsecular Challenge to Stakeholder Theory   106
    The Contributions of Practical Theological Methodology   111
    Conclusion   119

CONTENTS

7 What Is the Anabaptist Concept of *Gelassenheit* and How Can It Renew the Theme of Transformation for a Postsecular Context? | 120

    What Is the Ethic of Triangulating Love Developed in the New Testament and Christian Tradition?   121

    How Does the Anabaptist Tradition of *Gelassenheit* Develop the Theme of Triangular Love?   125

        Eckhart's *Gelassenheit*   125

        Early Anabaptist Spirituality   128

    What Are the Implications for the Theme of Transformation?   133

    Conclusion   140

8 How Can a *Gelassenheit* Model Strengthen Evangelical Reflexivity? | 141

    A *Gelassenheit* Epistemology for Faithful Practice   143

    The *Gelassenheit* Model Explained   147

    The *Gelassenheit* Model in Action   155

        Narrative One: Fulkerson's Congregational Study   156

        Narrative Two: A Personal Experience   158

    Gelassenheit Spiritual Practices   161

        Prayer   163

        Giving   166

        Sabbath   167

    Conclusion   169

Conclusion | 170

    Contributions   172

    Limitations and Areas for Future Research   175

Bibliography | 177

Foreword

It is a pleasure, as well as a privilege, to introduce this book and its author to what should be a very wide audience.

First, the author. Drew Yancey is uniquely well-equipped to write this volume. A successful entrepreneur and businessman in the US, Dr. Yancey was and is rooted in a commitment to renewing evangelical Christianity, a commitment informed by an impressively thorough critical theological education. While many people carefully cultivate living within their own comfort zones and within the echo chambers of their own tribes, reinforcing their own pre-existent view of the world, Dr. Yancey has a restless, questing intellect which is not content with taken-for-granted truisms. This set him off on a research journey to explore how evangelical Christianity might better engage with the worlds of business and the market. While maintaining his business practice, Yancey decided to undertake another full-time activity as a researcher—at a public, non-confessional university in a European country three thousand miles away! To help him with this, he employed as an adviser a liberal theologian in an unfamiliar discipline, practical theology. Practical theology is basically the critical, reflective study of the relationship between beliefs and actions in relation to professional practices, in Yancey's case, that of business management.

Once in the world of practical theology, Dr. Yancey chose to explore the important issue of how evangelical thought and practice might be appropriately transformational in the context of late capitalist and postsecular, consumerist culture characterised by rational instrumentality and individualism. Arguing, controversially perhaps, that evangelical thought and practice have both shaped and been unwittingly shaped by capitalism, Yancey tries to show the limits and possibilities of evangelical engagement so that it is more radically Christian, committed to scriptural faithfulness and transformational love. He does this by showing the defects in contemporary market structuring of society which encourages individualistic self-interest, unwittingly supported by individualistic religious thought, and by examining the obstacles in evangelical thinking which obscure a more creative and critical involvement.

Having diagnosed the problem, Yancey suggests positive ways forward—by moving backwards to recover aspects of the communal pietistic tradition with their roots, surprisingly, in Meister Eckhardt's notion of *gelassenheit*, the practice of detachment. Yancey concludes his exploration showing how detachment might allow contemporary evangelicals to change their thinking and practices in practical ways to affirm a more wholistic, loving view of the world, cultivating a communal and embodied critical reflexivity. This is to restore some of the radical good news of gospel for a dying and unequal world dominated by unbridled consumption mediated through western enterprise that is unmitigated by effective Christian critique and practice.

This bold, complex, imaginative and wide-ranging book is intellectually and practically demanding and challenging. It is erudite, and the argument it outlines is carefully adumbrated, crossing disciplinary boundaries as well as business and religious practices and ideologies. It might be very uncomfortable reading for those who cannot imagine that their faith commitments and practices have any kind of negative effects on the world or require revision. But Yancey's message is a constructive, positive one for them, as for all its readers. He offers here a fuller vision of evangelical theology and practice which opens up new vistas for faithful understanding and engagement that are prophetic, encouraging, even exhilarating!

I see this book as a significant addition to the literature of practical theology and Christian cultural dialogue. It augments and expands the under-developed field of evangelical practical theology whose voice and insights are so badly needed, not only by evangelicals themselves, but also by other Christian believers, theologians and ethicists. *Inter* alia, Yancey shows that ideas and traditions do not, and cannot, exist in hermetically-sealed isolation from each other, and that the past cannot be separated from the present. This is very good news for all those who care about truth as well as about the contribution that Christianity can make to wider society and culture. I very much hope that it will not just be Christians who will benefit from Dr. Yancey's learning and insights. Theorists and practitioners of business management and the responsibility of enterprises to wider society will find much to learn in terms of method and content from the reflexive experience and knowledge embodied herein, particularly in relation to stakeholder theory and its limits. As a piece of outward-facing public theological work, the book is potentially transformational for business as much as for ways of working with tradition, church and theology.

Christian theology and practice in general and evangelical theology and practice in particular have helped to shape the capitalist world we live in, for better and for worse. Christian business people and theologians are part of the problem, and so we must become part of the solution to heartless and loveless exploitation of the limited human and material resources available to us in God's world. Drew Yancey's book will help us to take another intellectual and practical step on this urgent journey. I commend it wholeheartedly to its readers.

—Stephen Pattison

Acknowledgments

There are two people without whose guidance this book would not be possible. Dr. Pattison, thank you for the wisdom, insight, and companionship you have provided every step of the journey. I have cherished not only the answers you have given but even more the critical questions you have raised. The discipline of practical theology is forever enhanced by your contributions, and I count myself blessed to have been your student. Professor Gomes, thank you for taking a risk by supervising a student outside your program. Rare is the combination of humility and intelligence that you possess. You are the very model of interdisciplinary scholarship. I have been blessed with extraordinary supervisors, and I am profoundly grateful.

I have also been supported by the insights and valuable critiques from readers and reviewers who agreed to review a draft of the book. To Professors Graham, Kidwell, Miller, Chung, and Turpin, thank you sincerely for your time and feedback.

To all the faculty, staff, students, and alumni of the University of Birmingham, thank you. You are a remarkable community and have marked me indelibly.

Introduction

> Man has almost constant occasion for the help of his brethren, and it is in vain for him to expect it from their benevolence alone. He will be more likely to prevail if he can interest their self-love in his favor.
>
> —Adam Smith

> By this we know love, that he laid down his life for us, and we ought to lay down our lives for the brothers. But if anyone has the world's goods and sees his brother in need, yet closes his heart against him, how does God's love abide in him?
>
> —1 John 3:16–17

Contemporary American evangelical theology has a problem. In response to the dynamic growth of the global economy, it has been on a quest to integrate Christian faith and capitalistic enterprise. The effort to show that faith and work are not meant to be isolated from each other has focused on a central theme of transformation.[1] It expresses that capitalistic enterprise provides a platform for Christians to fulfill the call of God and live faithfully to the message of Jesus' death and resurrection presented in the Bible by (a) harnessing the material powers of enterprise to advance human flourishing for the common good and (b) sharing the gospel and engaging in personal conversion where opportunity allows to spread the kingdom of God.[2]

---

1. Miller, *God at Work*, 11.
2. Smith, *Evangelicalism*, 203–10.

In this traditional scheme, Christian faith is portrayed as harnessing the good of western consumer market capitalism without being affected by its excesses. When the theme of transformation was formalized in the twentieth century, this made relative sense. Evangelical Christianity still exercised significant sociopolitical influence in American public life and market capitalism's growth was relatively stable and predictable.

Times have changed. The phenomenon of postsecularism has challenged contemporary American evangelical theology's integrative vision that enterprise is a vehicle for moral and spiritual transformation. A set of trends suggesting a resurgence of religious beliefs in market form, postsecularism challenges integration by extending the instrumentalizing reach of consumer market capitalism into virtually every domain of human life, including religious expression. This poses two problems for the traditional theme of transformation. First, it has facilitated a decline in identification with institutionalized forms of Protestant Christianity, weakening the influence of evangelicalism in American public life. Second, it has facilitated a rise in less traditional forms of implicit religion that conceive of spirituality in more materialistic and individualistic terms. Human relationality is grounded in self-interested market exchange purposed for maximizing utility. This instrumentalized conception of spirituality runs counter to a prominent ethical thread in the Christian Scriptures. There, moral and spiritual transformation is grounded in the triangulating love of God and the regular resisting of the human tendency to seek individual and material gain at the expense of others (Eph 5:2; John 13:34; 15:13; Mark 8:34–35; Rom 5:8).

The theme of transformation needs a critical revision addressing the challenges of postsecularism. That is the subject of this book. Postsecularism has shown market capitalism to be more than merely an economic system. It is a "cultural system that wields a powerful influence on human valuing, relationship, and meaning-making."[3] Consumption moves beyond acquiring basic material necessities and "into the realm of meaning-making and valuing in a structured system."[4] Consumption, like religious faith, often evinces deeper and more profound longings.[5] It "implies a faithful dependency that orders the self at a primary level."[6]

Late capitalism's postsecular growth has been polarizing. It has contributed to measurable increases in standards of living and life expectancy,

---

3. Turpin, *Branded*, 30.
4. Tanner, *Theological Reflection*, 32.
5. Miller, *Consumer Religion*, 144.
6. Turpin, *Branded*, 40.

especially among those in extreme poverty.[7] But it has also imposed "negative pecuniary externalities" in the form of rising income inequality, environmental damages, and increasing social displacement.[8] Early market capitalism was premised on the belief that the rational pursuit of self-interest (what Adam Smith called "self-love") was the best way to maximize economic benefit. For Smith, human participation in broader society would incentivize an enlightened self-interest that limited greed and the violation of others' rights.[9] The radical prioritization of consumption in western "cultures of enhancement" undercut this check.[10] The autonomized consumer is accessing an ephemeral market for goods and services for self-making that minimizes human interaction and inhibits sociality. Left unchecked, this commoditized and instrumentalizing view of the self can disintegrate individuals from the "living human web" and erode social well-being.[11]

To articulate a postsecular theme of transformation, evangelical theology needs a more nuanced account of how Christian faith integrates with consumer market systems. Specifically, how embodied Christian practices can reinforce the formation of thick relational collectives that are necessary for human flourishing, but that increasing instrumentality has eroded. How can contemporary American evangelical theology reconstruct the theme of transformation for a postsecular context that counters the individualist-materialist excesses of consumerist spirituality? That is the focus of this book.

For American evangelical faith communities, this need is urgent and opportune. It is urgent because the polarizing effects of rapid consumer capitalist growth reverberate inside American evangelical hearts and church walls. Close historical analysis showed that American evangelicalism has not evolved unaffected by postsecular consumerist spirituality—rather, it has helped create it. The Protestant-derived, individualist-materialist ethic of the early 1900s nourished a postindustrial economic boom that emphasized free market enterprise.[12] Adjusting to a consumerized religious marketplace, American evangelicalism differentiated from others through consumerist friendly efforts such as the megachurch movement and self-help gospels.[13]

---

7. McCloskey, *Bourgeois Equality*, 5–8; Sachs, *End of Poverty*, 1–2.

8. Barrera, *Economic Compulsion*, 19.

9. Wright, "Adam Smith and Greed," 46.

10. Latimer, "All-Consuming Passions," 162–64.

11. Miller-McLemore, "Living Human Web." See also Taylor, *Malaise*; Rogers-Vaughn, *Caring for Souls*.

12. Dyck and Schroeder, "Management, Theology," 706.

13. See Einstein, *Brands of Faith*.

Complex questions of faith and practice problematize the living out of scriptural, spiritual, and moral transformation within immersive postsecular consumerist narratives. Rational instrumentality is everywhere, and participation in its systems is inevitable for most evangelicals. How should the evangelical commitment to Christian love shape its participation? What does detachment from internalized material possessiveness look like in liturgical practice and ecclesial life? Where can Christian conviction in enterprise provide ways to overcome relational individualism? How do evangelical missionary efforts reflect intrinsic love?

These are tensions with which I am intimately acquainted. As a professional business executive rooted in the American evangelical tradition, I have experienced the highs and lows of the quest for integration. I helped lead the sale of a fourth-generation family company for millions of dollars, funds of which have been used for a variety of transformative efforts including development work in Africa. I have also been involved in the closure of a company that resulted in the loss of jobs, serious harm to relationships, and a crisis of personal identity. In both, I have struggled to resist the inner hold of material wealth, to bear the burdens of entrepreneurial self-making, and to pursue sacrificial love in my relationships at home and church.

My lifelong involvement with American evangelicalism has both resourced and intensified these struggles. I have found the evangelical commitment to the *kerygma* of the Christian scriptures and intimate personal faith to be clarifying and transformative. At the same time, the lack of critical reflection on how broader sociocultural norms and practices implicitly shape evangelical theological conviction has stunted my faith. Evangelical theology highly values completely integrated belief systems, but often the ambiguities of practice mean "being a self who faiths may not be as tidy as we imagine."[14] The quest for integration and spiritual transformation must extend beyond propositional assent to doctrine because the narratives of consumerist spirituality are often most alluring at affective and liturgical levels.[15]

However, it is also opportune. The postsecular diffusion of religious expression into spheres not generally seen as religious has opened doors for public dialogue about the theological and spiritual dimensions of capitalistic enterprise. New fields of inquiry, such as organizational spirituality, are grappling with the destabilizing effects of capitalism's instrumentalizing forces. This creates opportunities for religious traditions such as evangelical Christianity to exemplify the intrinsic dimensions of human spirituality.

---

14. Turpin, *Branded*, 46, 49.
15. See McClure, *Partial Faiths*.

How, then, can contemporary American evangelical theology achieve a postsecular renewal of the theme of transformation that counters the individualist-materialist excesses of consumerist spirituality? The answer is not a non-individualist, non-materialist, non-consumerist spirituality. Rather, I contend in this book that it is a *reflexive* spirituality, that is, a spirituality that regularly interrogates its own practice.[16] A reflexive spirituality "nurtures not only dispositions to see but also capacities to discern."[17]

I am positioned in this approach within the discipline of practical Christian theology, the branch of theological inquiry focused on "critical and constructive reflection on the praxis of the Christian community's life and work in its various dimensions."[18] A central focus for practical theology is strengthening theological reflexivity. Since all action is worldview guided, critical self-awareness about the assumptions, processes, and forces shaping the formation of theological beliefs and embodied rituals are important.[19]

Practical theology resists the tendency in the western tradition to bifurcate belief and practice. It argues for a strong link between religious beliefs, practices, and ethics. Christian traditions—doctrine, liturgy, spiritual practices, forms of life—are always contextually embedded and bound by practice. This was true of Jesus' earliest followers, and it is true of every community of faith since (cf. Acts 1:1–2; 1 Clem 7:2–3; 1 Cor 11:23, 15:1–3; John 21:24–25; 1 Thess 2:13). The articulation of transformative Christian faith in and to a postsecular context is, therefore, a theological imperative.[20] At the same time, Christian tradition "should be prepared to engage in an open exchange of ideas and debate with different cultural disciplines, values, images, and worldviews."[21] Even more important now, when postsecularism has revived globalized and interconnected expressions of religion. "Theology cannot reveal all that one needs to know adequately to respond to contemporary situations and issues"; other disciplinary perspectives must be utilized.[22]

Drawing on these values, I will be arguing that contemporary American evangelical theology can achieve a postsecular renewal of the theme of transformation through a *reflexive retrieval of the past* guided

---

16. Stoddart and Johnson, "Retail Faith."
17. Flanagan, "Sociology in Theology," 189.
18. Anderson, *Shape of Practical Theology*, 32.
19. Graham et al., *Theological Reflection*, 21.
20. Bevans, *Models of Contextual Theology*, 3.
21. Graham et al., *Theological Reflection*, 138.
22. Woodward and Pattison, "Pastoral and Practical Theology," 15. See also Huyssteen, *Shaping of Rationality*.

by *interdisciplinary engagement*.[23] This book will articulate a constructive model for strengthening theological reflexivity. This model addresses two dimensions of theological reflexivity. First, it addresses a conceptual inconsistency in the common articulation of the theme of transformation by restoring a scripturally faithful relational ethic of triangulating love. Second, it provides a way for individuals and congregations to critically interrogate, for the purposes of shaping faithful practice, instrumentalizing tendencies that inevitably emerge.

In summary, this book is a critical, constructive conversation in Christian ethics and practical theology. The reflexive spiral starts implicitly with an understanding of my own context in American evangelicalism. I provide a description of evangelical theology and practice, then problematize this by showing the theoretical and practical limitations faced. Finally, I draw on resources from tradition to expand and develop both theology and practice. I now turn to a fuller description of its argument and methodology.

Shape of the Argument and Research Methodology

Positioned within the discipline of practical theology, I argue for a postsecular renewal of the theme of transformation as, first, a reflexive retrieval of the past. Streaming into the American evangelical quest for integration are Christian traditions rich with reflection on the relationships between wealth, enterprise, and triangulating love. Much of it predates the western tradition's substantial emphasis on relational individualism.[24] Mining this heritage is essential because relational individualism as an unqualified good is precisely what needed to be reevaluated.

Two figures—Augustine and Aquinas—loom in the triangular love tradition and have primarily been the focus of evangelical scholarship. However, there is a neglected third figure, the medieval mystic Meister Eckhart, whom I demonstrate offers unique insights. Eckhart emphasized the sacramental nature of triangulating love expressed through the spiritual practice of *gelassenheit* (detachment). When one yields to God's mysterious and often uncomfortable work of detachment from instrumentalizing excesses, the affections of the heart and soul are realigned back to God through the way of the cross.

Concerned by increasing individualism and materialism, the early Anabaptist communities of fifteenth- and sixteenth-century south Germany

---

23. Buschart and Eilers, *Theology of Retrieval*, 5.
24. Weaver, *Self Love and Christian Ethics*, 19.

appropriated mystical *gelassenheit* into a lived relational ethic that manifested in transformative acts. For contemporary American evangelical theology, a retrieval of early Anabaptist spirituality's mystical *gelassenheit* enabled it to counter consumerist narratives that the ever-more consumption of goods and services produces spiritual transformation.

Second, I argue that a reflexive retrieval is guided by interdisciplinary engagement. For contemporary American evangelical theology, stakeholder theory within the field of organizational management represents an ideal interdisciplinary dialogue partner. Stakeholder theory has emerged in the field of business ethics as the dominate heuristic for understanding the transformative role of enterprise in shaping human and social good. It holds that enterprise is transformative when it focuses on maximizing long-term value for all its stakeholders, not just profits for shareholders.

In trying to hold up this core framework against the forces of postsecularism, stakeholder theory faces remarkably similar issues to contemporary American evangelical theology. I show that the instrumentalizing excesses of postsecularism have pressed stakeholder theory to better capture the social dimensions of enterprise. This provides contemporary American evangelical theology an opportunity to demonstrate the limits of capitalistic enterprise's contributions to human flourishing and the crucial contributions that theological perspectives can make.

Together, my proposition is that contemporary American evangelical theology can achieve a postsecular renewal of the theme of transformation by critically: (a) engaging stakeholder theory to establish the limits of capitalistic enterprise's contributions to human flourishing; and (b) appropriating the Anabaptist tradition of *gelassenheit* to reconstruct the theme of transformation around a scripturally-faithful relational ethic of triangular love. The argument unfolds in two parts: In part one (chapters 1–4), I elaborate the problem facing contemporary American evangelical theology. In part two (chapters 5–8), I unpack the resolution.

This is a closer look at both parts. Part one elaborates the problem facing contemporary American evangelical theology by evaluating its essential facets. This begins in chapter 1 by positioning my own practical theological method within the diverse landscape of the discipline of practical theology. I do this, first, by detailing how the discipline links together practice, ethics, and public theology. Analyzed here are the discipline's key historical developments, core methodological framework, and the primary contemporary trajectories. Second, I show how contemporary practical theological methodology informs a strengthening of American evangelical reflexivity, specifically, how contemporary critical trajectories within the discipline can draw out the ways that evangelical spiritual practices have been affected by the diffusion of consumer capitalist ideology into non-market contexts.

In chapter 2, I anticipate and address early objections to reflexivity that might arise in contemporary American evangelical theology. I focus on two potential roadblocks: first, American evangelical theology's allegiance to foundationalism and second, its concern to safeguard scriptural authority.

In chapter 3, I introduce and overview the theme of transformation. Capitalism's dynamic growth has resurfaced a long-standing theological debate in contemporary American evangelical theology about the nature of the kingdom of God and the responsibilities of Christians to transform society. I describe the current state of transformational thinking in American evangelicalism, where it comes from, and why it matters to evangelical theology and religion. By charting its development, I show that sociohistorical variables have factored heavily, not just theological ones.

In chapter 4, I widen the lens to analyze postsecularism as a substantial disruption in the American religious landscape in which the theme of transformation has evolved. After overviewing postsecularism, I define the nature of postsecular consumerist spirituality and then relate it to contemporary American evangelical theology. I show that as American capitalistic enterprise has become more intensely consumeristic and instrumentalizing, it has obscured the intrinsic goods of human flourishing that are necessary for spiritual transformation. This is an opportunity for contemporary American evangelical theology because it reconfigures the public sphere to allow for more meaningful dialogue about the theological and religious aspects of capitalistic enterprise, but also a dilemma because it exposes that American evangelicalism itself has contributed to the development of the materialistic and individualistic aspects of postsecular consumerist spirituality.

The problem facing a postsecular renewal of the theme of transformation, then, is how to account for both. Shifting to the resolution in part two (chapters 5–8), I propose that a postsecular renewal involves an interdisciplinary engagement in the public sphere that subjects evangelical theology to critical correlation. Stakeholder theory within the field of organizational management represents an ideal interdisciplinary dialogue partner, and I introduce stakeholder theory on its own terms in chapter 5.

I show that in trying to hold up its framework against the forces of postsecularism, stakeholder theory faces remarkably similar issues to contemporary American evangelical theology. In chapter 6, I argue that the instrumentalizing excesses of postsecularism have pressed stakeholder theory to reconceptualize the social dimensions of enterprise. This provides contemporary American evangelical theology an opportunity to demonstrate the limits of capitalistic enterprise's contributions to human flourishing.

In the final two chapters, I build on this layer to propose a second element to a postsecular renewal of the theme of transformation: a contextualized retrieval of the Christian traditions. Streaming into the American evangelical quest for integration of faith and work is a rich heritage in the Christian traditions of grappling with the instrumentalizing tendencies of wealth and enterprise in the face of the triangulating love of God. In the late fifteenth century, early South German Anabaptist communities appropriated Eckhart's practice of mystical *gelassenheit* to counter what they perceived as increasing individualism and materialism. Like contemporary American evangelical theology, these Anabaptists were concerned to show how Christian faith can be transformative and they represent an ideal source of retrieval. In chapter 7, I show how Eckhart's mystical *gelassenheit* was appropriated by early Anabaptism. In chapter 8, I show how contemporary American evangelical theology can use this appropriation to construct a model for strengthening reflexivity.

The Intended Audience and Need for the Research

Having identified the research topic as interdisciplinary, it is important to discuss its intended audience and research need. The book addresses two major streams. The first and primary stream is academic Christian theology, particularly constructive practical theology. Secondarily, is stakeholder theory in the field of business ethics. While these two major streams address quite similar questions about the relationship between human values, theological and religious belief, and the global economy, they have never been brought into significant synthesis, not simply for the sake of comparison, but for constructive proposals. Practical theology and ethics have primarily focused on church life to the neglect of secular organizational life. The sparse attention paid to capitalism has tended to be in the form of systemic critique, not necessarily to help capitalists and entrepreneurs think about their work. However, then, stakeholder theory and business management have not substantially dealt with action-guiding ideologies and identity, especially the experience of religious, identity-forming communities.

The primary audience is academic Christian theologians, particularly constructive practical theologians. From the standpoint of the primary audience, there are four gaps I am filling: (a) the need for constructive, practical theological ethics; (b) the need for evangelical practical theologies; (c) the need for scholarly research on the theme of transformation in American evangelical theology; and (d) the need for contemporary reappraisals of early Anabaptist spirituality's use of *gelassenheit*.

First, is the need for constructive theological ethics in the discipline of practical theology. This book is fundamentally a work of constructive theological ethics residing in the discipline of practical theology. Though a highly pluralistic field contemporary practical theology sustains a fundamental concern for the integration of theory and practice.[25] Among the five main currents Heitink identifies, I am working from the empirical-analytical current. Highlighting the relevance of social scientific research, this current desires to "make theological concepts operational . . . and seeks to link in an open manner quantitative and qualitative research."[26]

In trying to operationalize the theological theme of transformation, I am specifically pursuing *constructive* practical theology. While constructive theology has emerged primarily in systematic theology as a method for relating traditional Christian doctrines to contemporary questions of faith and ethics, there has been comparatively less effort using constructive theology in the discipline of practical theology.[27] This is striking given that questions of faith and ethics are at the heart of practical theology's concern for integrating theory and practice.

By pursuing a constructive, practical theology within the empirical-analytical current, I am challenging the silos imposed by the traditional theological encyclopedia by generating theological reflection that pulls from all four forms: historical, systematic, biblical/exegetical, and practical. The goal is to contribute to a more effective harmonizing of belief and practice in a specific faith tradition, namely contemporary American evangelical theology.

Second, is the need for evangelical practical theologies. Contemporary practical theology's emergence as a discipline has been robust, but it has spread very little into evangelical theology. Simply, "evangelicals have never found an established footing within the established guilds of practical theology."[28] The bulk of the engagement from evangelical theologians with practical theology has come from a single individual (Ray Anderson) at a single institution (Fuller Theological Seminary).

Evangelical theology has tended to regard with suspicion post-Kantian continental philosophical and theological movements (including

25. Osmer, *Practical Theology*, 241.
26. Heitink, *Practical Theology*, 174.
27. Quite insightfully, constructive systematic theology seeks to reframe the concept of doctrine, not as traditionally understood fixed propositional constructs but rather theological geographies that guide Christians as they strive to make sense of the complex terrain of faith. See Jones and Lakeland, *Constructive Theology*. Pattison's *Saving Face* comprised a rare example of constructive practical theology.
28. Root, *Evangelical Practical Theology*, 95.

Schleiermacher), viewing them primarily as attacks on the normative authority of the Bible. If practical theology is going to see greater activity from evangelically influenced scholars, it must deal with the obstacle that "evangelical practical theology has lacked constructive interdisciplinary models."[29] This research study utilized specific frameworks within practical theology to construct an interdisciplinary model for strengthening reflexivity within evangelical theology that advances the integration of theory and practice.

Third, is the need for scholarly research on the theme of transformation in contemporary American evangelical theology. The theme of transformation is one of the primary conceptual apparatuses by which both contemporary American evangelical theologians and laypersons understand the effort to integrate religious faith and professional work. Yet, its expressions in evangelical theologies and lay evangelical faith communities have never been critically compared.

Fourth, is the need for contemporary reappraisals of early Anabaptist spirituality's use of *gelassenheit*. Some of the earliest Anabaptist communities to emerge in the Reformation were in south Germany. They are often categorized with the Rhineland mystic spirituality movement because of the appropriation of Meister Eckhart's emphasis on God's love by figures such as Thomas Müntzer and Hans Denk.

Eckhart's theology of love is most clearly expressed in the concept of *gelasseneheit*, representing one of the most significant but under-researched articulations of triangulating love in the Christian traditions. In light of the phenomenon of postsecular consumerist spirituality, the practice of *gelassenheit* has renewed relevance. This book addresses this gap by providing an analysis of Eckhart's scheme in its utilization by early Anabaptist spirituality to demonstrate its contemporary relevance to theological discussions about consumerist spirituality.

The secondary audience extends twofold: stakeholder theory in the field of business ethics and postsecular theory in the field of sociology of religion. There are two gaps I intended to fill: (a) the need for robust theological engagement with stakeholder theory and (b) the need for diagnostic comparisons between postsecular theory and stakeholder theory.

First, is the need for robust theological engagement with stakeholder theory. It has quickly emerged as the dominant heuristic in the field of business ethics for understanding the relationship of capitalistic enterprises with their broader constituencies. It calls for a shift away from prioritizing shareholder profit as the focus of an enterprise's value to its ability to profitably serve all its stakeholders (e.g., vendors, customers, employees, society, environment). This shift has opened the door for meaningful challenges to the individualist and materialist excesses of capitalistic enterprise. Oddly,

---

29. Root, *Evangelical Practical Theology*, 95.

while recent scholarly discussions in stakeholder theory have involved a number of interdisciplinary partners including sociology (e.g., Jones and Wicks, "Convergent Stakeholder Theory,"), psychology (e.g., Bridoux and Stoelhorst, "Microfoundations for Stakeholder Theory") and philosophy (e.g., Arnold, Beauchamp, and Bowie, *Ethical Theory and Business*), theology has been largely absent.[30]

Second, is the need for diagnostic comparisons between postsecular theory and stakeholder theory. Like stakeholder theory, likewise, postsecular theory in the discipline of the sociology of religion has emerged as a dominant heuristic for understanding the implications of capitalistic enterprise for its field, displacing an entrenched one. It has overturned secularization theory's long-held consensus that the economic and social modernization of western society would displace religion to contend that religious expression has not entirely dissipated but rather shifted.

With the scope of this book, stakeholder theory and postsecularism are brought together and critically analyzed as a secondary audience to fill a void in both fields of study, which have so far lacked critical comparison. I intended to show that in both theories a relational individualist ethic is operative that posits a social self and an individual self in terminal opposition and that practical theological methodology can provide a helpful reframing of these categories that offers more explanatory power.

Conclusion

In this introductory chapter, I have established that this book is a critical evaluation of the theme of transformation in contemporary American evangelical theology. I have shown it is necessary because of the postsecular growth of consumer market capitalism, which has weakened evangelicalism influence on American public life and intensified individualist and materialist conceptions of spirituality. As contemporary American evangelical theology seeks to integrate Christian faith and capitalistic enterprise in a postsecular context, it needs to revise the theme of transformation around a relational ethic that reflexively resists the instrumentalizing tendencies of consumerist spirituality and recovers a scripturally faithful triangulating ethic. Because of its focus on the indissoluble links between theology, religious practices, ethics, and public engagement, the discipline of practical theology is optimally aligned to address these concerns. I now turn to a fuller unpacking of the discipline and my position within it.

---

30. Miller, "Organizational Research as Practical Theology," 1–4.

Introduction to Part One

For a postsecular revision of the theme of transformation, we must first lay some conceptual groundwork to elaborate the problem facing contemporary American evangelical theology. Having overviewed the research question and argumentation and delimited its scope in the introduction, I now move into part one and a definition of key concepts. This begins in chapter 1 with an articulation of the practical theological methodology framing my research. In chapter 2, obstacles to evangelical theological reflexivity are analyzed. In chapter 3, I overview the theme of transformation in contemporary American evangelical theology. Finally, in chapter 4, I analyze postsecularism as the broader sociohistorical context in which the theme of transformation has emerged.

1

What Practical Theological Method Is Being Utilized?

A recent edited volume with contributions from major American evangelical insiders contemplates the state of the movement after Donald Trump's election to the American presidency in 2016. It starts bluntly: "Evangelicalism in America has cracked, split on the shoals of the 2016 presidential election and its aftermath, leaving many wondering whether they want to be in or out of the evangelical tribe."[1] The dynamic and uneven growth of capitalistic enterprise is at the heart of this splitting. A divided vote in American evangelicalism was symptomatic of growing racial tensions spurred by socioeconomic disruption across the country:

> A middle-class, underemployed, white American, perhaps living in Appalachia or the Rust Belt, may believe failed immigration policy or enforcement has disrupted their "God-given right" to work, which makes it difficult to support welcoming the alien or stranger. An African American or Latino American living in Los Angeles or New York may view huge rallies of white people as excluding or mistreating people who look like them and hear the rallies' language about God as abusive and its "good news" as unrecognizable.[2]

For contemporary American evangelical theology to renew a transformational vision of enterprise, it must confront these fractures. To do so will require a reframing of the relationship between religious belief and practice. Historically, American evangelical religion has emphasized individual belief systems and doctrinal propositions as the basis for forming and sustaining communities of faith. In short, that the right theological beliefs produce morally sound practice.

1. Labberton, *Still Evangelical*, 1.
2. Labberton, *Still Evangelical*, 7.

However, what the 2016 election exposed is that the complexities facing American evangelical efforts to integrate Christian faith and capitalistic enterprise are "more about social location than theology proper."[3] The strengthening of theological reflexivity—taking an evaluative stance toward its own beliefs and practices—requires American evangelicalism to interrogate not just its own theological propositions, but also how they are implicitly shaped by sociopolitical-economic contexts and manifested in embodied spiritual practices.

The dynamic growth of consumer capitalism makes this no easy undertaking. One of the markings of present-day consumer capitalism is the diffusion of consumer markets and ideology into non-market contexts (including Christian churches). The reach of instrumentalizing forces extends into daily consumer life, but subtly. To draw out these forces, consumer capitalism's political and social power structures and how they shape religious practice must be analyzed.

These are questions germane to the discipline of practical theology and its distinguishing focus on the practice of Christian beliefs. In its relatively short history, the discipline of practical theology as broadened its focus of inquiry from primarily the practices of clerical ministry to how belief, tradition, and practice intersect complex human experience within the daily life of faith communities.

The purpose of this chapter is to provide a fuller framing of the book by locating myself within the diverse landscape of practical theology. I do this, first, by overviewing the discipline to show how it links together practice, ethics, and public theology. Key historical developments that created these links are highlighted, and then the contemporary state of the discipline is analyzed in terms of its core methodological framework and the four primary trajectories that express it. Second, I relate contemporary practical theological methodology to the strengthening of American evangelical reflexivity. Specifically, how the transforming praxis and neo-Aristotelian trajectories in contemporary practical theology can be applied to draw out the ways that evangelical spiritual practices have been affected by capitalism's diffusion.

I proceed, first, by elaborating how consumer capitalism's diffusion has shifted religious expression. Then, I show how the transforming praxis and neo-Aristotelian trajectories are best suited to draw out the effects of these shifts. Finally, I contend that these practical theological trajectories affirm a strengthening of theological reflexivity that functions not in isolation, but

---

3. Labberton, *Still Evangelical*, 15.

in interdisciplinary engagement with fields such as management ethics undergoing similar shifts.

Before proceeding, I should briefly elaborate on how I am using the term *evangelical* throughout this dissertation. The word evangelical transliterates εὐαγγέλιον, "good news" or "gospel."[4] Historically, it designates Protestants who emerged from the Reformation "strongly emphasizing the redeeming work of Christ, personally appropriated, and . . . spreading the good news of that message."[5]

I generally adopt this conventional usage, although it is important to note that evangelicalism has undergone significant demographic transition within the last century. According to *World Christian Encyclopedia*, over 90 percent of evangelicals were concentrated in Europe or North America in 1900, whereas today the number of evangelicals in Europe and North American is exceeded independently by those in Africa, Asia, and Latin America.[6] Thus, contemporary evangelicalism is best understood as a set of multi-faceted movements and denominations sharing common convictions.[7] A widely cited summary of these shared convictions is Bebbington. He identified four critical theological emphases of evangelicalism: personal conversion, the hermeneutical priority of the Bible, missional activism, and the death and resurrection of Jesus.[8]

For this book, I focus on contemporary American evangelicalism. This is not out of a desire to narrowly define the meaning of the word "evangelical," as can be the case among conservatives in the tradition.[9] Rather, it is

---

4. On occasion, and mostly by non-evangelicals, the term "fundamentalist" is used as a synonym for "evangelicals." I avoided the terms "fundamentalist" and "fundamentalism," not because they are historically insignificant but rather because they are used today in primarily pejorative contexts. Again, the historical background is relevant here. Marsden noted that the term was "invented in American in 1920 to apply to militant evangelicals," conservatives who were "willing to take a stand and fight" (Marsden, *Understanding Fundamentalism*, 1). In this sense, the term applied to more than just a certain type of evangelical but any denomination (e.g., Baptist, Methodist) that was operating on the far political right. Today, "fundamentalism" has broadened and can be applied to far-right religious adherents outside Christianity—for example, Islamic fundamentalism. For a helpful comparison of fundamentalism in Christianity, Islam, and Judaism, see Antoun, *Understanding Fundamentalism*.

5. Knoll, "What Is 'Evangelical'?," 10.

6. Barrett et al., *World Christian Encyclopedia*, 13–14.

7. This is partly self-imposed. As McGrath noted, "The history of evangelicalism in the United Kingdom and the United States is frequently dominated by debates over who is in and who is out, not to mention who has the right to draw the somewhat contested boundaries in the first place" (McGrath, "Evangelical Theological Method," 26).

8. Bebbington, *Evangelicalism in Modern Britain*.

9. Greggs, "Opening Evangelicalism," 5.

because the diffuse and varied nature of contemporary evangelicalism means that with a topic like the global enterprise—itself diffuse and varied—there are too many social, economic, and political variables to speak generally. There are even substantial differences between evangelicalism in America and the UK. American evangelicalism, for example, has more often been associated with conservative political ideology and entrapped in so-called "culture wars."[10] As I show in later chapters, this feature of contemporary American evangelicalism bears heavily on its quest for integration.

Overview of the Discipline

Throughout western history, theology has been commonly associated with the supernatural, transcendent, sacred, and spiritual while practice is associated with the everyday, common, material, and embodied. Contemporary practical theology challenges this as a "function of Enlightenment dualistic thinking, which arbitrarily exalts thought and cognition as modes of knowledge and perception over more embodied kinds of knowing and being."[11] Practice and theology belong together because practices are central to human being and knowing. They sustain life and create meaning, whether explicitly or implicitly theological. Through "inhabited action-guiding worldviews" humans navigate a complex network of material and structural relationships and social practices.[12] Thereby constituting a living human web that bear religious and theological import beyond mere religious ideas and texts.

If theology is tied to practice, then it must also be to ethics. However, ethics are conceived of more broadly than in the Eurocentric model, which has pervaded western history. It emphasized detached moral abstraction: deducing the right ethical theory from revelatory text or doctrine for application to hypothetical cases.[13] Allegedly controlled for here were the fallacies of human subjectivity and particularity. However, a focus on practices reveals a deeper, indissoluble union between subject and object. Moral-ethical reasoning, in practical theology, is inherently a hermeneutical circle in which we

> have a duty to test what we claim normatively against what others live. For ethics to offer constructive insights and norms for

---

10. Bean, *Evangelical Identity*.
11. Bennett et al., *Research in Practical Theology*, 57.
12. Pattison, *Challenge of Practical Theology*, 7.
13. De La Torre, "Ethics," 337.

shaping social relations and values, it has to demonstrate that it has first taken the complexity of reality and lived experience into account. Moral claims lack force if they jump too quickly into prescription without taking a full enough view of the complexity of the issues at stake.[14]

Finally: if theology, practice, and ethics belong together, then it all plays out in public. Western modernization has tended to drive a wedge between public and private domains, relegating theological and religious expression to the latter as a form of subjectivity. Practical theology labors to show that there is only one realm of human experience and no domain exists in a pure or isolated state. The increasingly fragmented, disparate, and diverse nature of public life might not recognize the value of theology and religion as a sustaining force, but sometimes the role of public theology is to "challenge that agenda and its priorities."[15] A public facing practical theology seeks spaces of shared meaning across all domains, and "to do this, it cannot simply be applied to situations; it must, at least in part, take flesh within them."[16] This demands reflexivity; a self-aware posture helps to guard against creating a "purportedly perfected system of theological or ethical thought" that fails to acknowledge that "no theological statement fully conveys divine being and action. Our understandings of revelation are never final or complete."[17]

How did the discipline of practical theology come to link together practice, ethics, and public engagement? I will answer this question by charting key historical developments that have shaped the field and then analyzing its methodological core and contemporary trajectories.

Key Historical Developments

Miller-McLemore differentiates four uses of the term "practical theology"[18]: an activity of believers seeking to sustain a life of reflective faith in the

---

14. Scharen and Vigen, *Ethnography as Christian Theology*, 67.
15. Forrester, *Christian Ethics and Practical Theology*, 80.
16. Scharen and Vigen, *Ethnography as Christian Theology*, 66.
17. Scharen and Vigen, *Ethnography as Christian Theology*, 69.
18. Miller-McLemore, "Practical Theology," 1471. As a term, "practical" theology is often compared and contrasted to "pastoral" theology, with North American (and largely Reformed) usage tending to emphasize the contrasts between the two and British (and largely Anglican) usage tending to downplay them (Woodward and Pattison, "Pastoral and Practical Theology," 1–3). Pastoral theology is an older term that stems from the discipline's origins in clerical ministry. In recent times, the terms have blended far more than they have diverged, and their nuances are due more to preference than

everyday; a curricular area in theological education focused on ministerial practice; an approach to theology used by religious leaders and by teachers and students across the curriculum; and an academic discipline pursued by a smaller subset of scholars to sustain these first three enterprises.

I am especially focused on the last usage. Woodward and Pattison offer a helpful standard definition of academic practical theology: "A place where religious beliefs and practice meets contemporary experiences, questions, and actions and conducts a dialogue that is mutually enriching, intellectually critical, and practically transforming."[19] As an academic discipline, practical theology is relatively young.[20] Its origins are typically identified with German theologian Friedrich Schleiermacher, who near the end of the eighteenth century divided theology into three fields: philosophical theology, the root of the tree; historical theology, the stem or body; and practical theology, the crown.[21]

Schleiermacher was an important transitional figure, contemporaneous with the birth of the modern German research university model and the Enlightenment. Practical theology for Schleiermacher was the crown of theology in that it welded together both ecclesial concern and scientific inquiry.[22] He wrote:

> Without an ecclesial interest neither the feelings nor the excitations of mind and heart just mentioned will arise, and without a scientific spirit no deliberative activity—that is, none that will be guided by prescriptions—arises either but rather the sort of motivation that is disinclined toward cognition and disdains rules.[23]

Practical theology is not derivative—merely an application of dogmatic or systematic theology. It stands by itself as a reflective theory of practice that was always mediated through the experience of the subject. Schleiermacher's views were shaped by his broader conception of religion and Christianity.[24] The Enlightenment was well underway in continental Europe, and modernist intellectuals were turning their attention from theology and religion to rationalist utilitarian philosophy and ethics. Descartes had set an early tone by seeking epistemic certainty through a project of complete skepticism led

---

substance. Since practical theology has a more formal connection to and development within the academy, I use it throughout.

19. Woodward and Pattison, "Pastoral and Practical Theology," 7.
20. Penzel, "Schleiermacher and Practical Theology," 3.
21. Schleiermacher, *Outline of Theology*.
22. Sleeth, "Schleiermacher," 45.
23. Schleiermacher, *Outline of Theology*, 97.
24. Grab, "Practical Theology."

by the supposed universal value of reason.[25] Knowledge needs a universal foundation, and the grand pursuit of the Enlightenment project should be to find one. The Cartesian scheme prioritized *episteme* or *theoria* (theoretical and propositional knowledge) as the purest form of knowledge. This was a disembodied cognition that produced practice.[26]

Critiquing both the so-called rationalists and empiricists of early foundationalism, Immanuel Kant introduced a paradigmatic shift by asserting "knowledge emerges at the inner part of the data of the senses (the content) and the categories of the mind (the structure)."[27] The mind does not simply passively receive information, as the foundationalist epistemologies central to both Descartes and Locke asserted.

A leader in the German romantic movement, Schleiermacher applied Kant's "turn to the subject" to say that religion belonged to a realm of human subjectivity beyond the realm of theoretical knowledge. He defended religion as an irreplaceable dimension of human existence, not from the standpoint of its institutional forms but from the perspective of individual human nature itself. Appropriating Aristotle, Schleiermacher characterized practical theology as a *technik* that moved past mere mechanistic action to guiding principles "mediated through competence, freedom, and creativity."[28] Schleiermacher's ideas set the tone in continental Europe and the broader western tradition for the discipline's early emphasis on equipping clergy for ministerial work.[29] His disciple, Carl Immanuel Nitzsch, intensified this focus by describing the research domain of practical theology as the praxis of the church, and on equal footing with the other theological disciplines.

Into the twentieth century, two fundamental movements broadened the discipline's emphasis on practice from the clerical and into everyday human experience. The first was correlational theology, which evolved primarily in liberal Protestant and Catholic circles in Europe and North America. This maintained that insights from Christian revelation should be correlated with the pressing issues of human existence brought to the surface by existential and psychological analysis. Paul Tillich, the movement's leading voice, wrote in his *Systematic Theology*:

> The Christian message provides the answers to the questions implied in human existence. These answers are contained in the

25. Broughton, *Descartes's Method of Doubt*.
26. See Saul, *Voltaire's Bastards*.
27. Clark, *To Know and Love God*, 55.
28. Woggon, "Deliberate Activity," 8.
29. Dingemans, "Practical Theology," 82.

revelatory events on which Christianity. . . . Their content cannot be derived from questions that would come from an analysis of human existence. They are "spoken" to human existence from beyond it.[30]

The philosopher, herself tasked with the study of being and human finitude, posed the existential questions, for which the theologian, herself tasked with the study of Christian revelation, sought to correlate responses. Tillich was not primarily talking about strict empirical correlation but rather a posture of interpreting the general relationship between theology and human experience.[31] Developing Tillich's ideas and then intensifying them, Catholic theologian David Tracy contended that for theology to remain relevant in a pluralistic world that privatizes faith, the domains of Christian revelation and human experience needed to be in mutual dialogue to revise each other.[32]

The second major influence came from liberation theology, which extended correlation perspectives to second and third world contexts. Beginning in the 1960s, a wave of contextual theologies emerged that were attuned to socioeconomic structures and injustices.[33] European theologians began to speak more frequently about political and public theology. German Gert Otto wrote a two-volume work called *Practical Theology* to analyze the effects of religion on society. A student of Otto's, Andrea von Heyl unpacked the implications of the Frankfurt school's reinterpretation of Freud and Marx for the field of practical theology. Asian American theology too began to call for liberation from social oppression.[34] In 1969, American James Cone published *A Black Theology of Liberation* that articulated liberationist tones from the American civil rights movement.

Perhaps most prominently, Gustavo Gutierrez called for a "theology of liberation" throughout Latin America as "a critical reflection on Christian praxis in the light of the Word."[35] Despite gaining political independence from European colonizers a century before, south and central America continued to be plagued by economic poverty, social inequality, and political unrest. For many Latin American theologians (particularly in the Catholic church), Marx's socioeconomic analysis held explanatory power in accounting for these struggles.

30. Tillich, *Systematic Theology*, 66.
31. Miller, "Organizational Research as Practical Theology," 15.
32. Tracy, *Analogical Imagination*, 51.
33. Cahalan and Mikoski, *Opening the Field*.
34. See Phan, *Asian American Theology*.
35. Gutiérrez, *Theology of Liberation*, 13.

Drawing on a Hegelian model of history, Marx argued that human societies were shaped through the struggle of the classes within them. In capitalist systems, this struggle manifested as a conflict between the bourgeoisie ruling class that controlled the means of production and the proletariat working class that enabled production by selling labor for wages. Marx's historical materialism contended that these internal class contradictions would eventually result in capitalism's self-destruction, as the working class developed a class consciousness that would propel political revolution and emancipation and the gaining of power to establish a communist (classless) society marked by the free association of producers.

Marxist-influenced thinkers developed a "dependency theory" to explain the realities in Latin America: "Developing counties continued to experience a disadvantageous relationship with the industrial west, in terms of trade and other forms of neo-colonialism."[36] Across the west, liberation theologians called for breaking free from this dependence with a "preferential option for the poor" that prioritized value guided action (praxis) over doctrine. Progressive streams in the Catholic church began efforts in adult literacy programs, health care initiatives, and church community outreach. In the areas of economic justice, poverty, and human rights, political activism was understood as the domain of the practically oriented theologian, not just through the efforts of Gutierrez in Peru, but Leonardo Boff in Brazil, and Jon Sobrino in Spain. Theology is a form of "talk about God" in which the social context of a believer demands practices of liberation and solidarity.

Thus, theology "is not the rational exploration of divine revelation to increase its intelligibility" but a "rational exercise that follows upon the action of the poor and searches for an understanding of God's revelation that discloses its redemptive and liberative power."[37] Read through these lenses, the Bible provided not just a typology but a mandate for such action. In the Old Testament, it was the exodus Israelites who broke free from the social and economic oppression of Egypt and Babylon. In the New Testament, it was Jesus who overcame social sin and called his followers to break free from Rome.

Correlation and liberation influences helped spark an identifiable renaissance in practical theology starting in the 1970s throughout Europe, North America, South America, and Asia.[38] Thought centers arose at the University

---

36. Graham et al., *Theological Reflection*, 242.

37. Baum, "Impact of Marxist Ideas," 180–82.

38. Particularly in the UK, this renaissance in part involved a critique of the ways that North American correlational approaches stunted the radical implications of liberationist approaches for social ethics. See Woodward and Pattison, *Pastoral and Practical Theology*; Stoddart, *Advancing Practical Theology*.

of Chicago, Princeton Theological Seminary, and Emory University, among others. Several thinkers set the pace for the contemporary shape of the discipline in North America: Don Browning (University of Chicago), Richard Osmer (Princeton Theological Seminary), and Charles Gerkin (Emory University). On the European front, pivotal academic institutions included Cardiff University, University of Birmingham, and Catholic University of Nijmegen (Netherlands). Among European contemporary practical theologians, Elaine Graham, John Swinton, Stephen Pattison, and J. A. van der Venn are prominent.[39] In Asia and South America, the Graduate School of Practical Theology in Icheon, Korea and Faculdade Luterana de Teologia (Brazil) and theologians such as Yoo-Kwang Hyon (South Korea), Leonardo Boff (Brazil), and Daisy Nwachuku (Nigeria) to name a few.

This renaissance strengthened the link between practical theology and public theology. Public theology in the western tradition has traditionally focused on exploring corporate, political, economic, and social dimensions of religious belief and practice.[40] For the bulk of the twentieth century, the primary concerns of public theology were around rational and apologetic defenses of Christian doctrine, reflecting its strong base in mainstream Protestant and Reformed denominations in North American and the UK.[41] The influx of liberation theologies pressed for more critical and contextual approaches that extended beyond ecclesial borders. Practical theology's growing emphasis on the religious nature of practices across the private and public domains aligned well.

Greater interdisciplinary engagement also contributed to the link. For example, Browning worked from the social sciences to construct an integrative hermeneutic for moral deliberation that accounted for the emotional and social complexities of human living.[42] For Browning, practical theological reason needs to make itself communicable to a skeptical public while at the same time raising questions about the alleged objectivity and neutrality of the social sciences.

Modern practical theology, accordingly, found a natural home in postmodernism's skepticism of modernity's knowledge claims. Postmodernity catapulted the discipline into ever-widening explorations of the integration of theory and practice in the midst of capitalism's global expanse:

---

39. Gerben Heitink, another important Dutch practical theologian, has written what remains the benchmark survey of the discipline's historical developments and contemporary trendlines. See his *Practical Theology*.

40. Graham, *Rock and a Hard Place*.

41. Stackhouse, *Public Theology and Political Economy*.

42. Browning, *Fundamental Practical Theology*.

> Postmodern practical theologies seek to be deeply responsive to the general Western cultural situation. . . . Capitalism was recognized as having extended its global reach . . . and the complex dynamics of globalization became a major object of attention. Theologically informed discernment about the victors and victims of a consumer capitalism that had come to seem inevitable was recognized by the theological academy as essential work.[43]

Postmodernism has generally been skeptical about universalizing accounts of rationality and human nature. Postmodern practical theologies have reflected a diversity of perspectives and research interests. Schweitzer and Osmer, for example, focused on postmodern perspectives for religious education and pastoral care,[44] Graham on theological method and feminist theology,[45] and Althaus-Reid on LGBTQ and gender inequalities.[46] In all, postmodernism has imprinted two features on practical theology's distinguishing focus on practice. First, that theory (theological or otherwise) is often insufficient in surfacing the full range of practices that give significance and meaning to human life. Second, human experiences are always contextually bound and thus often best understood in their particularity or specificity.

Contemporary Trajectories in Practical Theology

Of all the theological fields, then, practical theology "gives the most attention to studying and engaging the present context directly. It seeks to learn from the present context, as well as to guide and even transform the present context."[47] To do so requires that theology is tied to practice and ethics in a public facing posture that explores critical questions about human relationships and social well-being. The contemporary state of the discipline is situated in a globalized milieu. In so far as its starting point is the everyday and ordinary, it is also a diverse field that sometimes lacks clear disciplinary boundaries.[48]

---

43. Beaudoin, "Postmodern Practical Theology," 204.
44. Schweitzer, *Postmodern Life Cycle*; Osmer, *Practical Theology*.
45. Graham, *Transforming Practice*.
46. Althaus-Reid, *Indecent Theology*.
47. Osmer, "Empirical Theology," 67.
48. Ward, "Introducing Practical Theology." This has led to greater reengagement with historical, systematic, and mainstream theology, all of which have sought distinctive representations of the relationship between belief and practice. See Lee, "Practical Theology."

Are there any common themes across the spectrum? Having noted key historical developments that shaped the formation of the discipline, I now turn to an analysis of its methodological core and manifold trajectories. Bennett et al. helpfully outlined several theses that capture the core of contemporary practical theological methodology.[49] First, the theology of practical theology is instantiated within action, praxis, performance, and practice. Human activity is contextual, normed, and capable of embodying social goods. By nature, practices are value laden and generally oriented toward some *telos* or objective. Practical theology, then, focuses on human context and the realities of lived experience as the places where Christian discipleship and theology occur. Practical theology cannot be applied doctrinal theology because "theology does not simply end in practice, but starts there, too."[50] Practical theologians are not simply interpreters of enshrined texts and traditions but "critical inhabitants of action-guiding world-views" that interrogate and interpret how socially and relationally embedded beliefs and values facilitate faithful practice.[51]

Likewise, practice is theological because it bears implicit values that strengthen or impair virtue. Though the western tradition has isolated theological activity to written and read scriptural texts—a tendency deeply influenced by the Cartesian legacy—theology is *first* performed and enacted only then written down and systematized. Orthodoxy (right believing) codified through doctrinal statements or propositions is "and inadequate way of framing theological understanding since it overlooks the necessity of divine incarnation with the particular, immediate and concrete."[52] However, orthopraxis (right action) denotes a truer integration of theory and practice that ignites transformational change. We perform orthopraxis guided by and inhabiting theological traditions (including sacred Scriptures), but hermeneutically improvised.

Second, practices build worlds, both symbolic and material. Practices—contextual and relational with no exceptions—are necessary for humans to build worlds of meaning and social relations. In its primary form, theology is a language of practice, enacted and embodied in the sacred and mundane alike. Like any language, meaning is facilitated by convention and routine. Practice is *habitus*—not by dull repetition but a dialectic of "preoccupied, active presence in the world."[53] Practices shape character as

49. Bennett et al., *Research in Practical Theology*, 60–80.
50. Bennett et al., *Research in Practical Theology*, 64.
51. Pattison, *Challenge of Practical Theology*, 77.
52. Bennett et al., *Research in Practical Theology*, 65.
53. Bourdieu, *Theory of Practice*, 52.

a *phronesis prudential* (practical wisdom) governed by and perfected in a vision of excellence normed in the community.[54] They are likewise *poesis*, creatively enlivening the everyday to reveal sacred value.[55]

Third, religion is more than "belief." All of this pushes religion beyond a "belief in" something, only a matter of cognition. It is a "complex system constituted by the practices of belonging, believing and behaving . . . as a form of 'lived experience.'"[56] Religion as cognitive belief and propositions is a paradigm largely shaped by Western Protestant and Catholic traditions that prioritize the interpretation and analysis of written texts to the neglect of the myriad of other artifacts (e.g., rituals, images, material culture) that express material and symbolic practices and rituals. To analyze Christian theology, then, is to recognize that the "church does not speak only in its sermons . . . and theological tomes" but also "in the manner of its being . . . the church shows its vision of things quite as much as it states it."[57]

Fourth, practices are value laden and revelatory—as practices build worlds, so they (and we) perform our truths. One of the effects of postmodernism is the fragmentation of meaning. According to Bennett et al., "if notions of virtue and good cannot be metaphysically or ontologically grounded . . . they may instead be realized in and through practice, and specifically, the regular habits by which we orient ourselves toward the good and the virtuous."[58] Religious practices like prayer, forgiveness, and hospitality can embody wisdom and value, even if they cannot be reduced to words or instantiated in texts.[59] Indeed, the scriptural texts and traditions are themselves a byproduct of practice. Theological inquiry always exists amid practices, which are performed and communicated within a complex network of instructional patterns and power structures. Part of practical theology's task is to draw out and surface the hidden presuppositions within the conduct of practice.

In contemporary practical theology, four trajectories have solidified as the dominant ways that practical theologians go about interrogating and assessing practice. They all share postmodern skepticism toward Enlightenment-based understandings of scientific empiricism, shifting

---

54. MacIntyre, *After Virtue*.
55. Walton, *Seeking Wisdom*, 7–9.
56. White and Hopkins, *Social Gospel*, 71.
57. Biggar, *Behaving in Public*, 80.
58. Bennett et al., *Research in Practical Theology*, 72.
59. See Bass et al., *Christian Practical Wisdom*.

the study of practice from objective, inductive, and neutral to reflexive, dialectical, and engaged[60]:

a. *Hermeneutical trajectory*: Representatives include James Fowler, Don Browning, and Martina Kumlehn. This trajectory understands practical theology as ultimately a hermeneutical activity and heavily factors in developments in philosophical hermeneutics such as Gadamer and Ricoeur.

b. *Transforming praxis trajectory*: Representatives include Elaine Graham, Mary McClintock Fulkerson, and Thomas Beaudoin. This trajectory draws heavily from liberation theology and critical social/poststructural theories. It places practical theology's emphasis on contributing to individual and social transformation through the critical engagement of power structures, discourses, and everyday practices.

c. *Neo-Aristotelian trajectory*: Primarily rooted in an American context, representatives include Craig Dykstra, Dorothy Bass, and Dianna Butler Bass. This trajectory draws heavily from appropriations of Aristotle in contemporary moral philosophy, especially through MacIntyre. It places emphasis on fostering character in moral and religious communities through virtue oriented practices, against modernity's overly individualistic and utilitarian frameworks that have eroded such capacities.

d. *Confessional trajectory*: Representatives include Ray Anderson, John Swinton, and Deborah van Deusen Hunsinger. This trajectory draws heavily from neo-orthodoxy as seen in Barth and Bonhoeffer. It places emphasis on supporting faith communities' performance of gospel witness through confessional forms.

My Position within Contemporary Practical Theological Methodology

Having overviewed the discipline through its key historical developments, core methodology, and dominant trajectories, I would now like to position myself within the field for this research project's reflexive evaluation of contemporary American evangelical perceptions of enterprise. The dynamic and uneven growth of capitalistic enterprise has challenged contemporary American evangelical theology's efforts to integrate Christian faith with capitalistic enterprise. As consumer capitalism has diffused into

---

60. Osmer, "Empirical Theology," 55–65.

non-market settings, it has shifted and fragmented spirituality toward consumer-oriented practices. For American evangelicalism, this raises the need to understand better how such forces have shaped its own spiritual practices and how a reframing of the relationship between theological belief and practice might be necessary to foster materially and spiritually transformative alternatives.

I proceed, first, by elaborating how consumer capitalism's diffusion has shifted religious expression. Then, I show how the transforming praxis and neo-Aristotelian trajectories are the most suited to draw out the effects of these shifts. Finally, I contend that these practical theological trajectories affirm a strengthening of theological reflexivity that functions not in isolation, but in interdisciplinary engagement with fields such as management ethics that are undergoing similar shifts.

Capitalism's Diffusion

I understand my positioning in reference to broader developments in religion, economics, and western society. From the end of World War II to the early 1970s, western capitalism experienced a period of enormous and rapid expansion. This time saw the rise of multinational corporations, mass communication, information technology, and international financial markets. A core feature of this expansion has been the proliferation of consumer market systems across global and social borders. As a result, consumer consumption has become an ever-more personal dimension of human experience.[61]

Later in the book, this phenomenon is analyzed in detail. Here, it is enough to note that the nature of capitalism's growth has challenged the consensus view for much of the nineteenth and twentieth century that economic and social modernization would eventually eliminate religious expression. That has not been the case—in many places, religious expression has intensified. What has occurred (particularly in the American context) has been a noticeable shift in religious expression—away from traditional mainline Protestant Christianity and toward more individual and material expressions of spirituality.[62]

Of note here is the effect that these trendlines have on spiritual and religious practices, particularly in American evangelicalism. As capitalism's mid-twentieth-century growth in America gained momentum, American evangelical fundamentalism's backing of corporate power "played a key role in creating institutions that would tie together conservative theology and

---

61. Perez, *Technological Revolutions*.
62. Fuller, *Spiritual but Not Religious*.

free market economics."[63] Many conservative Christian business leaders understood consumer markets as a mechanism to sustain a link between their own subculture and the broader sociopolitical order.[64] Conservative evangelical Christian opposition to the New Deal, for example, was grounded in the belief that a literal reading of the Bible supported free market capitalism as a sanctified economic system.[65]

As the language of spirituality has become more common in the late western world, so too has been the adoption of consumerism as a form of spirituality in which practitioners "make meaning, create identities, and participate in communities through acts of consumption."[66] In response to the increasingly diverse religious landscape and the growing influence of market capitalism, American evangelicalism adopted and modified features and products of the consumer market to stay relevant.[67] Churches and religious organizations ramped up the marketing of religiously themed products and services, formed alternative institutions specifically for sports and leisure (e.g., YMCA), and focused on broadcast activities in television and radio. This commodification of religious organization also included the emergence of the megachurch movement, which integrated a seeker-friendly consumer market style with elements of the prosperity gospel.[68]

A shift in American evangelical spiritual practices followed. Historically, American evangelicalism has been rooted in a conception of the Christian life as primarily a personal relationship with God. By placing belief in Jesus as a personal savior, the sinner is saved from God's judgment and called to share the gospel so that non-believers can also be saved. Discipleship is fundamentally a spiritual transformation that occurs inside a person and is expressed in moral obedience to biblical rules. Therefore, American evangelical spiritual practices have generally focused on individualized expressions: daily "quiet times" in personal Bible reading, prayer, sharing one's faith, and individual church attendance.[69] The "faith at work" movement that emerged in the 1980s largely affirmed these practices with an emphasis on workplace evangelism, moral duty, and individual hard work and excellence as expressions of godliness.[70] Largely,

---

63. Logan, "Commerce, Consumerism, and Christianity," 5.
64. Hammond, "God Is My Partner."
65. Grem, *Blessings of Business*.
66. Glover, *Paying Attention to God*, 11.
67. Moore, *Selling God*.
68. Marie, *Selling Christianity*.
69. Chan, *Spiritual Practices*.
70. Miller, *Consumer Religion*.

liturgical rituals in other Christian traditions were dismissed as secular and, in some cases, non-biblical.

Beginning in the latter twentieth century, calls arose within American evangelicalism to expand the individual focus of spirituality to include broader social concerns, including liturgical practices represented in Protestant, Catholic and Orthodox traditions. A large gathering of global evangelical leaders in the 1970s drafted "The Lausanne Covenant" and affirmed that evangelism and sociopolitical involvement were bound together. Progressive evangelicals such as Sider and Wallis called for more evangelical involvement in serving the poor and healing racial and social-class divides.[71] There was a growing influence from the charismatic Pentecostal movement (especially by the global south) that emphasized spirituality as an experiential reality.[72] More American evangelicals began to read spiritual writers such as Richard Foster who explored and affirmed practices within non-Protestant and Catholic sacramental and liturgical traditions such as Ignatian prayer.[73]

The cross-fertilization of spiritual practices has contributed to a more ecumenically aware evangelicalism with a deepened sensitivity to the social and relational dimensions inherent to theological practice. At the same time, the adoption of an eclectic set of spiritual practices devoid of strong communal centers and removed from their traditions has contributed to fragmented spiritualities.[74] This is reflective of broader shifts in religion and Western society. Wuthnow observed that the American religious landscape more generally has moved from a spirituality of dwelling to a spirituality of seeking. If the first speaks of being grounded in the firmness of home, tradition, and institution, the second speaks of fluid, consumer-like identities that are forged through negotiation, searching, and selecting. The postsecular milieu has exposed the deficiencies of both:

> Habitation spirituality encourages dependence on communities that are inherently undependable and fosters an idolization of particular places to the point that energies gravitate too much to those places rather than being deployed to the full round of human needs in a complex world. A spirituality of seeking in contrast is invariably too fluid to provide individuals with the

---

71. Sider, *Rich Christians*; Wallis, *Call to Conversion*.
72. Jenkins, *Next Christendom*.
73. See, for example, Seddon, *Gospel and Sacrament*.
74. Miller-McLemore, "Practical Theology."

social support they need or to encourage the stability and dedication required to grow spiritually and to mature in character.[75]

A spirituality focused on a reflective retrieval of wise practices presents an alternative. According to Wuthnow, it would "require individuals to engage reflectively in a conversation with their past, examining who they have been, how they have been shaped, and where they are headed."[76]

The data suggest that American evangelicalism is experiencing the effects of these shifts. For the bulk of the last thirty years, affiliation with American evangelicalism has held steady—at 40 percent in the 1970s compared to 41 percent at the turn of the century. During this stretch (especially in the 1980s and the rise of the "religious right" and "moral majority"), conservative evangelicalism remained a powerful political force. However, rapid changes are afoot, driven by generational turnover and a changing political order. Younger generations are leaving traditional religion faster than ever—according to the Pew Foundation, 23 percent of Generation X Americans (born between 1965 to 1980) claim no religious affiliation. That number rises to 34 percent of older millennials (born between 1981 to 1989), and to 36 percent of younger millennials (born between 1990 to 1996).

In the 1970s, research suggested that conservative evangelical American churches were growing faster than other denominations partly because of their comparatively more considerable emphasis on theological doctrine, which created a stickiness with members.[77] Now, that facet seems to be working in the opposite direction. Only 8 percent of young Americans identify as evangelicals. A 2015 Pew Research report found that one-third of white Americans raised in evangelical households depart the faith in adulthood, and nearly half of white evangelical Protestants under thirty say that their church should adjust traditional beliefs and practices or adopt modern beliefs and practices.

Intertwined here are dramatic shifts in socioeconomic and class perspectives. A 2018 Gallup survey found that fewer than 45 percent of young Americans have a favorable view of capitalism, representing a twelve-point decline since 2010. This has correlated with a growing racial wealth gap. A 2017 *New York Times* study found that for every $100 in white family wealth, black families hold just $5.04. A study in the same year by the Institute for Policy Studies showed that between 1983 and 2013, the wealth of the median black household declined 75 percent, and the median Latino household declined 50 percent (from $4,000 to $2,000). At the same

75. Wuthnow, *After Heaven*, 16.
76. Wuthnow, *After Heaven*, 16.
77. Kelley, *Conservative Churches*.

time, wealth for the median white household increased 14 percent from $102,000 to $116,800.

These shifts raise essential questions about the future viability of American evangelicalism's effort to integrate Christian faith and capitalistic enterprise. Is evangelicalism's espousal of capitalist systems as morally and spiritually transformational in need of revision? Is so, how can evangelical faith communities rejuvenate embodied spiritual practices?

Practical Theological Assessments

In assessing these questions, two trajectories in contemporary practical theology are drawn on throughout this book: transforming praxis and neo-Aristotelian. They are both necessary because, in complementary ways, they help surface consumer market capitalism's entanglements for spiritual practice. My purpose here is not to delve into their contributions in full detail but to capture the contours as a way of previewing them.

For surfacing the structural influences of late capitalism that can impose oppressive social dimensions within faith communities, the transforming praxis trajectory will be called upon. Critiquing and building on classic Marxism, critical social theorists (including the Frankfurt school) in the mid-twentieth century raised concerns about the ill social effects of capitalism's rapid growth—automation of labor, wage stagnation, and economic inequalities. Adorno argued that such concentration of social control in big government and big business in late capitalism could devalue individual freedom to resist oppression.[78] At the heart of this critique was a call for a better nuanced analysis of social forces. The present state of a society cannot be taken for granted. It needs critical lenses built on conceptions of human nature and values that can discern social inequalities and power imbalances. Among the most prominent, Habermas's theory of communicative action contended that capitalist markets' commodification of everyday life acts is technical rationality that colonizes deep forms of action, experience, and social organization necessary for robust living.[79]

At issue here is the structural logic of capitalism. Adam Smith championed an enlightened self-interest that would protect against greed and corruption. His argument was developed in the context of "small businesses marked by personal relationships in towns and villages in eighteenth-century England," but are now applied to "giant corporations whose revenues exceed those of small countries, as well as to large scale structural adjustments that

78. Adorno and Horkheimer, *Dialectic of Enlightenment*.
79. Osmer, "Empirical Practical Theology."

affect the economies of whole nations."[80] Capitalism sees the invisible hand of the market as translating selfishness and greed into common good. However, is this in and of itself not a form of religious idealism?

Economic globalization has a way of obscuring power differential under the guise of the workings of consumer markets, but intensifying them at the same time. This "soft power" is a form of top-down assertiveness that

> often find expressions in ways that are harder to see, for instance through lower paychecks, hidden prejudices that make it more difficult to get jobs or fair treatment before the law, and even the sort of romanticization that seeks to shape other people according to our fantasies.[81]

Indeed, one of the fundamental challenges to the logic of capitalism is the consensus data that greater material prosperity "is not matched by greater happiness, but is accompanied instead by greater social and individual distress, manifested, for example, in increasing crime and ill-health, such as depression."[82]

For much of its history, Western theology has tended "to affiliate itself with dominant processes of globalization and the mostly economic and cultural processes that undergird them."[83] Drawing on its liberationist influences, the transforming praxis stream of practical theology makes the point that this weakens theology's ability to offer a critique of its excesses. It also misaligns theology with a core scriptural theme—material wealth and power structures can be abused to harm others, with the vital point that the liberating God is on the side of the disenfranchised. American evangelicalism historically has accounted for socioeconomic inequalities individualistically.[84] The transforming praxis trajectory shows that this is an insufficient theological lens and that moral and spiritual transformation (especially in economic contexts) demands attention paid to structural forces.

There is abundant data to suggest that religion and spirituality can contribute to overall social and personal well-being as a form of spiritual and social capital.[85] Central to this contribution is religion's ability to foster strong relational collectives that connect members to each other and

---

80. Rieger, *Reconfigure the Common Good*, 45.
81. Rieger, *Reconfigure the Common Good*, 45.
82. Graham, "Virtuous Cycle," 247.
83. Graham, "Virtuous Cycle," 247.
84. Emerson and Smith, *Divided by Faith*.
85. For example, Eckersley, *Culture, Spirituality, Religion*; Swinton, "Spirituality and Mental Health."

broader community.[86] Contrasted with the profoundly utilitarian and instrumental ethic underlying consumer capitalism, faith communities can serve as outposts of intrinsicality.

However, then this demands that religion and spirituality synthesize belief and action. Drawing on Atherton, Graham posited a practical theological perspective of "performative faithful capital" where "belief and practice are indivisible, something also encapsulated well in understandings of *praxis*, as value-driven, value-directed action, or of *phronesis*, or practical wisdom."[87] Here, a vital link is established between communitarian ethics and virtue ethics—and between the transforming praxis trajectory and the neo-Aristotelian trajectory, the second significant trajectory that informs my positioning in the discipline of practical theology.

If the transforming praxis trajectory enables the critical analysis of the social structures and forces of capitalism's diffusion, the neo-Aristotelian trajectory enables a critical analysis of how consumer capitalism can influence conceptions of human flourishing. In part, the growth of capitalistic forces has sparked a revival in virtue ethics. In contrast to Kantian or utilitarian traditions in moral reasoning, virtue ethics has focused on the qualities that mark moral agents. Virtue based approaches have tended to reference back to Aristotle's conception of the good life as the pursuit of happiness, or *eudaimonia*.[88] For Aristotle, every person acts toward some desired end. A virtuous person is a person with proper character traits, developed and nurtured through habits in the context of a community. In the Christian intellectual tradition, both Augustine and Aquinas adopted Aristotle's basic notion into Christian theological frameworks that conceptualize the good life as fulfillment in God through the practice of the core of virtues of faith, hope, and love (and empowered by divine grace).

Spearheading a revival of virtue ethics in the twentieth century was the work of moral philosopher MacIntyre. Humans are *telos*-oriented, and virtues are the means by which we strive. Practices are

> any coherent and complex form of socially established cooperative human activity through which goods internal to that form of activity are realised in the course of trying to achieve those standards of excellence which are appropriate to, and partially definitive of, that form of activity, with the result that human

---

86. Putnam, *Bowling Alone*.
87. Graham, "Virtuous Cycle," 227. See also Atherton, *Transfiguring Capitalism*.
88. Anscombe, "Modern Moral Philosophy."

powers to achieve excellence, and human conceptions of the ends and goods involved, are systematically extended.[89]

For MacIntyre, the central problem of modernity is that it has undermined intrinsically valuable forms of life. In place of integral communities and embedded individuals creating meaning in their lives by finding place and purpose in those communities, "modernity has substituted the incoherent set of possibilities for money-making and power-wielding."[90]

Money and power are inherent to any set of practices, but the contradiction of capitalism's ideology is the instrumentalizing of them as ultimate ends and external goods, rather than as resources that "can be organized for the sake of goods internal to practices."[91] Crucially ignored in instrumentalizing schemes, according to MacIntyre, is fundamental human finitude. Human flourishing is a relationally bound pursuit because intrinsic goods like love and friendship are necessarily manifested in relationships. These virtues of acknowledged dependence "enable agents to appreciate human vulnerability and to respond with appropriate forms of care."[92]

MacIntyre's work has catalyzed a variety of critical ethical approaches across disciplines (including business ethics) that assess the potentially harmful effects of consumer oriented capitalism on human flourishing.[93] At its individualist and materialist excesses, consumption amounts to a spirituality (attachment) with liturgical features (buying), but to deficient ends.[94] It envisions human *telos* as acquirable through products and services, with minimal relational and social dimensions.

Contemporary practical theology's understanding of practice owes much to MacIntyre.[95] The neo-Aristotelian trajectory as seen in MacIntyre and virtue approaches generally are necessarily corrective to the deceptions of consumerist spiritualities that human flourishing can be acquired like one acquires products and services in consumer markets. Cavanaugh pinned the unfulfilled promises of "free market" consumerism to a misconception of freedom. In free market ideology, freedom is defined negatively as freedom *from* (interference and external coercion), resulting in an economic model based on sheer individual want and arbitrary desire. This leaves out crucial questions about what drives consumer desires and toward what

89. MacIntyre, *After Virtue*, 187.
90. Noonan, "Capitalist Modernity," 191.
91. Knight and Blackledge, "Revolutionary Aristotelianism," 44.
92. Cobb, "Acknowledged Dependence," 26.
93. Garcia-Ruiz and Rodriguez-Lluesma, "Cosumption Practices," 511–15.
94. Rittenhouse, *Meaningful Lives*.
95. Bennett et al., *Research in Practical Theology*, 64.

ends they are directed. Only on the surface are consumers in this system attached to "things." In actuality, they are detached, restlessly cycling through goods and services that are offered in ephemeral markets that depersonalize sources of production.

"Human relationships fall away from the process of buying products," such that "relationships become more direct between ourselves and our things."[96] Yet, in the Christian traditions, there are offerings of an alternative conception of freedom wherein genuine freedom is not freedom *from* constraint but freedom *for* human flourishing. Both Augustine and Aquinas, for example, conceived of human freedom in terms of the spiritual capacities to pursue union with God, where the ability of an agent to choose is a necessary but not sufficient condition. Right human desire guided by virtues mark the way. For Cavanaugh, this enables a twofold counterforce: first, a non-arbitrary means of critiquing injurious features of consumer markets; and second, a remedy outside the centralized power of the state, as far as faith communities can foster materially and spiritually transformative alternative practices.

The Role of Reflexivity

As is explored throughout this book, the transforming praxis and neo-Aristotelian trajectories within practical theology offer rich ways to resource contemporary American evangelical theology's effort to integrate Christian faith and capitalistic enterprise. However, *how* they do so is just as important. To repeat a critical point made in the introduction, the answer to the individualist-materialist excesses of consumerist spirituality is not a non-individualist, non-materialist, non-consumerist spirituality. Instead, it is a *reflexive* spirituality that nurtures capacities to discern.

This stems from pedagogical convictions within contemporary practical theology itself. Like many other disciplines that deal in human values, contemporary practical theology often involves complex moral reasoning and human experience. Apart from reflection on and in action, preconfigured protocols are insufficient. Experiential learning must be built in. Extending the work of influential advocates such as Schon, for more than three decades practical theology has emphasized the importance of reflection.[97] More recently, however, calls for a movement beyond reflection have been identified on the grounds that reflection is ultimately a reinforcement of

---

96. Cavanaugh, *Being Consumed*, 45.
97. Schon, *Reflective Practicioner.* See also Graham et al., *Theological Reflection.*

the "binary divide of subject and object."⁹⁸ The risk that reflection runs is that it becomes overly individualized and objectifies the "other." Reflexivity calls attention to the embodied multiplicities of self-in-relation to the other, hopefully as a means of deeper engagement with others.⁹⁹

According to Bennett et al., if

> reflection suggests looking thoughtfully at something—usually at some length, perhaps with the benefit of hindsight, and with a critical eye, then being "reflexive" suggests additionally looking thoughtfully at one's own self—at what I am like, at how I see what is outside of myself, how I affect it, or how my seeing of it affects how I present it.¹⁰⁰

This is quite critical for contemporary American evangelical theology's relationship with capitalistic enterprise. The two do not stand apart from each other—their shared historical lineages and the subterranean ways that the values of capitalistic enterprise operate demand of American evangelicalism, a reflexive posture as much as a reflective one.

Inherent to practical theology's emphasis on reflexivity is a commitment to interdisciplinarity. Reflexivity instills an epistemic obligation to look beyond the boundaries of one's own familiar networks toward the unfamiliar in pursuit of interdisciplinary dialogue. Bridge theories should be constructed between disciplines while at the same time respecting the integrity of reasoning strategies within each discipline. Huyssteen called this a "transversal reasoning"¹⁰¹ that is not about arbitrarily opening ourselves up or closing ourselves off to other viewpoints, but rather it is about what it means to discover an epistemic space that allows for the kind of "interdisciplinary critical evaluation that includes a critical self-evaluation and optimal understanding. . . . The fragile public space created in interdisciplinary dialogue is the practical theologians' ecotone, which provides for a wide reflective equilibrium."¹⁰²

Interestingly, both poststructural and neo-Aristotelian influences have found root in critical approaches to business and management ethics. Modern business management evolved in the early twentieth century with stress on productivity and output. Frederick Taylor, an engineer by trade, provided one of the first management theories.¹⁰³ The innovation of Taylor's system

---

98. Canning, "Reflective Practitioner," 11.
99. Veling, "In the Name of Who?"
100. Bennett et al., *Research in Practical Theology*, 34.
101. Huyssteen, *Shaping of Rationality*, 421.
102. Muller, "Postfoundational Practical Theology," 2.
103. See Taylor, *Principles of Scientific Management*.

was the idea that efficiency could be enhanced by analyzing workflows.[104] He challenged the prevailing assumption that an increase in the intensity of a laborer's work automatically equaled an increase in economic value. Using several time and motions studies, Taylor argued that the focus of management should be on an optimization of the workflow process. Thus, Taylor argued for a management bureaucracy in an organization that was devoted to training employees and controlling outputs.[105]

Capitalism's rapid industrial growth had created a need for better management systems and Taylor's ideas spread quickly. However, they did not go unchallenged. A vocal critic was Max Weber. Like Taylor, Weber espoused a bureaucratic organizational control equipped with standardized procedures and a focus on efficiency.[106] However, as a sociologist, Weber diverged from Taylor by warning of the social dangers of an excessive individualist-materialist emphasis, like the one manifested in the Protestant work ethic. It was an "iron cage" that reduced human workers to output figures, degrading their moral basis and autonomy.[107] To break free from the shackles, what is needed is the "articulation of alternative moral points of view upon which to develop a new paradigm for management."[108]

However, it was not until societal attitudes in the United States toward business began to change in the 1960s that critical approaches began to emerge in the business ethics guild. De George pointed out a few of the primary drivers of this shift: a growing distrust of the partnership between business and government as expressed in the military-industrial complex that played itself out in World War II, the Cold War, and Vietnam; the surging economic dominance the United States was imposing on the world stage, leading to the emergence of multinational conglomerates and widespread consumerism; and the awakening of the environmental consciousness in response to the rise of innovation in the chemical industry.[109]

The increased attention paid to corporate activity prompted two critical reactions, the first being the introduction of the idea of "corporate social responsibility" by corporations as a means of combating the negativity.[110] Alongside this, there was the increased involvement of business schools and academic thinkers (in business and in philosophy, theology,

---

104. Drucker, *Management*, 181.
105. Littler, "Understanding Taylorism," 198.
106. Clegg, "Moral Philosophy of Management," 867–69.
107. Weber, *Protestant Ethic*, 181.
108. Dyck and Schroeder, "Management, Theology," 707.
109. De George, *History of Business Ethics*.
110. Cheit, *Business Establishment*.

and sociology as well) in the theorizing about the ethical concerns in the modern corporation.

The emergence of stakeholder theory (which is analyzed in detail in later chapters) is representative of this shift. Critical ethical approaches were a direct challenge to the dominant free market paradigm at the time, encapsulated by the "shareholder theory" set forth by Nobel laureate economist Milton Friedman. He contended that the sole purpose of an enterprise was to maximize shareholder profits within legal limits. R. Edward Freeman, a philosopher by training who was teaching at the Darden School of Business at the University of Virginia, directly challenged this perspective. The volatile growth of market capitalism, he contended, required broader ethical analysis about how an enterprise could maximize value for all its stakeholders, not just shareholders.

As stakeholder theory has dislodged shareholder theory as the dominant paradigm, both poststructural and neo-Aristotelian variations have emerged. Solomon, for example, represented a strong neo-Aristotelean account. For Solomon, business ethics has suffered for some time from a false distinction of domain that economics focuses on systems (where amoral determinative causes are at play) while ethics focus on individual behavior (where moral voices are at play). This has unduly severed a narrow view of individual ethical behavior within an organization from the broader view of how businesses as organizations systematically affect societies, when in fact, they belong to and need each other. An emphasis on character, for Solomon, corrects this and

> fills the void between institutional behaviorism and an excessive emphasis on free will and personal autonomy that remains oblivious to context, the reality of office work, and the force of peer and corporate pressures. . . . It provides a locus for responsibility without sacrificing the findings of 'management science.'[111]

For Aristotle, it was important to think of the individual as a member of the larger community (the *polis*), for "what is best in us—our virtues—are in turn defined by the larger community, and there is, therefore, no ultimate split of antagonism between individual self-interest and the greater public good."[112] Looked at this way, business ethics meaningfully engages on the ground reality, shifting "the critical focus from oneself as a full-blooded person occupying a significant role in a productive organization to an abstract

---

111. Solomon, "Victims of Circumstances?," 44.
112. Solomon, "Corporate Roles, Personal Virtues," 73.

role-transcendent morality that necessarily finds itself empty-handed" when applied to real corporate settings.[113]

With its focus on theological practices as *telos*-oriented and contextually embedded, practical theology is a future oriented discipline. Yet, "this dimension . . . is not always acknowledged in research endeavors."[114] A reflexive interdisciplinary posture of transversal reasoning can help. In drawing parallels between developments in business ethics and practical theology for the purposes of application to contemporary American evangelical theology, I am focused on innovating new links between disciplines, rather than merely describing known links. The dynamic and uneven growth of capitalistic enterprise has sparked significant reevaluation in the fields of academic business ethics and practical theology. A practical theological interdisciplinary model of what Berg and Ganzevoort called "designing-creative" enables the practical theologian to "not so much prepare for what may happen, but to envision what we want to see happen . . . to facilitate a transformation that fosters love, justice, healing, growth, and harmony."[115]

Conclusion

Where American evangelicalism evolves from the fundamental shifts sparked by the 2016 election of Trump is unclear. What is clear is "a self-contained evangelical spirituality is in danger to itself."[116] According to Gillett, "if a spirituality is not broader than the very essentials of evangelicalism it rarely survives well the transmission from one generation to another."[117] A starting point for this book is that a revisioning of the integration of Christian faith with the forces of capitalistic enterprise is crucial for the future viability of contemporary American evangelical theology. Understood through the perspective of the discipline of practical theology, this amounts to a reframing of how religious belief and practice interact to foster embodied spiritualities.

The concern of this chapter has been to shape the contours of the practical theological methodology that guide this book, with a central concern for the link among theology, practice, and ethics. I did this, first, by providing an overview of the discipline of practical theology, charting its critical historical developments, core methodology, and dominant contemporary

---

113. Solomon, "Corporate Roles, Personal Virtues," 74.
114. Berg and Ganzevoort, "Art of Creating Futures," 182.
115. Berg and Ganzevoort, "Art of Creating Futures," 182–83.
116. Chan, "Spiritual Practices," 250.
117. Gillett, *Trust and Obey*, 31.

trajectories. Then, I positioned myself within these trajectories, explaining that I drew particularly on the transforming praxis and neo-Aristotelian steams to assess capitalism's diffusion into nonmarket contexts and the effects on evangelical spiritual practice.

2

What Are Potential Roadblocks to Contemporary American Evangelical Reflexivity?

Before proceeding to a substantive analysis of the theme of transformation, on the heels of last chapter's emphasis on practical theological reflexivity, I first want to take up potential initial obstacles to the exercise of reflexivity in contemporary American evangelical theology. The exercise of theological reflexivity within faith communities often encounters resistance not from without, but within. For American evangelicalism, which places a premium on integrated belief systems, exploring the ambiguities of practice might be unsettling, especially since, as McGrath observes, "there is widespread agreement within the evangelical theological community that evangelicals have not paid adequate attention to the issues of theological method."[1] The purpose of this chapter is to anticipate early objections to reflexivity that might arise in contemporary American evangelical theology. I focus on two potential roadblocks: first, American evangelical theology's allegiance to foundationalism; and second, its concern to safeguard scriptural authority.

Foundationalism

Contemporary American evangelical theology has historically grounded its theological methodology in epistemic foundationalism. This is to secure an alleged objective rationality for the construction of a comprehensive Christian worldview. I argue in this chapter that such a scheme inhibits the strengthening of theological reflexivity because it underemphasizes natural

---

1. McGrath, "Method," 10.

human epistemic limits. Recognition of these limits is essential for the postsecular exercise of theological reflexivity. They are also scriptural.

A brighter spotlight on the theological method requires practical theologians to thoroughly engage philosophical concepts and categories. If the theological method is defined as how thinkers think about God and related themes, then philosophical epistemology bears heavily. Epistemology is the branch of philosophy focused on account of knowledge: its defining components, its substantive conditions or sources, and its limits of justification.[2]

Contemporary American evangelical theological perceptions of enterprise have been formed in an epistemological environment based mainly on foundationalism, which posits a reliable account of epistemological justification. The central epistemological tension in contemporary American evangelical theology has been the extent to which it requires classical foundationalism. I argue that a theological method contextualized to a postsecular study of contemporary American evangelical theology mandates an epistemology that incorporates a broader concern for non/post-foundationalist positions than has generally been the case.

In contemporary philosophy, the epistemological positions on the justification of knowledge are generally subdivided among four main options: (a) foundationalism, which understands the justification for knowledge in basic, universal, and unquestioned foundational beliefs that give rise to contingent beliefs; (b) coherentism, which understands the justification for knowledge in terms of the coherence of beliefs to one another in a system or web of belief;[3] (c) reliabilism, which understands the justification for knowledge in terms of the reliability of the belief-forming process; and (d) pragmatism, which shares and critiques each of the others and understands the justification for knowledge in terms of the consequential goals, ends, and norms that beliefs support.[4]

As discussed in the previous chapter, Descartes was a beginning point for modern Western philosophy. His quest for epistemic certainty sought a project of complete skepticism and was led by the supposed universal value of reason. Even though most who followed him diverged from his version of foundationalism, Descartes was a beginning point for Enlightenment inquiry because he set in place a foundationalist agenda.

While a foundationalist agenda carried the Enlightenment project for some time, its initial cracking began soon after its inception, with Kant. It is difficult to overestimate the long-term effects of Kant on perceptions about

---

2. Moser, *Oxford Handbook of Epistemology*, 2.
3. Quine and Ullian, *Web of Belief*, 3–8.
4. Audi, *Epistemology*, 206–36.

the role of the mind in framing knowledge claims for broader Western philosophy, especially Protestant thought from which American evangelicalism was eventually derived. Critiquing both the so called rationalist and empiricists of early foundationalism, Kant asserted "knowledge emerges at the interpart of the data of the senses (the content) and the categories of the mind (the structure)."[5] In other words, the mind does not simply passively receive information, as the foundationalist epistemologies central to both Descartes and Locke asserted. Over time, Kant's turn to the subject became entrenched in western philosophy and theology.

As North American Christian theology began to grapple with Kant in the nineteenth century, a divide emerged between liberal and conservative theologies along epistemological lines. Trying to preserve foundationalism, liberals appealed to "universal human experience of the religious" while conservatives "devised a foundationalist theological method that appealed to an inerrant Bible, the veracity of which was thought to be unimpeachable by the canons of human reason."[6] As American evangelical theology formally developed into the twentieth century, it did so from this conservative line.

This is clear in the emphasis that modern and contemporary American evangelical theology has placed on the concept of "worldview."[7] It expresses a conceptual objective "to provide a comprehensive explanation of reality that is rooted in the Word of God" over and against modernity's secularizing forces that squeezed religious belief out of public life and reduced it to the realm of personal piety.[8] Two figures factored strongly. One was nineteenth- and twentieth-century Dutchman Abraham Kuyper. Lamenting the "storm of modernism" that had taken hold of both America and Europe, Kuyper argued that two "life systems," modernism and Christianity, were in heated battle.[9] In defense, Christian theology cannot survive with an atomistic approach but instead must demonstrate the comprehensive superiority of the Christian view of the world.

The other was Francis Schaeffer, who was enormously influential to lay audiences with his trilogy of publications emphasizing the rational order of

5. Clark, *To Know and Love God*, 55.

6. Grenz, *Renewing*, 112.

7. The English word *worldview* is derived from the German word *Weltanschauung*. There is consensus that *Weltanschauung* was coined by Kant. See Naugle, *Worldview*, 58. The term itself played a limited role in his thinking, but because of the broader influence of his epistemology it "evolved rather quickly to refer to an intellectual conception of the universe from the perspective of a human knower" (Naugle, *Worldview*, 58).

8. Naugle, *Worldview*, 5.

9. Kuyper, *Lectures*, 11.

Christianity.[10] For Schaeffer, "The Christian system is a unity of thought . . . and this system is the only system that will stand up to all the questions that are presented to us as we face the reality of existence."[11] These reactionary sentiments have sustained a defense of rational totality, which by its very nature, gravitates toward a strong form of epistemic foundationalism.[12] Thus, North American evangelical theology, with very few exceptions, has sought to defend a theological method deeply rooted in foundationalism.[13]

However, this raises an intriguing question. Why is it that outside evangelicalism the demise of classical foundationalism has been declared as "the closest thing to a philosophical consensus in decades"?[14] The answer lies in the arrival of postmodernism. It has challenged evangelical theology's close association with the "universal rationality of the Enlightenment."[15]

Postmodernism cannot be distilled to a single movement and is "a highly complex phenomenon encompassing a variety of elements."[16] Its central challenge to foundationalism was an "incredulity toward metanarrative."[17] Instead of understanding reality as existing "out there" and to which human language and perception correspond, reality is constructed by social and cultural conventions particular to the speaker. "As a result, no simple, one-to-one relationship exists between language and the world. Nor can any single description provide an accurate 'map' of the world."[18] This struck at the heart of evangelical theology's comprehensive worldview project and prompted a counter-reaction. Particularly, conservative contemporary American evangelical theology has tended to rebuff any accommodation

---

10. Schaeffer, *God Who Is There*; *He Is There*; *Escape from Reason*.
11. Schaeffer, *God Who Is There*, 176.
12. Henry, *Fortunes*, 163.
13. One of the few exceptions was Bloesch, *Essentials*. There were evangelicals such as Moreland and DeWeese who criticized classic foundationalism as being overly ambitious but still wanted to preserve some soft foundationalism. See Moreland and DeWeese, "Premature Report," 81–108. To be clear, I am not trying to construct a strawman by arguing that contemporary evangelical theology largely supports classic foundationalism in order to tear the strawman down. Rather, I am acknowledging as part of my argument that even though most contemporary evangelical theologians would not want to defend classical foundationalism, there is still substantial support for what has been termed "modified" or "soft" foundationalism. See, for example, Carson, *Gagging of God*, who called for a chastened foundationalism.
14. Westphal, "Reader's Guide," 11.
15. McGrath, "Theological Method," 33.
16. Grenz, *Renewing*, 108.
17. Lyotard, *Postmodern*, xiv.
18. Grenz, *Renewing*, 108.

of postmodernism, claiming that its relativist epistemology represents an attack on foundational "objective truth claims."[19]

However, I contend that contemporary American evangelical theology's reaction against the relativism of postmodernism ignores the contributions brought to the theological method by post/non-foundationalist epistemologies, specifically pragmatism. Unquestionably, there are extensions of postmodern ideology that undermine the basic structures of evangelical theology and indeed theism in general. For example, deconstructionist applications nihilistically eliminate any transcendent concept of the divine.[20] However, to dismiss the entire postmodern epistemic apparatus is to miss a fundamentally crucial theological point: as finite beings, humans have epistemic limits that prevent absolute foundationalist certainty.

A nuanced reading of postmodern epistemology shows that the philosophical lineage of pragmatism drawn from Wittgenstein through Rorty benefits evangelical theological method by providing a healthy dose of epistemic humility.[21] This acknowledgment of the limits of human knowledge has resonance not only philosophically, but perhaps more crucial for evangelical theology, scripturally. Consider the claims of absolute certainty tucked within classical foundationalism read against the backdrop of the story of the garden in Genesis 1–3, a text usually seen by evangelical theology as systematically imperative. They appear eerily similar to the first and ultimate "sin" of humanity in Genesis 3:1–7: an absolute claim on knowledge by creatures that is reserved only for the Creator.[22]

What are the related contributions of Wittgenstein and Rorty? First, Wittgenstein demonstrated that a classic referentialist account of language, in which words have fixed meanings that "name" objects and refer to realities outside the account, underplays contextuality.[23] Much as Kant critiqued classic foundationalism for underemphasizing the human mind's role in shaping knowledge, Wittgenstein critiqued it for not giving an adequate account of how language and context determine meaning. Language use is practiced within a broader context of a language game or form of life that provide rules for playing. Meaning is "bound up with use, and use is relative to the conventions of a community of practitioners."[24]

19. Groothuis, *Truth*, 69.
20. See Caputo, *Hoping*.
21. Smith, *Who's Afraid of Relativism?*, 29.
22. Smith, *Who's Afraid of Relativism?*, 29; Ansell, "Call," 40–43; Enns, "Sin," 104.
23. See Wittgenstein, *Philosophical*.
24. Smith, *Who's Afraid of Relativism?*, 46. I agree with Milbank on this point, though not his entire project built on it. This "linguistic turn" represents a "theological turn" that returns theological methodology to a more "orthodox" Christian account. See Milbank, *Word*, 84–90.

Second, in developing Wittgenstein, Rorty critiqued Western epistemological inquiry's long-held concern for the "transaction between the 'knowing subject' and 'reality.'"[25] If Wittgenstein and other pragmatists are correct that language is decidedly determinative and not merely representative, then the search for grounds of knowledge in privileged representations is heading in the wrong direction entirely.

For Rorty, rationality and epistemic justification are partly a matter of sociological conditioning and practices as far as they are determined by what "society lets us say."[26] Epistemology becomes a consideration of human social practices more than it is a foundational search for correspondence between internal conditions of knowledge and external "reality." This demands that it be more attuned to the "contingency and particularity of human finitude, to the conditions of creaturehood."[27]

At times, Rorty and Wittgenstein pushed their philosophical innovations to frontiers that are admittedly difficult to reconcile with classical Christian theism (to say nothing of contemporary evangelical theology). Wittgenstein, for example, distinguished life of faithful belief in God from any conscious reality of a deity after death, about which he remained skeptical. Rorty embraced the religious and spiritual components of human beings only when stripped of any metaphysicality.[28] However, what if one approached the postmodern sentiments of Wittgenstein and Rorty with a purpose of appropriating pragmatic and coherentist insights for sound theological method?[29] Having critiqued contemporary American evangelical theology's over reliance on classic foundationalism as a compromise of epistemic humility, I want to close this discussion by briefly highlighting an example of a post/non-foundationalist epistemology that harmonizes with central evangelical theological convictions.

The example is reformed epistemology, which emerged from the writings of America philosophers Plantinga and Wolterstorff. Its central thesis is that religious belief can be entirely rational without any appeal to evidence or argument. Classic foundationalism, according to Plantinga, fails on two fronts. First, it misses the fact that many beliefs are taken by rational humans as rational but do not share the features of foundational or properly basic beliefs, such as the world has existed for more than five minutes

25. Rorty, *Philosophy*, 9.
26. Rorty, *Philosophy*, 170–74.
27. Smith, *Who's Afraid of Relativism?*, 84.
28. Rorty and Vattimo, *Future*, 55–59.
29. As Smith recalled, Augustine approached Plato in the manner of the Hebrews plundering Egyptian gold for the glory of God. See Smith, *Who's Afraid of Relativism?*

or other persons exist. Second, it is self-referentially incoherent in that it presupposes a foundational criterion for rationality that cannot be proved by the same standard. Instead of supposed underlying foundational beliefs, warrant is conferred to religious beliefs in reformed epistemology by reliable belief-forming processes. In both critiques, reformed epistemology is surfacing a core problem for any evangelical theological method that strives for foundationalist certainty: how does one account for the role of experience in the formation of religious belief?

Contributing to the desire for epistemological certainty in contemporary American evangelical theology, I contend, is a misconstrual of the nature of experience. Going back to at least the time of John Wesley in the late eighteenth century, it has been common to identify four normative sources for theological and doctrinal development: scripture, tradition, reason, and experience.[30] This framework has generated suspicion toward the formative role of experience among some conservative evangelical theologians.[31]

This is precisely where I want to draw attention in analyzing the contributions of a model like reformed epistemology to a theological method contextualized to twenty-first-century American enterprise. The positioning of experience alongside Scripture, tradition, and reason fails to identify the precise nature of experience. It is not merely a "source for theology . . . but the primary lens through which human beings access any and all scientific, moral, or theological knowledge."[32]

In the introduction, I noted that as market capitalist societies become increasingly modernized, religious expression has not disappeared as secularization theory predicted but rather shifted away from mainline traditional Protestant belief and toward more individualized and materialized spirituality, reflecting the pull of consumerist capitalism. In a classic foundationalist model of theological methodology, it is difficult to account for this shift credibly. If theological belief is only a matter of securing universal, rational foundations, then the intensive and extensive immersions of capitalism should have no bearing on the nature of belief. There are no grounds for critiquing, for example, the capitalistic excesses of individualism and materialism. However, in an epistemological model such as reformed epistemology, this experience can be accounted for and critiqued precisely because it acknowledges that experience plays a decisive role in shaping religious belief.

30. See Thorsen, *Wesleyan Quadrilateral*.
31. Ramm, *Evangelical Heritage*, 13; Crisp, "Faith and Experience," 68.
32. Scharen and Vigen, "Theological Justifications," in *Ethnography as Christian Theology*, 63.

A theological methodology grounded in a post/non-foundationalist epistemology scripturally-sound creaturely limits meaningfully contributes to contemporary American evangelical theology's integrative quest. It does so by providing a mechanism for interrogating how its own belief systems and faith practices have been implicitly shaped by consumerist instrumentality.

Scriptural Authority

In the previous section, I contended that a theological method contextualized to postsecularism requires an epistemology that incorporates a broader concern for non/post-foundationalist positions than has generally been the case in American evangelical theology. In this part, I explain how a post/non-foundationalist epistemology affects perhaps the most prominent theological theme associated with the evangelical theological method: the authority of Scripture.

The authority of Scripture represents one of Bebbington's four central features of classical evangelicalism. For American evangelicalism, it has featured prominently in disputes over the doctrine of inerrancy and postmodernism, even serving as a proxy for the various political and social "culture wars" that have marked American public discourse on the Bible.[33]

If a high authority of the Bible is commonly associated with American evangelicalism, so too is the criticism that evangelical understandings of biblical authority have often amounted to "biblicism," or the idolization of the written text.[34] The charge has various iterations. In critical biblical scholarship, the term generally refers to an approach to reading the biblical texts "literally" that ignores historical and cultural factors, metaphorical use of language, or the premodern perspective of the ancient writers.[35] In sociology, it has been defined "as an interpretive tradition mediated by a complex set of sociocultural practices and textual ideologies."[36]

Evangelical biblical scholars are generally apt to defend these criticisms as misunderstandings of what they mean by "literal," not a wooden literalism, but one that seeks the plain reading of the text according to

---

33. Setzer and Shefferman, *Bible*, 95–108. Knoll made the astute observation that while contemporary American conservative evangelical theology has coalesced around a narrow understanding of scriptural authority, American Christianity was itself an inheritor of a rather diverse set of models of biblical authority from seventeenth-century Europe. See Knoll, *Word*, 25–145.

34. Stackhouse, "Evangelical," 47.

35. Crook, "Miracles"; Crapanzano, "Literalism."

36. Juzwik, "Biblicism," 335.

normal conventions of interpretation. For example, Klein et al. pointed out that the contemporary evangelical emphasis on a literal hermeneutic dates back to at least the time of the Reformation. The grammatical-historical method arose as a contrast to what can be loosely called the allegorical approach, which was the dominant hermeneutical approach during the first millennium of church history.[37]

A broader issue here for the theological method is not so much whether contemporary evangelical theological readings of the scriptural text amount to biblicism, but rather whether the concept of Scripture operative within contemporary evangelical theology readings is epistemically consistent. Conservative evangelical defenses of scriptural authority often work off the assumption of a "fixed text."[38] The Bible is treated as an established and unchanging document that contains the contents of God's revelation, which then exercises unilateral and non-conditioned authority over Christian conduct and practice. In its reliance on a classic foundationalist epistemology that underplays the role of language in the hermeneutical process, I assert that the concept of a completely fixed text is untenable.

Contemporary American evangelical theological readings of Scripture grounded in a theoretical fixed text are seeking a universal foundation on which to rest scriptural authority, but is such a foundation possible? Already, if revelation is mediated through a historically situated person such as Jesus of Nazareth and then witnessed to in a historically situated set of texts such as the New Testament corpus, then an ahistorical universal foundation is untenable. Huyssteen explains: "What we are calling 'revelation,' and what we are interpreting as God's revelation, shares in the ambiguities of history and is therefore by necessity part of the limited, fallibilist form of all of our knowledge."[39] Moreover, pervasive oral traditions in Middle Eastern cultures during the biblical period make the concept of an original fixed-text implausible.[40]

---

37. Klein et al., *Biblical Interpretation*. An allegorical hermeneutic can be seen in early figures such as Philo and, at times, by the biblical writers themselves. The use of the Old Testament by New Testament writers presents, in my opinion, a serious challenge to the strong emphasis placed on a "literal" hermeneutic in conservative evangelicalism. At the very least, New Testament writers seem to stray with some frequency from a literal hermeneutic. As Hays said, "Let us not deceive ourselves about this: Paul would flunk our introductory exegesis course" (Hays, *Echoes*, 181).

38. See Treier, *Scripture*.

39. Huyssteen, "What Makes Us Human?," 152.

40. See Dunn, *Jesus Remembered*; Ehrman, *Misquoting Jesus*. This is different from saying that there is not vast manuscript support for the textual transmission process that produced modern interpretations of scripture. See Blomberg, *Can We Still Believe?*

Is a theological method possible that values the evangelical priority for Scripture but also accounts for the shortcomings of a fixed-text approach and moves beyond classical foundationalism? Vanhoozer's canonical-linguistic approach represents a convincing method, and it serves as the basic model from which I operated on the question of scriptural authority.[41] Vanhoozer applied Plantinga's account of warrant "to stretch his insight into human interpretative faculties" and the proper role of scriptural authority.[42] A truly biblical evangelical theology, for Vanhoozer, is one that seeks alignment with the central narrative of redemption found within Scripture more than it does with foundationalism. Following Sternberg, Vanhoozer argued that such a theology encompassed the "redemptive-historical substance of the biblical text . . . and the redemptive-hermeneutical form."[43] Thus, two levels were present: the drama of redemption (God speaking to the reader in and through the biblical text) and the drama of reading (the subsequent response of the reader).[44]

A dramatized theology is Vanhoozer's way of countering the heavy foundationalist and propositional approaches in modern evangelical theology that tended to reduce revelation to doctrinal propositions. On this, Vanhoozer showed influence from Barth and Balthasar. Barth posited God's self-revelation in Jesus Christ as a starting point for theology, which effectually subordinated the form of God's revelation in Scripture to the God revealed in Scripture.

Balthasar similarly argued that divine revelation is not a fixed object of examination but a movement of action by God in the world.[45] By attending to Barth and Balthasar, Vanhoozer stressed, evangelical theology can see that it does not need to "choose between God as speaker and God as an actor. Nor should we choose between theology as solely propositional or solely personal."[46] Here, language is a form of action that can refer to both history and subjective experience, but in a way that shapes those realities as much as it portrays them.

Applied to perceptions of enterprise, a keen benefit is gained by contemporary evangelical theology construing the relationship between language and scriptural authority in this way. One of the residues of economic intensification has been the tying of human identity to professional status.

---

41. Vanhoozer, "Voice."
42. Vanhoozer, "Voice," 87.
43. Vanhoozer, "Voice," 65. See Sternberg, *Poetics*.
44. See also Barton, "Interpretation."
45. Balthasar, *Theodrama*, 25–50.
46. Vanhoozer, "Voice," 73.

According to Michaelson et al., "In the human quest for meaning, work occupies a central position.... Most adults spend the majority of their waking hours at work, which often serves as a primary source of purpose, belongingness, and identity."[47]

For contemporary evangelical theology to engage this milieu in which consumer capitalism pivotally shapes human value, it must incorporate a dynamic concept of scriptural authority that does more than enlist theological propositions for cognitive assent. Such an account terminally divorces text and action. By incorporating a canonical linguistic account of scriptural authority that invites the reader/interpreter to partake in the narrative of revelation that emerges from the text, evangelical theology is better equipped to reflexively examine the consumer capitalistic narrative operating within enterprise, particularly those features that are determining conceptions of human value. Briggs polished the point: "Text and action are bound together, we might say, in transforming the reader . . . such a text requires long slow perseverance with regard to reading and living, which is surely what any reader of the Bible we have before us should expect."[48]

Conclusion

The concern of this chapter has been to anticipate and assuage early objections that might arise in contemporary American evangelical theology to the objectives of strengthening theological reflexivity. Analyzing its allegiance to foundationalism and its concern for scriptural authority, I demonstrated that the core evangelical values underlying these concerns did not need to be compromised to engage the concept of reflexivity more meaningfully. Setting the stage, I now turn to a formal analysis of one of the dominant expressions of the quest for integration in contemporary American evangelical theology, the theme of transformation.

---

47. Michaelson et al., "Meaningful," 1.
48. Briggs, "Bible Before Us," 25.

3

What Is the Current State of Transformationalist Thinking in Contemporary American Evangelical Theology?

In keeping with the focus of part one to elaborate the challenge facing contemporary American evangelical theology, I shift from a discussion of theological methodology to perceptions of capitalistic enterprise. In this chapter, I introduce the theme of transformation as a central conceptual lens for contemporary American evangelical perceptions of enterprise. In chapter 4, I detail postsecular consumerist spirituality as the broader context in which the contemporary articulation of the theme of transformation has emerged.

Over the last thirty years, American Protestant Christianity, including evangelicalism, has paid increased attention to how Christian faith integrates with enterprise.[1] This is reflective of a broader cultural sensibility and interest for religion and spirituality in the workplace.[2] The theme of transformation has emerged as a dominant conceptual lens for articulating integration. It expresses the notion that capitalistic enterprise provides a platform for Christians to fulfill the call of God and live faithfully to the message of Jesus' death and resurrection presented in the Bible by: (a) harnessing the material powers of enterprise to advance human flourishing for the common good and (b) sharing the gospel and engaging in personal conversion where opportunity allows to spread the kingdom of God.

This book amounts to a critical analysis of the theme of transformation in light of the phenomenon of postsecularism. It has challenged contemporary American evangelical theology to show how Christian faith and

---

1. Miller, *Work*.
2. Grabill, "Observations," 203.

practice can integrate with capitalistic enterprise and still be spiritually transformative. The first step in this analysis was to get a better understanding of what the theme of transformation is and how it developed, which is the focus of this chapter. I address three questions: (1) What is the theme of transformation? (2) Where did it come from? (3) Why is it significant for evangelical theology and religion?

The premise of this chapter is that capitalism's dynamic growth has resurfaced a long standing debate in contemporary American evangelical theology about the nature of the kingdom of God and the responsibilities of Christians to transform society. While theological variables are essential to the debate, so too are sociohistorical ones. Both need to be assessed.

What Is the Theme of Transformation?

The theme of transformation represents a spectrum of thought, not a singular point. It codifies the consensus within American evangelicalism that Christians should be involved in utilizing the sphere of capitalistic enterprise to transform it for the sake of human flourishing and the kingdom of God. However, the literature of contemporary American evangelical theology contains two different transformational approaches: hard transformation and soft transformation. Both share reformed heritages and central theological convictions but differ in how they construe the responsibility of transformation and the role of local faith communities in the effort of transformation.

The hard transformational perspective, heavily influenced by Kuyperian Neo-Calvinism (KNC), speaks about integrating faith and work from the standpoint of God's worldwide kingdom rule in all areas of life and emphasizes the Christian's responsibility to work toward the transformation of enterprise for the common good.[3] Alternatively, the soft transformational perspective, heavily influenced by the two kingdoms perspective (TKP), speaks about integrating faith and work from the standpoint of God's unique kingdom rule through Christ (as opposed to his general kingdom rule over humanity) and emphasizes the Christian's responsibility to live faithfully in the sphere of enterprise as part of a common human kingdom (which may or may not involve transformation as part of the redemptive kingdom).[4] I

---

3. McIlhenny, "Third-Way," is one of several who use KNC to designate Kuyperian Neo-Calvinism and the "TKP" to designate Two Kingdoms Perspective.

4. Many within the TKP have criticized Kuyperian Neo-Calvinism's use of the concept of transformation on the grounds that it is applied too broadly (VanDrunen, *Two Kingdoms*, 15). However, nearly all TKP adherents would say that Christians have

give a synopsis of each perspective, then highlight their approaches to the "business as mission" (BAM) movement to illustrate their differences.

Hard Transformation

Among contemporary American evangelicals, the influence of the hard transformation school of thought has been prolific. It prolongs a legacy that includes the prominent Dutch figures Herman Dooyeweerd and Abraham Kuyper and the French Reformer John Calvin.[5] In hard transformation, the integration of faith and work is typically cast from the standpoint of God's worldwide kingdom rule in all areas of life. It emphasizes the Christian's responsibility to be involved in the transformation of enterprise for redemptive good.

The primary influence on hard transformation is KNC, which has tended to prioritize two theological values.[6] First, the sovereign rule of God in all domains of life means that there is no distinction between "sacred" domains and "secular" domains for Christians.[7] Second, the cultural mandate of Genesis 1:28 directs Christians to pursue the redemptive transformation of all spheres of culture through the exercise of God-endowed gifts.[8] These theological values are sustained by a reading of the Bible through a tripartite thematic narrative of creation, fall, and redemption.[9] In this logic, everything has been created good, including the full range of human cultures, but evil has also corrupted everything, so everything must be redeemed by Jesus Christ. Therefore, all cultural labor is potential kingdom work, including in capitalistic enterprise.[10]

New Testament scholar Wright's use of the creation-fall-redemption scheme to criticize Platonic duality has marked contemporary American evangelical theology.[11] For Wright, the Western theological emphasis on individual salvation and the privatization of the realm of faith amount to a

---

some level of involvement in transforming the world around them, which is why I have chosen to use the designation of "soft transformation." The TKP is also commonly called two kingdoms theology.

5. VanDrunen, *Two Kingdoms*, 16.
6. Goheen and Bartholomew, *Living*, 16.
7. See Schaeffer, *God*; Moore, *Touchdown*.
8. Lewis and Demarest, *Integrative*, 36.
9. Sometimes, a fourth and final element of "consummation" is added (e.g., McKnight, *Kingdom Conspiracy*, 24).
10. VanDrunen, *Living*, 19.
11. See Wright, *Surprised*.

modern form of the Platonic dualism some New Testament writers were trying to combat. This dualism places spiritual immateriality in a higher order of reality (what might be called "heaven") and relegates material being to a lower imperfect order.[12] This goes against the grain of the understanding of the kingdom of God found in the New Testament documents, Wright contended. Jesus' resurrection from the dead comprised a hope for his followers that bridged the present physical world and the afterlife. For hard transformation, this validates broad Christian redemptive cultural engagement; not simply for the "salvation of souls" for a future heavenly state.

Applied to capitalistic enterprise, hard transformational thinking opposes any separation between a religious self and a working professional self:

> Many employees with strong religious convictions find themselves living in two separate worlds: the private world of family and church where they can express their faith freely and the public world where religious expression is strongly discouraged.[13]

Modernism is the culprit for the sacred-secular dichotomy by promoting a worldview in which verification, commerce, and scientific inquiry belong to public spheres of fact and reason while faith and religious moral conduct belong to privatized spheres. Christians are to counter this worldview with one in which "all lines of work should integrate spiritual and sacred aspects of work as illustrated by the Protestant work ethic and its concern for the common good, altruism, and self-sacrifice."[14]

Soft Transformation

On the other end of the transformation spectrum in contemporary American evangelical theology is soft transformation. It often speaks of integrating faith and work from the standpoint of God's unique kingdom rule through Christ, as opposed to his general kingdom rule over humanity. It emphasizes the Christian's responsibility to live faithfully in enterprise as part of the common or human kingdom. Whereas hard transformation thinking bears marked influence from KNC, soft transformation does from TKP.

TKP has two defining features. First, "natural and common laws or norms . . . are part of the created order and inscribed on the hearts of all. Such creational laws are distinct from special revelation in God's law to his

---

12. Wright, *Surprised*, 88–92; Wright, *People*, 253–60.
13. Kim et al., "Sacred/Secular Divide," 203.
14. Kim et al., "Sacred/Secular Divide," 207.

chosen people: they do not save."[15] Second, these norms are how God governs the various spheres of human life, including social, political, and economic. Thus, there two distinct realms in God's universal kingdom: a civil kingdom pertaining to temporal, earthly, provisional matters, and a spiritual kingdom pertaining to heavenly matters of ultimate eschatological importance.[16]

Soft transformation sees throughout Scripture a consistent pattern where God is covenantally bound to a select group of people while at the same time governing over all of humanity with common principles. For example, in Genesis 3:16–19 God issues a curse to the man and woman but sustains the promise of blessing. This is a common rule of humanity alongside the creation mandate to rule creation in Genesis 1:28. Moving through the course of redemptive history, there is an interplay between specific and common covenants. For example, a common covenant with Noah governs the distribution of justice among humanity (Gen 9:6), and a specific covenant with Abram and his offspring in Genesis 12, 15, and 17 to bring redemptive blessing to humanity.

As the community of Israel entered the promised land, they demonstrated a dual-kingdom pattern. Religious life was governed by cultic regulation but still allowed for political and economic partnership with neighboring societies (e.g., 1 Kgs 10:22; 2 Sam 10:2). Likewise, after exile from the land, they maintained what religious cultic practice they could while observing the social and cultural norms of the conquering nations (e.g., Jer 29). Similarly, in the New Testament. The coming of Jesus and his death and resurrection enacted a new spiritual covenant particularized to his followers, the church (Eph 2:11–12; Luke 22:2). Much like the exiles in Babylon, however, this spiritual institution is to practice certain rituals while respecting the social and economic authority in broader secular society (e.g., 1 Pet 1–2; Rom 13).

In the TKP scheme, a natural moral law governs common society in which everyone is under obligation by God to cultivate moral goods such as justice and equity. Here is an important distinction from a hard transformation in the context of capitalistic enterprise. Soft transformation argues for a moral legitimacy for enterprise that is not dependent on whether the gospel is verbally preached or individuals are being saved. McIlhenny illustrates:

> The job of a building engineer is to adhere to the norms of the physical universe and to offer a just price for his labors. His job title, which reflects what he does, has nothing to do with advancing the gospel or administering the sacraments. Indeed, all callings

---

15. McIlhenny, "Third-Way," 73.
16. VanDrunen, *Natural*, 26.

outside the church follow the goal of living in accordance with God's created order and exercising justice in some way.[17]

Hard and Soft Transformation Contrasted: The Example of BAM

One of the best ways to illustrate the differences between hard and soft transformation in perceptions of enterprise is with their contrasting perspectives on the role of local churches in the effort of transformation, for example, with the concept of business as mission (BAM).[18] It has emerged primarily in the field of missiology to designate businesses with a hybrid organizational structure (generally operating in foreign contexts). Typically, they are small-to-medium enterprises organized as for-profit entities but are expressly attempting to use the operation of the business as a platform for evangelistic missionary work.[19]

While both agree that the hybridization of ministry and enterprise has precedent in Scripture (e.g., Acts 18; 20), hard and soft transformation view the necessity of BAM differently. Working from a KNC paradigm that proposes that kingdom specific transformation should be taking place at all levels of society, a hard transformation has tended to look favorably at BAM as a vehicle for transformation. In the words of the 2004 Lausanne Committee for World Evangelism, "Ultimately, churches, mission agencies, and kingdom businesses have the same purpose: to bring glory to God's name among all nations."[20]

In contrast, soft transformation has challenged the underlying premises of BAM. First, that the structure of BAM reinforces a subterranean sacred-secular dualism wherein BAM is sacred and "business as business" is secular.[21] Second, BAM distorts "God's sovereign intent for his creation" by fusing the separate domains of business—and its common mandate from God—with the domains of church—and its specific redemptive mandate from God."[22]

---

17. McIlhenny, "Third-Way," 79.

18. "Micro-enterprise development" is another term often used synonymously with BAM, though the two are not the exact same. See Bussau and Mask, *Microenterprise*, 7–8.

19. Rundle, "Business," 66.

20. Tunehag et al., *Business as Mission*, 3.

21. Quatro wrote: "All of God's people image Him through their professional practice in business, regardless of whether the company for which they work intentionally evangelizes/disciples/develops the nations" (Quatro, "Flawed," 83).

22. Quatro, "Flawed," 81.

Table 1 summarizes the differing approaches to transformation:

Table 1

	Hard Transformationism	Soft Transformationism
AKA	KNC	TKP
Key influencers	Calvin, Kuyper, Dooyeweerd	Augustine, Luther
Shared beliefs	The kingdom of God has both present and future elements and Christians are called to serve the common good in some way	The kingdom of God has both present and future elements and Christians are called to serve the common good in some way
Theological emphases	(1) God's sovereign reign over all things (2) The ongoing relevance of the "cultural mandate" (3) A creation-fall-redemptive hermeneutic	(1) The presence of common grace and natural law throughout creation (2) The division of the kingdom of God into a civil realm that pertains to all and a spiritual realm that pertains to the redeemed (3) A covenant-specific hermeneutic
Contemporary Proponents	Wright, Stackhouse, Grudem	VanDrunen, Quatro
Integration of faith and work	Emphasizes God's worldwide kingdom rule in all areas of life and emphasizes the Christian's responsibility to be involved in the transformation of enterprise for redemptive good	Emphasizes God's unique kingdom rule through Christ (as opposed to his general kingdom rule over humanity) and emphasizes the Christian's responsibility to live faithfully in enterprise as part of the common/human kingdom (which may or may not involve transformation as part of the redemptive kingdom)
Attitudes toward BAM (and the role of the local church in mission)	Generally supports BAM as a strategic method for combining the redemptive focus of the local church with the frontier of enterprise	Generally criticizes BAM as a reinforcement of the secular-sacred dichotomy and a mixing of the civil realm with the redemptive realm of the local church

Where Does the Theme of Transformation Come From?

In this overview of the theme of transformation, I defined the current state of transformational thinking in contemporary American evangelical perceptions of enterprise as a distinction between hard and soft varieties. However, this current state did not emerge in a vacuum, and both varieties have distinct theological and sociohistorical roots. I briefly analyze these roots by looking at two critical pre-twentieth-century figures and two key twentieth-century figures.

Key Pre-Twentieth-Century Figures

Both KNC and TKP were profoundly influenced by the reformed tradition. Two pre-twentieth-century thinkers figured prominently: Abraham Kuyper, representing a post-Reformation synthesizer; and Martin Luther, representing the classic reformation benchmark.

It goes without saying that Abraham Kuyper has been enormously influential on hard transformation and KNC.[23] Kuyper was a nineteenth and twentieth-century Dutch theologian with wide-ranging social influence. He was the founder of the Reformed Churches in the Netherlands, the Anti-Revolutionary Party, and the Free University of Amsterdam, as well as holding the position of prime minister from 1901 to 1905. Part of Kuyper's historical significance lies "in the fact that he represents an unusual blend of theological orthodoxy and cultural progressiveness," no doubt strengthened by the fact that he "was remarkably successful in realizing his political objectives."[24]

Kuyper's influence on contemporary evangelical transformational thinking can nearly be summed up in one concept that marks his work: "sphere sovereignty." The oddity of this is that he only formally spoke on the idea once, at a speech delivered for the founding of the Free University, and the picture he gave "was imprecise."[25] Sphere sovereignty expresses the idea that "each human activity has its rightful place or sphere in the creation, over which its norm for activity is sovereign, and should not be intruded upon by other spheres."[26] These spheres are each "animated with its own spirit" as "cogwheels" in "a great machine . . . spring-driven

---

23. VanDrunen, *Living*; Heslam, *Worldview*.
24. Heslam, *Worldview*, 4–5.
25. Bratt, "Sphere Sovereignty," 35.
26. Edgell, "Profit," 8.

on their own axles."[27] In a phrase often cited by contemporary American evangelicals, Kuyper famously declared "there is not a square inch in the whole domain of our human existence over which Christ, who is Sovereign over all, does not cry: 'Mine!'"[28]

Kuyper's effects on the Dutch neo-Calvinist movement and eventually on contemporary evangelicalism are tied to Kuyper's own complex sociohistorical milieu just as much as they are to his theology.[29] He was one of the first "significant reformed theologians to confront directly what is now called a post-Christian culture."[30] Therefore, it is not difficult to see why many American evangelicals confronting their own perceived post-Christian culture have drawn inspiration from Kuyper.[31] For Kuyper, the concept of sphere sovereignty strengthened this confrontation as part of a broader political philosophy of "pillarization," a way of hedging Christendom in the Netherlands against the onslaught of secularism.[32]

Social systems should be established, argued Kuyper, that recognized the common grace present in the cosmos and placed political rule not exclusively in the hands of an individual or the state, but in the intermediate pillars of universities, families, churches, and businesses.[33] God remained sovereign over all spheres, but delegated responsibility to each sphere such that they exist co-autonomously alongside each other.

For many Kuyperian influenced evangelical transformationalists, the concept of sphere sovereignty has informed the integration of faith and work, but often in disparate ways.[34] Hard transformationalists, for example, are apt to see in Kuyper's vision a common grace that is expendable to everyone but remains under the sovereignty of God a mandate to fully integrate the transformational agenda into workplace settings through intentional evangelism. However, soft transformationalists point to the sphere

27. Kuyper, "Sphere Sovereignty," 84.
28. Kuyper, "Sphere Sovereignty," 488. See Keller, *Endeavor*, 212.
29. For a helpful taxonomy of Neo-Calvinism's development, see Bratt, *Calvinism*.
30. VanDrunen, *Living*, 277.
31. Wolfe, "Evangelical," 10.
32. A defense of a sense of Christendom is alive in many quarters of American evangelicalism, representing yet another parallel to Kuyper. See Brown, *America*.
33. Kuyper, "Sphere Sovereignty," 166–69.
34. Kuyper's influence on the debate between KNC and TKP is complicated by the fact "that while he certainly addressed all of the major issues touching upon the two kingdoms doctrine, he did so with a very different set of terms and concepts" (VanDrunen, *Living*, 210). Keene offered a recent exploration of the implications of sphere sovereignty as expressed in both Kuyper and Dooyeweerd for university-centered and mission-driven transformational efforts. See Keene, *Kuyper*.

sovereignty paradigm as a reason for rebuffing a strong transformational agenda for business. The fact that work, home, church, government, business, etc., have been established by God as distinct and sovereign spheres with their own operating norms means that a business should not be run like a church, nor should Christians feel overly burdened to intentional evangelize in workplace settings.[35]

Any discussion of Kuyper's impact on contemporary evangelical theological perceptions of enterprise must also involve a discussion about the Protestant Reformation. Why? Because by drawing on Kuyperian themes, both hard and soft varieties of transformation in contemporary American evangelical theology make use of conceptual categories that were themselves made possible by the paradigm shifts that emerged out of Protestant Reformation. If hard transformation draws direct influence from Kuyper, then soft transformation draws direct influence from Luther. Specifically, we can identify two closely linked concepts of Luther's that shaped the theme of transformation in contemporary evangelical thought: vocation and two kingdoms.

In modern western Christian thought, few topics have attracted as much focus as a vocation.[36] Contemporary American engagements in evangelical theology with the concept of vocation have been broad.[37] Conceptual engagements with vocation have hardly been limited to Christian theology. Weber's analysis of the Puritan Protestant understanding of vocation, for example, sparked a wealth of scholarship in fields such as sociology of religion and management studies.[38] While this broad discussion is multi-faceted and deeply nuanced, a central feature is that Luther introduced a turning point in Western intellectual conceptions of the idea of vocation.[39]

---

35. "This is not to say that God has not ordained universal norms that transcend all spheres (e.g., admonitions against the love of money, or the command to love your neighbor as yourself), but it is to say that some God-ordained norms are constrained to specific spheres (e.g., the command to care for the poor, or the command to evangelize the nations)" (Quatro, "Flawed," 84).

36. Scholes, *Vocation*. "Vocation" comes from the Latin *vocatio*, meaning "call, summons." Thus, the word "calling" is also closely linked to "vocation" in contemporary usage. A scriptural text that is often cited in connection with both is from 1 Corinthians: "Only let each person lead the life that the Lord has assigned to him, and to which God has called him" (1 Cor 7:17).

37. See Novak, *Business*; Sherman, *Calling*; Goossen and Stevens, *Entrepreneurial*; Keller, *Endeavor*; Veith, *God*.

38. Roth and Schluchter, *Weber*. This is to say nothing of the explosion of research interests among psychology scholars and within the workplace spirituality movement over the topic of vocation (and the closely related topic of "calling"). See Duffy and Dik, "Calling."

39. Veith, *God*, 119–20.

Like much of Luther's theology, he is best understood in contrast to the medieval Roman Catholic thought of his time. About vocation, Luther sought to widen Roman Catholicism's narrow use of the term, which limited it to explicit ecclesial occupations in keeping with its understanding of bodily labor as a means of purification and development of virtue.[40] Stretching back to the time of Plato and up to the time of Luther, physical labor in the Western intellectual and religious tradition was generally associated with lower forms of human nature to be performed only if necessary for survival and higher forms of contemplation and leisure of the soul.[41]

Luther widened the concept to include everyone (not just the clergy) and all spheres (not just physical labor). For Luther, vocation is a "mask of God" that mediates the providential work of God through humans for the care of creation and distribution of gifts.[42] For the provision of daily bread, God provides through the vocations of farmers, millers, and bakers. For the provision of human life, God provides through the vocations of mothers and fathers, wives, and husbands. For the provision of bodily protection, God provides through the vocation of earthly government.

Critical for Luther was that every Christian enters a dualistic tension between two kingdoms (earth and heaven) with two competing powers (God and Satan, law and grace). To the degree that every Christian is called to navigate this tension by loving God and loving neighbor, Luther calls this his and her "vocation." Here we see Luther's doctrine of vocation closely linked to that of two kingdoms.[43] A "vocation is the specific call to love one's neighbor which comes to us through the duties which attach to our social place or 'station' within the earthly kingdom."[44]

Luther's initial espousal of vocation lacked the emphasis on active transformation that has come to define KNC, which accounts for his more direct influence on TKP. There was indeed a "static" element to Luther's concept of calling and vocation that contemporary expressions have moved well beyond. According to Chamberlain, "Lutheranism did not require a transformation of the world in a rationalized, ethical direction."[45] Vocation was a general term that applied to the various stations of the

---

40. See Calhoun, "Work."
41. Weber, *Protestant*, 56.
42. Wingren, *Calling*, 138–40.
43. Chamberlain, "Protestant," 5.
44. Hardy, *Fabric*, 46.
45. Chamberlain, "Protestant," 5. See also Troeltsch, *Social*, 610.

earthly kingdom, and thus, lacked the volitional and individual emphases of later evangelical reprisals.[46]

Key Twentieth-Century Figures

The influence of Luther and Kuyper on hard and soft transformation was mediated through two important twentieth-century figures who grappled with the rising force of capitalistic enterprise, albeit differently. First, was Walter Rauschenbusch, a foil along with the social gospel movement in early evangelical discussions. Second was H. Richard Niebuhr, whose *Christ and Culture* provided the vocabulary out of which the transformational language emerged. An analysis of each is in order.

Synonymous with the social gospel movement of the late nineteenth and early twentieth century, Rauschenbusch mixed theological academic in Germany training with pastoral work in New York City. At the time of his pastorate, rapid industrialization was imposing heavy social costs on American urban life. Rauschenbusch responded by articulating a utopic understanding of the kingdom of God that shaped the future of mainline American Protestantism and global liberation theology. For Rauschenbusch, every act of mercy and justice was "an extension of the reign of God in humanity, an incoming of the Kingdom of God."[47] Rauschenbusch argued that the Hebrew scriptures and the example of Jesus demand rectification of the social ills imposed by industrialization. Moral transformation requires moving beyond theological obscurity and into social and political action.

One of the great struggles for justice for a Christian moral vision was unchecked capitalism.[48] It has "generated a spirit of its own which is antagonistic to the spirit of Christianity; a spirit of hardness and cruelty that neutralizes the Christian spirit of love; a spirit that sets material goods above spiritual possessions."[49] As a social institution, the church must take an active role in combating social evils and "align itself with those values and forces in society that were on the side of the poor, the working classes, and the unemployed."[50]

Rauschenbusch's transformational ethic was situated within Protestantism and shared an evangelistic origin with American evangelicalism.[51]

46. Badcock, *Way of Life*, 44.
47. Rauschenbush, *Righteousness*, 67–68.
48. Beckley, *Passion*, 27–29.
49. Rauschenbush, *Righteousness*, 115.
50. Haight, "Mission," 243.
51. Hart, *Soul*, 72–79.

However, for most of the twentieth century, it constituted the foil against which evangelicalism cast its own transformational vision. Primarily, this was because Rauschenbusch adopted higher critical interpretive methods and rejected many metaphysical accounts of traditional Christian doctrine.[52] Many evangelicals believed that social gospel theology disposed of the authority of scripture reduced Jesus to merely a moral teacher and abandoned historically orthodox doctrines like substitutionary atonement and personal guilt.[53]

Heightening evangelical theology's criticism of the social gospel movement was its deepening attachment to Republican political efforts, beginning in the 1970s.[54] Whereas social gospel progressivism was increasingly identified with liberal platforms, evangelicalism was with conservative government ideology. Correspondingly, whereas progressivism tended to utilize communitarian ethical frameworks, conservative evangelicalism tended to emphasize individual moral responsibility.[55]

Evangelicalism's reaction against Rauschenbusch and the broader social gospel movement significantly shaped the theme of transformation in perceptions of enterprise. It intensified evangelicalism's emphasis on individual action and responsibility in articulating enterprise's contributions to human flourishing. For example, conservative evangelical Carl McIntire (founder of the Presbyterian church in America) vocally criticized Roosevelt's New Deal policies in the aftermath of the Depression. He argued it destroyed the American ethos of individual self-reliance, hard work, and free enterprise, which were essential to capitalism's capabilities.[56]

Throughout the growth of the faith at work movement, evangelicalism continued to conceptualize the relationship between the Christian gospel and secular business primarily through the lens of workplace evangelistic activity and individual ethical behavior. This meant that as evangelical theology conceived of moral and theological economic paradigms, it does so primarily highlight the moral primacy of free market enterprise above all other systems.

Where Rauschenbusch influenced evangelical transformation as a foil, another figure exerted direct influence: H. Richard Niebuhr. Entering the theological scene about thirty years after Rauschenbusch, Niebuhr

---

52. Rauschenbusch argued that his theological method was the result of "conceiving of Christian doctrine in social terms," which distinguished symbolic meaning from fundamentalist literalism (Rauschenbusch, *Social*, 8). See also Evans, *Kingdom*.

53. Weir, *Good Work*; Lewis and Demarest, *Integrative Theology*, 19.

54. Brown, *Christian America*.

55. Miller, *Evangelicalism*, 114–16.

56. Martin, "Evangelical Economic Rhetoric," 44.

experienced conditions substantially different. The apparent promise of social gospel transformation had been undermined by a devastating world war, a deep Depression, and the threat of a second world war. Niebuhr was sympathetic to the social gospel's objectives but was convinced that it was beset by "a weak understanding of the doctrine of sin and an overestimation of human agency."[57] Combining Barth's doctrine on God's absolute transcendence with Tillich's concept of being, Niebuhr emphasized a relational theological ethic that understood the human being as an entity always responding to external and internal influences.[58]

No doubt, his most prolific impact on evangelical theology continues to be his publication *Christ and Culture*. It established the categories that have shaped how evangelicals "think about the relationship of Christ and church to the world and culture."[59] Originally given as a series of seminary lectures, *Christ and Culture* attempted to defend Christianity's positive cultural contributions in the aftermath of World War II, when many secular critics were calling for a reappraisal of Western public religion.[60]

Niebuhr argued that belief in Christ and "loyalty to his cause involve people in the double movement from world to God and from God to world."[61] Culture is a composite of "language, habits, ideas, beliefs, customs, social organization, inherited artifacts, technical processes, and values."[62] He proposed three primary ways that Christians have related to culture: opposition (Christ against culture); agreement (Christ of culture); and synthesis (Christ above culture). Synthesis can take the form of either dualism (Christ and culture in paradox) or conversion (Christ transforming culture).

Niebuhr sought to balance the reality of God's transcendence with the relational nature of human finitude. His understanding of the kingdom of God departed from Rauschenbusch's ethnocentrism and asserted that God's sovereign rule was expressed in history, not relativized by it. This rule was distinctly linked to America's Protestant Puritan legacy.[63] Such a straightforward theological rubric and historical hermeneutic enormously influenced American evangelical readers.

---

57. Miller, *God at Work*, 27.
58. See Fox, *Niebuhr*.
59. McKnight, *Kingdom Conspiracy*, 229.
60. Diefenthaler, *Paradox*, xviii.
61. Niebuhr, *Christ and Culture*, 53.
62. Niebuhr, *Christ and Culture*, 32.
63. See Fox, "Divided Kingdom."

The effect carried over to transformational perceptions of enterprise. During his career, Niebuhr had attained significant political clout.[64] As Republican evangelicalism reached a political apex in the 1980s and 1990s, Niebuhr was cast as the ideal public theologian.[65] Conservative evangelicalism applied a "Christ transforming culture" rubric to the mounting culture wars, including over capitalism.[66] For the evangelical Christian trying to integrate personal faith into an increasingly secularized workplace, Niebuhr's categorization provided a lens to focus on individual morality as a means of transforming culture through enterprise.[67]

Why Is the Theme of Transformation Significant?

An overview of the development of the theme of transformation highlights its significance in American evangelical theology and religion. It is not the only way to express integration with capitalistic enterprise. The concept of using the professional workplace and capitalistic enterprise as platforms for spiritual and moral transformation has become a common way that evangelicals articulate integration. However, not all evangelicals share this conviction, and among those who do, I have shown that there is tremendous variety in how it is expressed.

The reason that the theme of transformation is significant is the tension it highlights in contemporary American evangelical theology's quest for integration. Adopting Niebuhr's Christ and culture framework, the traditional statement of the theme of transformation portrays a dichotomized relationship between Christian faith and capitalistic enterprise. Christian faith stands apart from capitalistic enterprise and transforms it morally and spiritually. The problem with this construal and Niebuhr's Christ-culture binary "is that Christ is already a cultural event. We have no access to a Christ who has not already been encultured."[68]

A closer look at the development of the theme of transformation has shown that its framework has been shaped not just by theological forces, but

---

64. While at Yale, Niebuhr was nominated to the Council of Foreign Relations and policy advisory roles with the US Department of State.

65. See Park and Reimer, "Revisiting." This was despite that Niebuhr had little interest in conservative evangelicalism and doubted its long-term relevance in American religious life. See Marsden, *Cultures*.

66. Curry, "Where Have All the Niebuhrs Gone?," 99.

67. See Siker, "Christ and Business."

68. Ward, *Christ and Culture*, 21.

social, historical, and cultural ones as well. These forces are not contextually neutral. All the key influencers on the theme of transformation were articulating theological positions that were themselves shaped by time and context. Including in their interpretation and application of scriptural texts, the readings involved an interplay of multiple hermeneutical horizons. Contemporary American evangelical theology's quest to integrate Christian faith and capitalistic enterprise must consider both how Christian faith affects the transformation of capitalistic enterprise, and how its own ability to be transformative has been affected by its entanglement with the culture of capitalism.

For example, is the theme of transformation's emphasis on individualism a result of pure theological doctrine? Does it reflect any underlying influence from sociohistorical variables that themselves need scrutinizing? The integration of Christian faith and capitalistic enterprise requires critical reflection on American evangelicalism's own situatedness. This is at the heart of a reflexive spirituality that can interrogate its own beliefs and practices.

In the last half century, the cultural grounds that gave rise to the theme of transformation have significantly shifted. Specifically, the phenomenon of postsecularism has changed both American evangelicalism's public influence and the nature of capitalistic enterprise's cultural force. A closer examination of the change is needed, and it is where I turn next.

Conclusion

The purpose of this chapter has been to understand better a dominant expression of contemporary American evangelical theology's quest to integrate capitalistic enterprise and Christian faith, the theme of transformation. I have shown that the current state of transformationalist thinking in contemporary American evangelical theology can be described as a spectrum with two poles. Hard transformation emphasizes the possibility of redemptively transforming enterprise for the kingdom of God while soft transformation emphasizes the responsibility to live faithfully within enterprise to serve the common good. I have also traced these poles back through their essential theological and sociohistorical lineages, including pivotal twentieth-century and pre-twentieth-century figures. In the next chapter, I broaden the analytical lens to analyze the postsecular shift that has taken place in American religious life that has served as the setting in which the theme of transformation in contemporary American evangelical theology has evolved.

4

What Is Postsecular Consumerist Spirituality and How Does It Impact the Theme of Transformation?

Part one focused on introducing the core concepts critical to the argument of the book. In chapter 3, I provided a detailed overview of the theme of transformation in contemporary American evangelical theology. To close part one, I now analyze the broader sociohistorical context in which the theme of transformation has evolved. The theme of transformation in contemporary American evangelical theology did not develop in isolation. Quite the opposite—its emergence can only be assessed as part of more substantive disruptions in the American religious landscape enacted by the dynamic growth of capitalistic enterprise.

The traditional framing of the theme of transformation portrays Christian faith as harnessing the good of Western consumer market capitalism without being pulled down by its excesses. This corresponded to the conditions of the mid-twentieth century, where evangelical Christianity still exercised significant sociopolitical influence in American public life, and market capitalism's growth was relatively stable and predictable.

Times have since dramatically changed. The instrumentalizing reach of consumer market capitalism has extended into virtually every dimension of human experience, including religious expression. Simultaneously, a decline in institutionalized forms of Protestant Christianity has weakened the influence of evangelicalism in American public life, and a rise in less traditional forms of "implicit religion" have intensified materialistic and individualistic expressions of spirituality.

This chapter analyzes this disruption, using as a central interpretive lens one of the most forceful (if not contentious) manifestations: the phenomenon of postsecularism.

Postsecularism does not represent a single idea or concept but rather a spectrum of "concerns and possibilities" about the failures of secularization theory to adequately capture the complex relationships between religion and western society in the latter half of the twentieth century.[1] Secularization paradigms theorized that religion would play a decreasingly influential role in the public domain as social and economic modernization increased. Yet, "rather than receding into the private realm as predicted under secularization theory, the meanings and expressions of lived religion—as identity, belief, practice, and cultural process—continue to be decisively public issues."[2]

Defining postsecularism is notoriously difficult, and any attempt must begin with the acknowledgement that it is a contested concept.[3] While most would agree that something like postsecularism exists, debate rages about precisely what it is. Even the most general assessment—that institutional religion has declined and secular materialism has increased—is too broad to be applicable to any one context. Attempts to employ postsecularism as a sociological description of empirical trends face the challenge of taking in an enormous amount of variegated data—for example, new visibility in religious faith and practice or the prominence of non-affiliated spiritual practice.

The American context presents even more complexities. From its founding, Christian religion has played prominently in American public life. Even though America's legacy of a "civil religion" has made it consistently more religiously affiliated than Europe, there has been a quantifiable decline in religious affiliation.[4]

Weighing in on the viability of postsecularism as a sociological description of empirical trends is not the purpose of this chapter. After all, I am not a trained sociologist. Instead, my objective is to assess any significant changes in the religious landscape in the American context that bear on contemporary American evangelical theological perceptions of enterprise while at the same time clarifying my own use of the category of religion as I make these assessments, recognizing the complexities of the issues involved.

---

1. Olson et al., "Retheorizing the Postsecular Present."

2. Berger, *Desecularization*, 2.

3. "Postsecularization," "postsecularism," and "postsecular theory" are often used interchangeably but have different nuances. Postsecularization generally "refers to the reemergence of religion in the public sphere, whereas postsecularism is associated with a normative position regarding the involvement of religious people, organizations, and ethics in public life" (Olson et al., "Retheorizing the Postsecular Present," 1422).

4. See Leezenberg, "Ethnocentric." The election of Donald Trump as American president in 2016 demands even more nuance given that more than 60 percent of self-identified evangelicals voted for Trump.

My thesis in this chapter is that postsecular trends undermine the traditional framing of the theme of transformation and by extension contemporary American evangelical theology's quest to integrate Christian faith and capitalistic enterprise. I demonstrate this by arguing the following. First, whatever else it has meant, postsecularism in the American context has facilitated a shift in religious expression: a decrease in traditional forms and an increase in non-traditional spiritual forms. Second, the dynamic growth of consumer capitalism has been at the heart of this shift, giving rise to a consumerist spirituality that portrays faith in increasingly individualist and materialist terms. Third, as American capitalistic enterprise has become more intensely consumeristic and instrumentalizing, it has obscured the intrinsic goods of human flourishing that are necessary for spiritual transformation. This is both an opportunity and a dilemma for contemporary American evangelical theology. An opportunity because it has reconfigured the public sphere to allow for more meaningful dialogue about the theological and religious aspects of capitalistic enterprise. However, it is also a dilemma because it exposes that American evangelicalism itself has contributed to the development of the materialistic and individualistic aspects of postsecular consumerist spirituality.

What Is Postsecularism?

Fundamentally, postsecularism is an attempt to explain two statistical trends.[5] First, there has been a decline in Americans' self-identification with mainline Protestant Christianity.[6] Second, there has been an increase in the

---

5. Though there is indeed import for the entire global stage, the thrust of the shift is in societies where consumer market capitalism and political democratization are either established or on the rise, especially since the categories and terminology used to describe postsecularism, government, enterprise, and religion are derived from western thought (Madsen, "Religion," 28–30). I focus my analysis on postsecularism in America.

6. See Brenner, "Identity"; Bass, *Christianity*, 13; Jones et al., *Religious*. The terminology here is important and complicated. According to Christiano et al., "The range of terms that have been used to describe religion in the United States since 1960 is as broad as the subject itself" (Christiano et al., *Sociology of Religion*, 85). I use the phrase "mainline Protestant Christianity" to designate all three of the generally recognized denominations within organized American Protestant Christianity: conservative (e.g., Southern Baptist Convention), moderate (e.g., United Methodist Church), and liberal (e.g., United Church of Christ). The growth of Pentecostalism is an anomaly. It is an outgrowth of traditional mainline Protestantism, but it also shares many features of new religious movements discussed below. See Robins, *Pentecostalism in America*; Jenkins, *Next Christendom*.

degree to which people identify themselves as "spiritual but not religious."[7] Together, these trends suggest that the general relationship between religion and contemporary society is not on the trajectory that nineteenth- and twentieth-century secularization theory predicted.[8] Rather than diminishing as Western society has become more economically and socially modernized as secularization theory predicted, some forms of religious expression are as abundant as ever.[9]

Assessing postsecularism, then, first requires an understanding of secularization theory. In basic form, "secularization theory anticipates the declining importance and presence of religion in individual lives, societies, and states."[10] While secularization theory is generally referred to under one umbrella term, Casanova was right to see three distinct components: (a) the decline of religious belief; (b) the differentiation of religious and nonreligious spheres; and (c) the privatization of religious commitments.[11]

Political secularization entails a legislated separation of church and state and an institutional firewall from religious entanglement, which clearly has transpired over the course of America's history. Economic and social modernization have increased the fundamental separation between church and state and lessened the influence of traditional religious authority in America. However, social secularization "refers to the everyday religious experience, practice, and belief and to the penetration of that everyday world by the secular market and secular values" and it is this component of the secularization that has garnered the greatest attention.[12] Increasing economic and social modernization has not eliminated this form of religious expression, but rather reconfigured it. This suggests "modernity and religion are not in a

---

7. Ellingson, "Spirituality," 257–60; Chaves, *American Religion*; Fuller, *Spiritual*, 1.

8. Habermas, "Notes," 5. The decline of secularization theory, while apparent on both sides of the Atlantic, has been more gradual in continental Europe than in America. This was not unexpected given that religion (specifically Christianity) has played a more formative role in the establishment of American society and government than among European countries. For a detailed discussion of the relationship between American and European perceptions of secularization theory, see Warner, "Convergence."

9. Berger, *Desecularization*, 2. Examples include movements such as the "Iranian revolution, the moral majority, the Pentecostal explosion, the post-socialist Buddhist revival, faith-based initiatives, communal violence, the politics of the veil, the inconclusive 'Arab spring,' and of course, 9/11" (Gorski et al., *Post-Secular*, 3).

10. Hershberger, *War*, 28.

11. See Casanova, *Public*. Turner further distinguished "political secularization" (the differentiation thesis, b and c) and "social secularization" (the commodification thesis, a). See Turner, "Post-Secular Society."

12. Turner, "Post-Secular Society," 141.

zero-sum relationship, in which the emergence of the former should inexorably lead to the disappearance of the latter."[13]

Secularization theory analyzed religious faiths through an interplay of the macro-level of society and the micro-level of the individual, a legacy of Enlightenment scientific positivism. Durkheim, for example, used the term *homo duplex* to describe a double center of gravity in each person between a lower individual state of ordinary ("profane") experience and emotions dictated by biological forces that is in tension with a higher social "sacred" state of experience and emotions dictated by society.[14] Two basic realities exist—individuals and society—and "between them, a primal opposition and divergence of interests operates."[15] In this scheme, religion was seen primarily as an abstract category of beliefs and doctrines exercised in private life and subjective experience. Its phenomenal forms (e.g., liturgies, rituals) were understood to be inessential.[16] Religious faith could be analyzed like any other social variable, but its influence on public life would decrease as society modernized.

In the 1960s, Berger and Luckmann initiated a paradigm shift in the study of religion.[17] There was a turn away from "questions of systems and functions toward a concern with the social processes the engender experience, knowledge, culture, and language."[18] This expanded the study of religion beyond formal religious organizations such as churches, denominations, and sects into "new religious movements."[19] In the classical tradition, religion was understood in its most natural sense as an institutionalized worship of a deity or higher power, but this shift subsumed religion under "a larger category of the sacred."[20]

Therefore, postsecular theory has come to refer to a diversity of interests and approaches to reframing the classical secularization paradigm. Most current work falls within four broad realms.[21] First, are those who find materialism and structuralism insufficient in and of themselves to fully describe

13. Giordan and Pace, "Mapping," 1.

14. Durkheim, "Dualism." See also Janssen and Verheggen, "Double Center"; Norris and Inglehart, *Sacred*, 5–8.

15. Smith, *You Are What You Love*, 57.

16. Mahmood, *Secularism*, 341.

17. Berger, *Sacred*; Luckmann, *Invisible*.

18. Beckford and Demerath, "Introduction," 4.

19. Christiano et al., *Sociology of Religion*, 39; Stark and Bainbridge, "Theory of Religion."

20. Beckford and Demerath, "Introduction," 70. In some ways, this shift was anticipated by Durkheim.

21. Olson et al., "Retheorizing."

reality and want to allow for religious, spiritual, or other-worldly experience to be recognized as a legitimate form of knowledge of the world.[22] Second, are those such as Taylor, Berger, and Connolly who advocate for normative and ethical alternatives to secularization theory.[23] Third, are those such as Asad who draw on poststructuralism and postmodernism as a means of deconstructing the category of religion itself in relation to the secular.[24] Fourth, are those who understand postsecularism to mean the persistence of religion or spirituality in places previously assumed to be secular.[25]

For the purposes of this chapter, this historical backdrop helps us see a conviction common to most all forms of postsecularism—that secularization theory's narrow definition of the category of "religion" faces significant conceptual limits.[26] Participation in mainline Protestant Christianity has declined, but this is only half the story. The emergence of phenomena such as new religious movements suggests that in other ways, religious expression is expanding across social spheres. This undermines conceptualizations of religion as predominately abstract intellectual assent and the hard boundary drawn between the public and private spheres.

In charting my own understanding of the category of religion, then, I am positioned within a broader critical movement away from monothetic approaches to defining religion, which seek to ascertain some universal core that explains all forms of privatized intellectual, religious assent.[27] This could be a belief in a supernatural, transcendent realm exercised through explicitly religious institutions or sacred rituals. Alternatively, it could be a sensemaking function that embraces "activities, ideologies, and structures

22. See McLennan, *Postsecular*; Bhaskar, *Science*.

23. See Taylor, *Sources*; Berger, *Canopy*; Connolly, *Capitalism*.

24. See Asad, *Genealogies*. Located especially within this stream are those such as Furani, who questioned the viability of the term "postsecular" even while affirming the insufficiencies of the secular paradigm. The current usages of postsecular generally attempt to challenge Enlightenment-driven appraisals of religion; yet, often this is done based "on a hegemonic premise whereby the secular marks difference from the religious, to which it remains exterior" (Furani, "Postsecular," 8). However, this can become a reassertion of the very secularity it seeks to overturn, especially reaffirming a Kantian distinction between the knowing self and knowledge. As Asad pointed out, the secular is an ontology and an epistemology before it is, conceptually speaking, a political doctrine (secularism), a sociological thesis, or a historical process (secularization).

25. Knott, *Location*.

26. Greil and Bromley, *Defining Religion*, 3; Pattison, "Religion"; Fitzgerald, *Ideoology*.

27. Saler, *Conceptualizing*. Critical theory-based approaches generally prioritize the "grounding of knowledge in historical context, critique through dialectical process, and identification of future potentialities for emancipation and self-determination" (Lunn, "Theological Reflection and Reflexivity," 951).

that seem to share features in common with religion although they are not always designated as such."[28] In both cases, religion is a thing in and of itself that can be isolated enough from its social and cultural masking to discern the essential element that makes it religion.

The monothetic categorization of religion is largely unique to eighteenth- and nineteenth-century western intellectual academics and was prompted by the breakdown in centralized ecclesiastical authority.[29] Evident here is that culturally constructed definitional efforts concerning the term "religion" have involved an element of power, as all definitional efforts do. The development of a differentiated category of religion in modern western society was not a blind, value free, inevitable historical process. It was shaped by historically contingent human actors exercising political and social will including, at times, coercive force.[30]

I am taking a critical approach that defines religion as primarily a tool for theory building. The objective is not to capture an alleged universal core but to establish internal coherence within a theoretical system to account for a "family of phenomena."[31] The category of religion cannot terminally separate the social and individual dimensions from each other without seriously compromising its explanatory scope. Religious expression is shaped by the complex social, political, cultural, and historical contexts in which it operates, and our analytic categories should reflect this diversity and by the interaction between the cognitive functions of a person and his or her surrounding environment. Cognitive schemes evolve through the course of selective interaction and "frame the way in which information is perceptually organized, stored, retrieved, and processed" to "make them meaningful and facilitate their processing."[32] As natural-goods-seeking persons, humans

---

28. Greil and Bromley, *Defining Religion*, 4. See also Johnstone, *Religion*, 7–9.

29. Harrison, "Religion"; McCutcheon, *Manufacturing*; Beyer, "Sensing Religion," 238.

30. In this case, power was exercised in favor of western Protestant Christianity and its conceptual categories, thereby resulting in the tendency to classify Eastern, poly/non-theistic Hindu and Buddhist religions as less developed and less significant. See Orsi, *Between Heaven and Earth*.

31. Saler, *Conceptualizing*.

32. McIntosh, "Religion-as-Schema," 5. These cognitive schemes are a complexity of not merely cognitive processes but also emotive and affective processes that can be described (at least partly) as precognitive and subconscious. See Houwer and Hermans, "Feelings." The challenging question regards the level of influence these different processes exert within the complexity. Despite a long trajectory in Western philosophical history that isolates cognition and reasoning functions from affective and emotive functions, developments in psychology of emotions and cognitive theory continue to point to the complexity with which emotive and affective functions affect the development of cognitive schemes, even as these developments raise important questions

are generally teleologically oriented around a desire for wellbeing, even if this *telos* is misconstrued or destructive.[33]

These qualifications clarify the presuppositions I carry with me as I analyze contemporary American evangelical perceptions of enterprise. First, I acknowledge that my utilization of the concept of religion is historically situated in a specific stream of modern western intellectual history, one that has involved the uses and abuses of power, especially within Protestant Christianity, which houses evangelical Christianity. Second, so situated, I am both accepting some features of this conceptualization and seeking to challenge others. I accept the basic framework that prevails in modern western society that understands religion as a fundamentally differentiated domain of social life. However, I challenge that any manifestation of this framework is absolute and I hope to show that, as it always has been subject to reconstruction, contemporary trendlines were collectively known as postsecularism and demand something of a fresh reconstruction.

By drawing out some of the entanglements involved in defining the category of religion, at this juncture, I hope to demonstrate that secularization theory, in predicting that political and economic modernization would reduce religious expression, depended on a narrow, differentiated concept of religion. It has explanatory power when applied to forms of traditional, institutionalized religious expression, but lacks explanatory power when applied to non-institutionalized religious expression.

If secular theory pitted "secular" against "religion," postsecularism recognizes that religion "nonetheless continues to exert influence in subtle, oblique ways that escape the secular understanding."[34] Having established that religious expression has not been entirely eliminated by the modernizing force of capitalistic enterprise but rather reconfigured, the features of postsecular religious expression can now be ascertained. If, as McGuire posited, "religion—rather than being a single entity—is made up of diverse, complex, and ever-changing mixtures of beliefs and practices, as well as relationships, experiences, and commitments," then our "analytic categories must be able to reflect this plurality."[35]

---

about how this interaction takes place. Space does not allow a meaningful elaboration, but for a balanced appraisal, see Sludds, "Emotions."

33. Smith, *Flourish*, 52–53.

34. Viswanathan, "Secularism," 480. Madsen reaffirmed the point well: Religion cannot "be separated from other forms of human life. . . . Ritual and myth at least are usually deeply blended into economic and political affairs" and the "extraordinary degree of separation that we know in North America and Europe today is a relatively recent development in one part of the world" (Madsen, "Religion," 36).

35. McGuire, *Lived Religion*, 185.

The Nature of Postsecular Consumerist Spirituality

Once it is established what postsecular religious expression is, describing its basic features is a much easier task. What does seem to be an unavoidable observation about postsecular trendlines, particularly in the American context, is the proliferation of religious subjectivities, especially through conceptions of spirituality. While modern continental Europe has tended to view itself as religiously secular, the United States has a longer history of a self-understanding as a "Christian nation." Its founding fathers envisioned a legal separation of church and state—but, importantly, sanctioned by God. This means religious expression from the beginning was structurally aligned with privatized expressions, and this basic sentiment has remained surprisingly resilient in American society even as so much else has changed. Thus, any strengthening of religiosity in the United States, however empirically vague, is best understood as a reemergence that still holds very tightly to a privatized conception of religion.[36] Perhaps the US context is best understood as late secular or, as Taylor described it, a flexible and responsive secularism where faith is one human possibility among others. US religiosity has become less active and more latent.[37]

In this section, I argue that postsecular religious expression in the context of contemporary American evangelical theology can be summarized as a latently consumerist spirituality that, because of its involvement with consumer market capitalism, has instrumentalizing tendencies. This is a problem. When not regularly checked against, rational instrumentality can obscure the fostering of intrinsic virtues such as love, friendship, and acceptance. Such goods are necessary for human wellbeing but dissipate when pursued for their utility.[38]

Spirituality in individuals and groups can be defined as "the experience and process of engaging with and managing significant relations and attachments with a variety of objects."[39] The fostering of a variety of relationships and attachments is essential for human survival. Specifically, humans seek spiritual experiences in pursuit of self-improvement, transformation, and transcendence.

The dynamic growth of consumer market capitalism has introduced a unique manifestation of spirituality: people who identify as spiritual and

---

36. Dias and Beaumont, "Postsecularism."
37. See Baird, "Late Secularism"; Taylor, *Sources*.
38. See McGilchrist, *Master*; Scruton, *Intelligent*.

39. Pattison, "Spirituality," 351. In this understanding, religious belief and practice are a part of general human behavior and a subset of the human pursuit and attachments.

not religious.[40] In this context, "religion indicates communal identity and interactions, authority, and tradition," whereas "spirituality indicates individual experience, novelty, and antiauthoritarian impulse."[41]

The substantial growth of the American middle class throughout the twentieth century was pivotal to the manifestation. Economic expansion and modernization meant that more members of the working class were "receiving incomes that enabled them to increase their consumption."[42] Religion was also pulled into this consumption.[43] The decision-making process that people used in their religious or spiritual lives took on the preference-driven process of other consumer choices such as buying a car or choosing a neighborhood in which to live.[44] Religious expression reflects a consumer lifestyle choice: low on obligation, highly individualistic, and highly subjective.[45]

In other words, this was a turn away from traditional mediums of experiencing the "transcendent" (such as liturgical practice), and toward commercialized mediums, which are inherently individualistic and materialistic. Consumer capitalism is contracting the sacred and transcendent of traditional religion inward, and consumerist spirituality is adopting the core features of enterprise itself.[46]

Given the original design of market capitalism, this is not altogether surprising. Consumer market capitalism is structurally calculated to achieve an efficient integration of supply and demand through a mechanism of self-interest. Utility is maximized when market actors take an instrumental approach to relating to other market actors. Capitalism's recent growth has extended the reach of instrumentality into various spheres of human experience.

However, this has far-ranging implications because consumption is not just an economic system, but a cultural and religious one that shapes human meaning and sociality. All forms of spiritual and religious practice

---

40. I am not suggesting that market capitalism's rapid growth was the only contributing factor, just that it was predominate. A plethora of social, cultural, economic, and geographic forces are at work, integrated with each other and not easily separable. See Albanese, *Nature*; Luke, *Civil*; Ruthven, *Divine*.
Part of the market pull was to increase the number of "offerings" from non-Christian religions (particularly eastern mystical).

41. Vries, "Why," 48.
42. Christiano et al., *Sociology of Religion*, 143.
43. See Einstein, *Brands*.
44. Christiano et al., *Sociology*, 40.
45. Turner, "Post-Secular Society," 138; Stark and Bainbridge, *Future of Religion*.
46. Luckmann, *Invisible*; Turner, "Post-Secular Society," 139.

involve physical and individual dimensions.[47] Indeed, consumer capitalism has advanced human wellbeing by increasing access to material goods that raise standards of living and life expectancy, especially among those in extreme poverty.[48] However, what appears to be setting postsecular consumerist spirituality apart is the intensity with which it emphasizes the material and individual dimensions for spiritual fulfillment. When analyzed with the integrative model of religion outlined above, postsecular consumerist spirituality envisions human *telos* as ultimately a product or service that can be instrumentally acquired through capitalistic consumer markets. The autonomous consumer is accessing an ephemeral and digitized market for goods and services for self-making that minimizes human interaction.

Herein lies the problem. By emphasizing the individual and material dimensions so strongly, this view of spirituality minimizes the relational and social dimensions that are also essential for the human pursuit of wellbeing, transformation, and transcendence. These social virtues, such as love, wisdom, and humility, are intrinsic in that they vanish if pursued for their utility. An attempt to grasp them by force of will "merely drives them away."[49] Thus, they are not acquired or experienced like consumer goods and services. They are gradually experienced and developed over long periods in the context of strong relational collectives.

Adam Smith argued that the social virtues would incentivize an enlightened self-interest in consumer exchange that limited greed and the violation of others' rights.[50] It appears that this check is being undercut by the nature of consumer capitalism's own dynamic growth. The radical prioritization of consumption in western "cultures of enhancement" has generated a commoditized and instrumentalizing view of the self that can disintegrate individuals from the "living human web."[51] Despite the digital interconnectedness that consumer capitalism has facilitated, a range of studies have documented a continued decline in the size of people's core network of close relationships.[52] The minimization of human sociality and intrinsicality can threaten the sustaining of deep symbols necessary to narrate the meaning of our lives beyond material terms.[53] Not surprisingly, one of the observed

---

47. Mises, *Theory*; Richins, "Valuing Things"; Woodward, *Understanding*.
48. McCloskey, *Bourgeois Equality*, 5–8; Sachs, *End of Poverty*, 1–2.
49. McGilchrist, *Master*, 161.
50. Wright, "Smith," 47.
51. Miller-McLemore, "Practical." See also Latimer, "All-Consuming Passions"; Rogers-Vaughn, *Caring*, 120–25.
52. Parigi and Henson, "Social Isolation in America."
53. Farley, *Deep Symbols*.

negative pecuniary externalities of late capitalism has been increasing social displacement and psychosocial disintegration.[54]

Here, we see the significance of postsecularism for contemporary American evangelical perceptions of enterprise. Western consumerism has reconfigured the religious and the political in late capitalism in a way that subverts the dichotomized relationship between Christian "faith" and "enterprise." This fundamentally challenges the traditional framing of the theme of transformation in which religious belief and practice stand apart from capitalistic enterprise and use it as a vehicle for moral and spiritual transformation while remaining unaffected by its excesses. Structurally, religion, state, and market remain differentiated spheres, but the market is increasingly shaping religious practice rather than the other way around. The result is a qualitative rather than quantitative transformation of the religious by the economic in which

> the tension between religion and the world has largely disappeared, or at least the tension has been eroded. Because religion is submerged in the circulation of commodities as a lifestyle choice, the capacity of religion to change societies is absent. . . . Religion as an agent of social change has been further compromised by the loss of any significant contrast between the sacred and the world. Religion has specialized in providing personal services and has therefore been competing with various secular agencies that also offer welfare, healing, comfort, and meaning. In this competition, religious groups have by and large taken over the methods and values of a range of institutions operating within what we can, for want of a more sophisticated term, call "the leisure industries."[55]

A narrow definition of religion as privatized propositional assent marginalized the relevance of theological and religious deliberation for public domains such as economics. So too, it blunted any critical consideration of the ways that consumerist capitalistic systems act as more than amoral mechanical operations, especially the coercive power structures that might be implicitly at work at social relational levels. Pushing back against this narrow definition enables critical consideration of such structures.

---

54. Barrera, *Economic Compulsion*, 19.
55. Olson et al., "Retheorizing the Postsecular Present," 142.

What Are the Implications of Postsecularism for Contemporary American Evangelical Theological Perceptions of Enterprise?

The purpose of this chapter has been to analyze the broader historical backdrop of postsecularism for the development of the theme of transformation in contemporary American evangelical theology. Thus far, I have shown that postsecularism challenges a narrow understanding of religion and spirituality as privatized propositional assent. By adopting features of capitalist enterprise, postsecular consumerist spirituality has implicitly obscured the intrinsic social and relational dimensions essential for spiritual and moral fulfillment. What remains to be demonstrated is how this bears on contemporary American evangelical theology.

It might seem that contemporary American evangelical theology is well-positioned to offer a corrective to instrumentality. Historically, religion has been a source for emphasizing the intrinsic dimensions of human experience and the necessity of resisting instrumentality for spiritual and moral transformation. Throughout the Christian traditions, the triangulating love of God has been seen as crucial. A prominent ethical thread in the Christian scriptures calls for the habitual resisting of instrumentalizing tendencies so that intrinsic human worth can be valued and relational communities can flourish. The human tendency to seek individual and material gain at the expense of others is transformed through the triangulating love of God expressed in Jesus of Nazareth into a non-possessive love of others (Eph 5:2; John 13:34; 15:13 Mark 8:34–35; Rom 5:8). "By pursuing God as the ultimate concern," human desire is transformed via God so that humans can value created things—including other humans—in their own right and love others intrinsically.[56]

In actuality, postsecular consumerist spirituality poses a fundamental paradox to contemporary American evangelical theology. It presents an opportunity by opening public space for dialogue about the religious, spiritual, and theological dimensions of enterprise. Alternatively, it challenges the traditional articulation of the theme of transformation in which Christian faith is portrayed as harnessing the good of western consumer market capitalism without being affected by its instrumentalizing excesses. I briefly explore both.

First, the opportunity. The postsecular diffusion of religious expression into spheres not normally seen as religious has created space for public dialogue about the theological and spiritual dimensions of enterprise.

---

56. Nieuwenhove, "Religious Disposition," 692.

At the popular level, this has been evidenced by media attention, such as the July 2001 cover story in *Fortune* entitled "God and business: The surprising quest for spiritual renewal in the workplace" and a 1999 cover story in *BusinessWeek* entitled "Religion in the Workplace." At a scholarly level, there has been a renewed interdisciplinary interest in subjects such as organizational spirituality.[57]

This reorientation has enabled both scholars of management and theology to point out where spirituality and organizational life intersect. Pattison, for example, spells out three ways in which modern management can be seen as "substantially religious activity": the faith assumptions of managers, the religious style and order of management, and the faith content and religious language found in management theory and practice.[58] He also suggested several benefits to management theory and practice were it to integrate theological thinking: (a) critical awareness of the use of language, metaphors, and myths; (b) the creative nature of faith; (c) a broad horizon for self-criticism; (d) critical understanding of transformational knowledge; (e) learning from other religious traditions.

Similarly, Greil and Bromley identified "quasi-religious corporations" as a facet of American organizational life.[59] They have arisen in response to the hegemony of the contractually organized public sphere of social life (structured principally by the economy and the state), over the covenantally organized private sphere structured principally by the family, community, and religion. These organizations

> promise to reintegrate work, politics, family, community, and religion through the formation of family-businesses that are linked together into a tightly-knit social network and legitimated symbolically by appeals to nationalism and transcendent purpose.[60]

For contemporary evangelical theology, the promise of this effort is that postsecular religious expression has opened the public sphere for refreshed dialogue, even for theology. Graham wrote:

> The postsecular represents the emergence of a new kind of public square in which religion is newly resurgent, and yet its legitimacy as a form of public reason continues to be hotly contested.... While the resurgence of religion is regarded by many as prompting a much-needed moral rejuvenation of secular

---

57. See Giacalone and Jurkiewicz, "Science"; Cadge et al., "Religion."
58. Pattison, "Faith," 37–39.
59. Greil and Bromley, *Defining Religion*, 135.
60. Greil and Bromley, *Defining Religion*, 135.

society, for others this new eruption of faith continues to represent a dangerous breach of the neutrality of the public sphere.[61]

While new visibility for religion and spirituality in public life presents an opportunity for contemporary American evangelical theology, it also presents a challenge. The reason is that postsecularism has shifted the conditions for public dialogue, requiring that contemporary American evangelical theology to offer a more reflexive account of how Christian faith can integrate with capitalistic enterprise for moral and spiritual transformation. Traditionally stated, the theme of transformation portrays Christian faith as harnessing the good of western consumer market capitalism without being affected by its instrumentalizing excesses. When the theme of transformation was formalized in the twentieth century, this made sense. Evangelical Christianity still exercised significant political and social influence in American public life. Moreover, market capitalism's growth was relatively stable and predictable.

Postsecularism has changed this. Both the decline in identification with traditional Protestant Christianity and the rise of individualist-materialist spirituality have weakened the public influence of evangelicalism. The mainstream public sphere can now be understood as post-Christian in that Christianity is no longer the majority "micro-sphere."[62] Globalization and interconnection have increased the diversity of perspectives, many representing non-traditional and minority groups that are, in fact, hostile to the legacy of traditional western Christianity. The destabilizing effects of capitalism's postsecular growth have extended the scrutiny to Protestant evangelical Christianity's ties to the instrumentalizing features of consumer capitalism.

A closer historical analysis shows that this scrutiny is warranted. There are three concerns at work. First, are the theme of transformation's imperialist and colonialist undercurrents. In the seventeenth and eighteenth centuries, American colonizers often defined their "transformational mission" in the new world in biblical terms. They were a "'chosen people,' on an errand in the 'wilderness,' creating the 'new Israel' or the 'new Jerusalem' in what was clearly 'the promised land.'"[63] As with the European colonization of Africa, American efforts integrated a God-sanctioned call for redemptive

---

61. Graham, *Rock and a Hard Place*, xviii.

62. McCallum, "Micro Public Spheres," 175–78.

63. Huntington, *Who Are We?*, 64. For an astute overview of the relationship of the "kingdom of God" to American colonialism, see Naveh, "Dialectical."

transformation with the imposition of Western cultural forms and economic value systems on the indigenous peoples.[64]

In this hermeneutic of colonization, there was an association between "whiteness" and civilized" and between "Indianness" and "uncivilized," and justification of such ideology from the Bible.[65] Puritan thinkers such as John Eliot and Cotton Mather expressed similar sentiments, continuing through the nineteenth century when "Christian mission agencies constituted the de facto arm of the US government's civilization project."[66] This hermeneutic drew from the Enlightenment myth of progress, a conception of "universal history as the ever-advancing development of human capacities" that has "has been fundamental to both to self-understanding of the modern West and its view of relations to the rest of the world."[67] The myth of progress figures heavily in evangelical espousals of American exceptionalism that America is a Christian nation ordained by God.[68]

Second, is the way in which American evangelicalism's emphasis on individualism and the free market fueled capitalism's modern expansion. Influentially, Weber saw a secularization of the Protestant work ethic in capitalism's early growth. Protestantism instilled in its adherents a distinct "ethic" and a sense of divine calling and election that fostered an individual mandate to hard work and to live frugally. For Weber, there was cause to be concerned about a secularized Protestant ethic so forcefully driven by a materialist-individualist "iron cage."[69] It could imprison workers in economic rationalization that degraded their moral basis and human autonomy.

The Protestant derived, individualist materialist ethic of the early 1900s nourished a postindustrial economic boom with an emphasis on free market capitalistic enterprise.[70] As noted in chapter 1, this harmonized with American evangelical theology's emphasis on individual responsibility and self-autonomy. With the rise of the evangelical Moral Majority and the Religious Right in the late 1970s and 1980s, a distinctly consumerist political-economic platform was materializing within conservative evangelicalism.[71] For example, evangelicals were highly supportive of President

64. See Mbiti, *African*.
65. Hawk and Twiss, "Only Good Indian."
66. Hawk and Twiss, "Only Good Indian," 52. See also Segal and Stineback, *Puritans*, 31–33. On the use of the Bible to justify slavery in American history, see Haynes, *Noah*.
67. McCarthy, *Race*, 3. See also Merrick, "Tracing," 105–11.
68. Parchami, *Hegemonic*; Bloom, *American*.
69. Weber, *Protestant*, 158.
70. Dyck and Schroeder, *Management*, 706.
71. See Brown, *Christian*.

Reagan's tax-cut and deregulation initiatives, which intended to incentivize consumer spending as a means of trickling wealth down from the wealthy to the middle-class and the poor.[72]

Third, is how contemporary American evangelicalism adopted the consumerist mentalities of postsecular spirituality. American evangelicalism adjusted to a consumerized religious marketplace by differentiating its "brand" from others.[73] An important manifestation was the "seeker-friendly" megachurch movement. It focused on constructing a Sunday church experience that appealed to the suburban middle and upper-class consumer. The continued success of megachurches is evidence that the categories of the "sacred" and "secular" are temporal and theorized. Evangelical megachurches have largely been able to sustain growth by

> its location on the postsuburban fringe of large cities, its fragmented, dispersed structure, and its focus on individualized spaces of intimacy such as small group meetings in homes, which help to interpret suburban life as religiously meaningful and create a sense of belonging.[74]

This subjective turn saw the Puritan Protestant ideals of self-sacrifice and moral-asceticism give way to a "fascination with the self and with human subjectivity."[75] The seeker friendly movement paralleled the emergence of new religious movements, even adopting the "religious" versus "spiritual" terminology.[76] A recent study, for example, found that almost 46 percent of minimally churched adults have an evangelical theological affiliation.[77]

What does all of this mean for contemporary evangelical perceptions of enterprise in the context of postsecular consumerist spirituality? It means that traditionally stated, the theme of transformation has not sufficiently accounted for the critical role that perceptual lenses, worldviews, and sociohistorical contexts play in shaping theological and religious belief. For the theme of transformation to remain viable in a postsecular context, it must acknowledge, and then overcome, the instrumentalizing forces that have marred enterprise-based transformational efforts in the past, some of which are still active.[78] According to Wilford, "far from

---

72. Nesmith, *New Republican Coalition*.
73. Einstein, *Brands of Faith*.
74. Wilford, *Sacred Subdivisions*, 33.
75. Hunter, *Evangelicalism*, 65–71.
76. See Heelas and Woodhead, *Spiritual Revolution*.
77. Barna and Kinnaman, *Churchless*, 73.
78. McCarthy, *Race*, 93; Merrick, "Tracing," 105; Hartz, *Liberal*, 285–86. Anecdotally, I can report that of the dozen or so primary sources of contemporary evangelical

spelling the end of religion, personalization, fragmentation, and compartmentalization serve as the social context within which religious organizations in civil society must adapt."[79]

The effects of conditioning factors on shaping theological belief is an even more critical consideration given that perceptions of enterprise entangle the perceiver in economic realities, increasingly forceful in their effect and yet decidedly conspicuous in their presence. To put it bluntly, "every member of an advanced society . . . is immersed in its economy—sometimes more than she knows, or wishes to admit," evangelicalism included.[80]

How, then, can contemporary American evangelical theology achieve a postsecular renewal of the theme of transformation that counters the individualist-materialist excesses of consumerist spirituality? The answer is not a non-individualist, non-materialist, non-consumerist spirituality. Rather, it is a *reflexive* spirituality that regularly interrogates its own practice and nurtures the capacity to discern.[81] An inner discipline subjects its own perceptional lenses to self-critique and self-scrutiny.[82] The conflicting or uneven implementation of theological notions across history warrants in the first place not a discarding of the categories, but the exercise of "practical public reason," or "moral discrimination that pronounces upon a preceding act or existing state of affairs to establish a new public context."[83]

For American evangelicalism, this represents a significant shift in how to publicly orient evangelical Christian faith. Reacting against liberal theological and philosophical movements, American evangelicalism throughout the twentieth century aligned around a classical foundationalist apologetics that sought to defend the rational totality of a supposed Christian worldview. The traditional articulation of the theme of transformation shared in this posture, articulating the relationship between Christian faith and capitalistic enterprise as transactional and compartmentalized.

Postsecular trajectories undermine this posture. Religion is increasingly visible in public life—but in ways starkly different than before: "Religious institutions are fragile; skeptics and critics of religion continue to question its very legitimacy as a respectable intellectual option and a legitimate influence in society; and yet, religion continues to be a significant

---

theology consulted for this section, not one contained a discussion about imperialism/colonialism.

79. Wilford, *Sacred Subdivisions*, 33.
80. Schneider, *Good of Affluence*, 1.
81. See also Stoddart and Johnson, "Retail"; Flanagan, *Sociology*, 189.
82. Werhane, *Moral*, 99.
83. Kidwell, "Righteousness," 95; O'Donovan, *Ways*, 7.

source of social capital, and comprises the strongest single stakeholder in the voluntary sector."[84]

As Graham continues, this means Christian traditions such as American evangelicalism must negotiate the "rock" of religious resurgence and the "hard place" of lingering secularism. So too, moving forward requires a mutually informing faithfulness to Christian tradition and openness to diverse and critical conversation in the public domain. This requires a shift from classical apologetics to an "apologetics of presence."[85] Centered on demonstrating how God's revelation through Jesus of Nazareth manifests in embodied social virtues such as love and friendship that contribute to human flourishing in ways that consumer markets cannot.

Contemporary American evangelical theology must contemplate, then, a postsecular renewal of the theme of transformation from a redefined position of power and influence that is no longer at the center but at the margins, where critical reflective practical wisdom displaces doctrinal articulation as a primary means of witness. In many ways, this is a return to scriptural *evangelical* Christianity.

Conclusion

The focus of this chapter has been to analyze the broader historical context within which the theme of transformation emerged in contemporary American evangelical theology. I did this by unpacking postsecular consumerist spirituality as a significant disruption in the American religious landscape enacted by the dynamic growth of capitalistic enterprise. It has facilitated both a decline in religious expression with regard to traditional forms of institutionalized religion and a rise with regard to a less traditional and more individualistic and materialistic form of implicit religious expression. By blurring the division between the supposed secular nonreligious public sphere and the private religious sphere, postsecularism has opened unique public space for dialogue about the transformative dimensions of enterprise but also challenges contemporary American evangelical theology's reflexive abilities.

---

84. Graham, "Rock and a Hard Place," 239.
85. Graham, "Rock and a Hard Place," 239.

Introduction to Part Two

Part one has elaborated the problem facing contemporary American evangelical perceptions of enterprise. This began in chapter 1 with an articulation of the practical theological method guiding my research. In chapter 2, potential obstacles to evangelical reflexivity were assessed. Chapter 3 overviewed the theme of transformation in contemporary American evangelical theology while chapter 4 analyzed postsecularism as the broader sociohistorical context in which the theme of transformation has emerged.

Having defined the problem as the need for a critical postsecular renewal of the theme of transformation that strengthens evangelical reflexivity, in part two, I now elaborate a resolution. It reflects my positioning within the discipline of practical Christian theology, where strengthening theological reflexivity is a core focus. The solution must address not just doctrinal consistency, but also the ambiguities of embodied spiritual practices.

5

What Is Stakeholder Theory?

Within organizational studies, stakeholder theory has emerged as a central framework for thinking about the moral dimensions of enterprise. For a postsecular renewal of the theme of transformation in contemporary American evangelical theology, it comprises an ideal dialogue partner. The place to begin is first to seek to understand stakeholder theory on its terms. That is the objective of chapter 5.

Like the theme of transformation, the emergence of stakeholder theory in the late twentieth century was not in a vacuum. Significant shifts were taking place in perceptions about the role of capitalistic enterprise in shaping human experience, prompting debates over the ways in which the financial and operational dimensions of a firm should determine its broader social functioning. In overviewing stakeholder theory, I first describe the stakeholder framework in relation to these debates. Then, I show how stakeholder's ethical framework has primarily depended on relational individualism, similar to the individualist model adopted by secularization theory.

The Stakeholder Framework

Stakeholder theory holds that the purpose of a firm is to maximize long term value for all its stakeholders. A stakeholder is "any group or individual who can affect or is affected by the achievement of the organization's objectives."[1] They are the groups without whose support the organization would cease to exist and include not just shareholders, but employees, customers, suppliers, society, government, and the environment.[2] It emerged in the late twentieth century in response to shareholder theory, which

---

1. Freeman, *Strategic Management*, 46.
2. Freeman and Reed, "Stockholders and Stakeholders," 89.

contended that the only responsibility of a firm is to maximize shareholder profits without violating any laws.

Conceptually, stakeholder theory is an effort to address three interconnected business problems: how value is created and traded, how ethics is connected to profit, and how to help managers think about management such that the first two are addressed.[3] An important conviction is that these problems are more effectively addressed with integrative vocabulary that captures the complex relationships between firms and their constituencies. A business can be seen through a financial lens as an income statement and balance sheet; through an operational lens as a supply chain or a distribution channel; through a customer lens as a product or service to be bought, and through a social/relational lens as a set of relationships among groups that have vested interest in its objectives and activities.[4] How executives and managers govern the interests of its various stakeholders determines the long-term success of the enterprise.

These ideas might seem obvious because stakeholder language has become so pervasive. However, that was not always the case. Modern business management evolved in the early twentieth century with stress on productivity and output. Frederick Taylor, an engineer by trade, provided one of the first management theories. The innovation of Taylor's system was the idea that efficiency could be enhanced by analyzing workflows.[5] He challenged the prevailing assumption that an increase in the intensity of a laborer's work automatically equaled an increase in economic value. Using several time and motion studies, Taylor argued that the focus of management should be on an optimization of the workflow process. Thus, Taylor argued for a management bureaucracy in an organization that was devoted to training employees and controlling outputs.[6]

Capitalism's rapid industrial growth had created a need for better management systems and Taylor's ideas spread quickly. Still, they did not go unchallenged. A vocal critic was Max Weber. Like Taylor, Weber espoused a bureaucratic organizational control equipped with standardized procedures and a focus on efficiency. However, as a sociologist, Weber diverged from Taylor by warning of the social dangers of an excessive individualist-materialist emphasis like the one manifested in the Protestant work ethic. It was an "iron cage" that reduced human workers to output figures, degrading

---

3. Parmar et al., "Stakeholder," 404.
4. Walsh, "Stock," 430.
5. Drucker, *Management*, 181.
6. Littler, "Understanding," 198.

their moral basis and autonomy.[7] To break free from the shackles, what is needed is the "articulation of alternative moral points of view upon which to develop a new paradigm for management."[8]

As an established concept, stakeholder theory is quite recent. The first use of the term was in the early 1960s by Stanford researcher Igor Ansoff describing corporate strategic planning. The long term goals of a firm, said Ansoff, should be the result of a balancing of the various (and sometimes conflicting) claims of the firm's stakeholders.[9] In this early understanding, stakeholder claims on an organization were primarily seen as one of several social factors that should be considered in the planning process. They were secondary to the long-term economic objectives of a firm, which should remain the central focus of strategic planning.[10]

Beginning in the 1970s, the growing field of business ethics solidified stakeholder language. De George points out a few of the primary drivers of this shift: a growing distrust of the partnership between business and government as expressed in the military-industrial complex that played itself out in World War II, the Cold War, and Vietnam; the surging economic dominance the United States was imposing on the world stage, leading to the emergence of multinational conglomerates and widespread consumerism; and the awakening of the environmental consciousness in response to the rise of innovation in the chemical industry.[11] Taylor suggested satisfying a firm's various stakeholders would become the dominant theoretical frame informing corporate strategic planning.[12] In 1975, Dill from the NYU School of Business published a critical article arguing that successful companies would be able to manage its dynamically changing stakeholder environment for "strategic prowess."[13]

By the early 1980s, the stakeholder perspective was firmly entrenched across business strategy and ethics. However, it was still without a *locus classicus*. All of that would change with R. Edward Freeman and his 1984 publication, *Strategic Management: A Stakeholder Approach*.

A philosopher by training, Freeman brought a broad perspective to stakeholder theory and synthesized earlier stakeholder notions. His was the first explicit attempt to create a stakeholder management approach,

---

7. Weber, *Protestant*, 181.
8. Dyck and Schroeder, "Management," 707.
9. Ansoff, *Corporate*, 34.
10. Freeman et al., *Stakeholder Theory*, 32.
11. See De George, *History*.
12. Taylor, "Future."
13. Dill, "Public," 59–64.

going from "an intuitively appealing description of a firm's theoretically underrepresented constituencies" to a "well-elaborated method of decision making in organizations."[14]

Freeman's central thesis was that the dominant story of managerial capitalism with shareholders at the center is no longer viable in a complex global society.[15] For most of the early period of the modern corporation, argued Freeman, the assumption was "businesses are to be managed solely for the benefit of shareholders. Any other benefits (or harms) that are created are incidental."[16] This focus on increasing shareholder wealth warrants scrutiny given the increasingly complex capital structures within the organization of corporations that separates management from ownership.

Freeman was directly confronting the shareholder/stockholder perspective, not without its own proponents particularly among free market economists, most notably, Nobel laureate Milton Friedman. He had written an influential *New York Times* essay in 1970 contending that maximizing shareholder profits within the legal limits was the fundamental responsibility of a firm's management. Anything that reduced shareholders' returns was a violation of this responsibility.[17] Friedman's reasoning was grounded in his liberal, moral, and economic philosophy, which put a high value on private property and free markets. Since "the corporation is an instrument of the stockholders who own it," it is the stockholders and their interests that have primacy and ultimate control.[18]

When managers pursue corporate social responsibility initiatives that leak out shareholder value, they are violating fundamental property rights essential to the proper functioning of capitalistic enterprise. This does not give managers license for evil since their endeavors for maximum shareholder return must conform "to the basic rules of the society, both those embodied in law and those embodied in ethical custom."[19]

For Freeman, the shareholder perspective served a purpose for a specific economic climate but was now in need of revision because economic and fiduciary circumstances have altered. Quite simply, "the world has changed so that the stability and predictability required by the shareholder approach can no longer be assured."[20] The majority view can no longer

---

14. Phillips, *Stakeholder*, 65–66.
15. See Bowie, "Kantian."
16. Freeman, "Managing for Stakeholders," 1.
17. Friedman, "Social Responsibility of Business," 6.
18. Friedman, "Social Responsibility of Business," 8.
19. Friedman, "Social Responsibility of Business," 8.
20. Freeman, "Managing for Stakeholders," 8.

commit a separation fallacy that separates "business" decisions from "ethical" decisions. At any point in its operation, a business is making decisions that have multi-dimensional outcomes for its stakeholders, and "there is no conflict between serving all your stakeholders and providing excellent returns for shareholders."[21]

Freeman saw in the separation fallacy a relic of Enlightenment scientific positivism. The naive modernist born dichotomy between the financial and operational aspects of business (its "public" and quantifiable concerns) and its ethical aspects (its "private" and qualitative concerns) is not only unrealistic but untrue. The separation fallacy needs to be replaced by what Freeman called "the integration thesis." Most business decisions or sentences about business have some ethical content or implicit ethical view. Most ethical decisions or sentences about ethics have some business content or implicit view about business.[22]

Stakeholder language provides integrative language for practitioners and theorists to reconceptualize the responsibilities of an enterprise that recognizes the humanness of organizations:

> Business is fully situated in the realm of humanity . . . human institutions populated by real live complex human beings. Stakeholders have names and faces and children. . . . As such, matters of ethics are routine when one takes a managing-for-stakeholders approach.[23]

As Freeman moved stakeholder theory to the forefront, many studies defended the financial soundness of the approach. For example, a stakeholder approach helps reduce business risk and create a more stable shareholder return, enhanced organization agility, and broader revenue streams through attractive joint ventures and partnerships.[24]

By the early 1990s, the stakeholder framework entered a period of increased diversity. Two different approaches, descriptive and normative, were materializing.[25] The descriptive approach was based on social science and focused on developing empirical models. The normative approach was based on ethics and focused on developing normative models. While utilizing different methodologies for different objectives, both remain focused

---

21. Freeman, "Managing for Stakeholders," 8.
22. Freeman, "Managing for Stakeholders," 5.
23. Freeman, "Managing for Stakeholders," 1.
24. Graves and Waddock, "Institutional"; Harrison and St. John, "Managing and Partnering"; Fombrun and Shanley, "Reputation."
25. See Jones and Wicks, "Divergent"; Donaldson and Preston, *Stakeholder*.

on a central question: "What kinds of stakeholder relationships are both morally sound and practicable?"[26]

The Relational Individualism of the Stakeholder Framework

An overview of the emergence of stakeholder theory shows that the contemplation of the moral and relational dimensions of enterprise is central to the stakeholder framework. It upholds that capitalistic enterprise has transformative potential "to contribute to the conservation and restoration of the natural world, to the development of human capabilities and to the enhancement of the freedom of future generations."[27] However, this transformative potential is only realized when managerial decision making within enterprise incorporates a broad view of a firm's stakeholders, integrating financial and operational ends with human and social ones.

Now, I want to show that the stakeholder framework has primarily adopted relational individualism to make its moral claims. In doing so, it mirrors a dichotomized model of the "individual" and the "social" like the one operative in secularization theory. Bucholz and Rosenthal argued that it is particularly the normative strand within stakeholder theory that has been deeply influenced by relational individualism, wherein, "individuals as well as institutions are isolatable units that have well-defined boundaries, can be considered as separate from their surroundings, and are not an integral part of the community or society in which they function."[28] According to Wicks et al., "One of the assumptions of this worldview is that the 'self' is fundamentally isolatable from other selves and from its larger context."[29]

The conceptualization of stakeholders into individuals or groups of individuals has far reaching implications because it takes place within a broader western cultural, scientific framework that has historically placed a high value on self-atomizing perspectives.[30] This atomized framework has origins in the scientific revolution that modified the ancient western tradition for applying moral and ethical reasoning to enterprise.

To see this, developments within contemporary stakeholder theory need to be briefly linked to their historical and philosophical lineages. In challenging the separation fallacy, Freeman and other early stakeholder

26. Jones and Wicks, "Divergent," 216.
27. Zsolnai, "Extended Stakeholder Theory," 37.
28. Bucholz and Rosenthal, "Contemporary Conceptual Framework," 138.
29. Wicks et al., "Feminist Reinterpretation," 479.
30. Schmuck and Sheldon, *Life Goals*, 2.

proponents called for more deliberate engagement with philosophical ethics. While not a comprehensive moral theory, the stakeholder perspective attempts to better integrate theory with practice to guide actual managerial decision making, often in areas where opposing organizational value systems, interpersonal conflict, social impact, and legal obligation are at play.[31] Therefore, it is encroaching on the realm of philosophical ethics, which deals "with substantive issues regarding moral values, principles, notions of well-being, and character."[32] Freeman wrote:

> Stakeholder theory represents a bridge between the normative analysis of the philosopher and the empirical/instrumental investigation of the management scholar. By being at once explicitly moral and requiring support from instrumental analysis, stakeholder theory offers a new way to think about management theory. To provide a defensible normative core, researchers need to be able to show that it is simultaneously defensible in terms of moral norms and principles as well as in terms such that enacting these norms and principles is likely to help the firm generate economic value to remain a sustainably profitable enterprise.[33]

Normative contemporary stakeholder theory is marked by a variety of proposals for what should constitute a normative ethical core.[34] My purpose here is not to enter the thick of this debate, but rather to point out that to justify their cores, the dominant proposals derive ethical philosophical lineages from post-Enlightenment relational individualism. The philosophical roots of business ethics are principled, in two forms: utilitarian-based ethics approaches and deontological-based approaches.[35] Both ethical approaches "provide guidelines to help people evaluate whether acts are morally right or wrong."[36]

As a form of consequentialism (also called the teleological approach), utilitarianism evaluates an action based on the extent to which it achieves a particular result. Right action is that which maximizes the good or minimizes the bad for the greatest number of people in a community. The term was coined by eighteenth-century legal philosopher Jeremy Bentham but found its most notable proponent in the thought of nineteenth-century

---

31. See Phillips, *Stakeholder Theory*.
32. Smith, *Normative Theory*, 42.
33. Parmar et al., "Stakeholder Theory," 411.
34. See Dienhart, *Business, Institutions, and Ethics*; Ross, *Right and the Good*.
35. Donaldson and Werhane, *Ethical Issues In Business*, 7.
36. Horvath, "Excellence v. Effectiveness," 500.

philosopher and economist John Stuart Mill.[37] Connecting the principle of utility to ancient notions of happiness, particularly in Aristotle and Augustine, Mill argued that if on reasonable grounds it is asserted that everyone desires happiness or pleasure, then morality is that which successfully results in the maximization of happiness for the greatest number.[38] An enlightened self-determination was the fundamental basis of human autonomy, expressing the idea that a "person is a bounded individual who is able to live her life freely in accordance with her self-chosen plan, and ideally *independently* from controlling influences."[39]

With its focus on outcomes, utilitarian approaches have been widely adopted within business ethics in general and stakeholder theory in particular.[40] Among contemporary stakeholder theorists, Gustafson represented a utilitarian approach. Challenging the misconstrual that utilitarianism in business ethics is synonymous with cost-benefit, profit maximization, and self-interest, he contended that a well-articulated utilitarian stakeholder approach emphasizes long-term outcomes:

> A company which follows this . . . will be concerned with fair treatment of employees, honest habits with customers and suppliers, and just policies because acting with justice, fairness, and honesty will, in the end, produce the greatest happiness for the many—through increased productivity, a strong reputation, and customer loyalty all leading to a positive outcome.[41]

Consistently throughout philosophical tradition, criticism of utilitarianism has centered on two aspects.[42] First, as far as utilitarianism seeks the good for the majority, it leaves open possibilities of injustice for the minority irrespective of consequences. Second, critics have noted the difficulty in prioritizing which "good" constitutes the maximal good. Contemporary business ethical criticism of utility generally follows these trails. For example, Hartman and Bowie leveled the charge of a majority bias undermining the rights of the minority while Paine underscored the detriment of trying to seek a meaningful definition of the common good in a compliance-based culture that utilitarianism can tend to foster.[43]

---

37. See Burns, "Happiness and Utility."

38. Mill, *Utilitarianism*, 81.

39. Dove et al., "Beyond Individualism," 152.

40. See DesJardins, *Business Ethics*; Elfstrom, *Moral Issues*; Frederick, *Companion to Business Ethics*.

41. Gustafson, "Utilitarian Business Ethic," 332.

42. Donaldson and Werhane, *Ethical Issues in Business*, 18–20.

43. See Hartman, *Organizational Ethics*; Bowie, "Kantian Approach"; Paine, "Organizational Integrity."

In contrast to utilitarianism is deontology, an alternative dominant ethical perspective that views the principles and rules guiding behavior as the focus of ethical concern, not the outcomes.[44] Generally, the deontological perspective is further divided into two forms. The first form comes through Kant. Seeking the fundamental grounds for which human actions are universally moral, Kant argued that goodness is ascribed to actions motivated by willfully free and reasoned decisions. Actions "are good because they are done for the sake of what is right and not because of the consequences they might produce."[45]

To arrive at the context in which pure goodness is done for pure reasons, Kant posited the idea of "the categorical imperative," which consists of principles that are intrinsically good and must be adhered to by all peoples in all circumstances. In contrast to hypothetical imperatives, which are temporally employed for the attainment of specific ends, categorical imperatives denote universal duty or obligation.[46]

For Kant, the ethical person is one who acts from right intentions. The concept of the categorical imperative functioned as a sort of litmus test for universal moral truths. In deciding whether a certain action was moral, it could be asked whether a world in which everyone acted on that principle was possible. Kant pointed to many examples to illustrate his point, one of which involved commerce. He proposed for consideration a man in dire financial straits who borrowed money and promised to pay, but in actuality, had no intentions to repay. To evaluate the morality of the man's actions, Kant reasoned, it should be asked whether a universal maxim could be logically constructed from the action—that all people should borrow money with no intention to repay. In this case, it cannot, thus, the "maxim would necessarily destroy itself as soon as it was made a universal law."[47]

Kantian-based approaches are numerous among contemporary stakeholder theorists, a notable one being Bowie. He saw in Kant's categorical imperatives substantial grounds for morally sensitive business practices. One of the most prominent regards the treating of stakeholders as persons. Essential to Kant's moral conceptualizing was the existence of individual free will, with

---

44. "Deontology" comes from the Greek word δέον, meaning "obligation" or "duty."

45. Donaldson and Werhane, *Ethical Issues in Business*, 5–7.

46. The fundamental categorical imperative for Kant was "to act only according to that maxim whereby you can, at the same time, will that it should become a universal law" (Kant, *Grounding*, 30). Additionally, there are at least two other maxims that qualified as categorical imperatives for Kant: treat human beings as an end and never a means, and act as if you were making laws for a kingdom in which you were both a subject and a sovereign (Kant, *Grounding*, 43).

47. Kant, *Grounding*, 30.

which moral agents could make deliberate decisions for moral reasons. Bowie argued: "Since human beings have free will and thus are able to act from laws required by reason, Kant believed they have the dignity of or a value beyond price. Thus, one human being cannot use another simply to satisfy his or her own interests."[48] Likewise, above all, this means a business firm is a moral community sustained by and dependent on humanized employer-employee relations that challenge hierarchical constraints.

The second form of deontological ethics is known as the contractarian perspective. It is an alternative to Kantian deontology in that it reasons not from categorical imperatives that all rational individuals should be able to agree upon, but from social contracts. This view received initial expression through Locke, who contended that universal ethical norms could be reasoned for by beginning with a state of nature in which there were no laws, states, or political conventions, and then seeking foundational rules rational people would use to govern communities.[49] For Locke, these rules function as protections against the violations of natural rights by governments.

A modern proponent of contract theory—one whose work has dramatically affected stakeholder theory—was John Rawls.[50] While utilizing the concept of a social contract to identify universal ethical norms, Rawls diverged from Locke's proposition of natural rights. Instead, he argued, if each person were behind a "veil of ignorance" about himself or herself—utterly devoid of a self-understandings about race, gender, age, etc., thus, incapable of self-favor—we could identify universally-applicable principles of justice by speculating about what principles to which such people would agree.[51]

This "justice as fairness" is grounded, first in the principle that "each person has the same indefeasible claim to a fully adequate scheme of equal basic liberties, which scheme is compatible with the same scheme of liberties for all," and second, that where social and economic inequalities do exist, "they are to be attached to offices and positions open to all under conditions of fair equality of opportunity and they are to be to the greatest benefit of the least-advantaged members of society."[52]

While pursuing a broader Kantian ethic, Freeman drew heavily from Rawls's conceptualization of justice as fairness, as his original stakeholder notions were formalized into normative forms.[53] More broadly, the deon-

---

48. Bowie, "Kantian Approach," 64.
49. See Wolterstorff, *John Locke*.
50. Hsieh, "Normative Study," 93.
51. Rawls, *Theory of Justice*, 118.
52. Rawls, *Justice as Fairness*, 302.
53. See Evan and Freeman, "Stakeholder Theory." Appropriation of Rawls has been

tological perspective's most significant criticism has been its inability to account for the seemingly valid presence of exceptions to general rules. If there are indeed universal moral norms that are true in all circumstances, how can they be general enough to apply to all circumstances, yet, specific enough to account for exceptional circumstances?[54]

An overview of the dominant ethical approaches within normative stakeholder theory clarifies the vital role relational individualism has played. While there is an excellent variety within the consequentialist and deontological camps for justifying normative cores, they take as an implicit starting point the Enlightenment-derived categories of the "individual" and the "social." I say implicit because answering the question, "What is the human person?" is not a fundamental objective of normative stakeholder theory. Instead, it is characterizing the relationship between an individual person or corporation and broader society. Yet, in utilizing these categories, a *de facto* account of what it means to be human is constructed.

This paradigm posits a dichotomized relationship between the individual and society. The theoretical individual is framed as "presocial, atomistic, autonomous, self-subsistent, self-determining, always seeking liberty and freedom, and valorized as representing the triumph of the human agent overall external forces of constraint and repression" while the social self, by contrast, is framed as "socially dependent, socially constituted, constructed, and determined, variable, transient, and morally illusory compared to the valorized individual."[55]

In the case of stakeholder theory, there is a dichotomized relationship between the realm of atomic corporate interests (and by extension, the individuals within a single corporation) and broader social stakeholder interests (and by extension, the community of individuals outside a single corporation).[56] Essential to this schema is the functional compartmentalizing of individual and social dimensions of reality. First, at the level of the

---

critiqued by some on what is determined to be "differences between business organizations and states that make it inappropriate to apply Rawls's theory to business organizations" (Hsieh, "Normative Study," 98).

54. Donaldson and Werhane, *Ethical Issues in Business*, 9.

55. Smith, *Flourish or Destruct*, 57.

56. Kluver et al. differentiated between two closely related approaches to human ontology in the context of management studies. *Homo economicus*, which drew from the human ontologies of Adam Smith, David Hume, and J. S. Mill, has been adopted as foundational to neoclassical economics in its view that humans are self-interested utilitarian maximizers of their individual preferences in ways that benefit larger society. *Homo heuristicus*, which incorporates evolutionary psychology, understands human self-interest as contextually shaped by certain heuristics developed within one's surrounding environment. See Kluver et al., "Behavioral Ethics."

individual, where a "private" and a "public" sphere is posited, and then at the level of the social, where domains such as "government," "education," "home," and "enterprise" are posited.

Like any attempt to capture the relationship between the individual and the social, this approach has definite explanatory appeal and excels at capturing certain elements of the flourishing human endeavor. It did not come to dominate the spectrum of western intellectual thought for no reason. In two key areas, it has held explanatory appeal. First, it helps explain the seemingly fundamental need for human beings to connect with other human beings.[57] Durkheim's original theory about the phase changes between individual and group states was based on observations of aboriginal groups that would gather together collectively throughout astrologically significant times of the year to partake in community liturgical rituals.[58] While the form of participation has obviously changed in most modern societies, Ehrenreich charted the historical evolution of individuals seeking group belongingness as a significant source of joy, from ancient aboriginal practices to modern weddings.[59]

Second, it helps explain the tangible effects that social structures and systems can have on human beings. Durkheim posited that some social realities operate independently from any one individual's control and cannot be reduced to mere biology or physiology, but that still have a coercive effect on individuals.[60] In other words, it is not just that individuals occasionally move toward a sacred collective to satisfy the need for belongingness and then return unchanged to an individual level. There is a reciprocal effect, such that the social level imparts change on individuality.

Applied to the stakeholder framework, this dichotomized model fits the trajectories of nineteenth- and twentieth-century developments in both western philosophical ethics and industrial capitalism. Early forms of relational individualism in utilitarian and Kantian ethics were optimistic about the abilities of human beings to rationally predict and control their material environments. This seems to fit the circumstances of the times. Mill, for example, was writing during the robust growth period of the Industrial Revolution, when material prosperity was spreading, and questions were being raised about the role of government in protecting private property and socializing outcomes.

---

57. See Baumeister and Leary, "Need to Belong."
58. See especially Durkheim, *Elementary Forms*.
59. Ehrenreich, *History of Collective Joy*.
60. Durkheim, *Elementary Forms*, 13. See also Allan, *Explorations in Classical Sociology*, 105.

However, coupled with large scale sociopolitical conflict, capitalism's continued industrial growth confronted this implicit optimism with the realities of growing income inequality, socioeconomic volatility, and world wars. Mid-twentieth-century business ethics, out of which stakeholder theory came, recognized a need to broaden management perspectives of the firm to deal more effectively with these social and relational disruptions. Yet, even as Freeman and others identified the separation fallacy as detrimental to the transformative potential of capitalistic enterprise, relational individualism has remained firmly entrenched.[61]

Conclusion

Capitalism's dynamic, globalized growth has heightened the need to consider together the ethical and moral dimensions of enterprise. Like American evangelical theology, stakeholder theory has emerged with a view of capitalistic enterprise as a transformative platform. Similarly, stakeholder theory believes that an integrative approach combining the financial and moral dimensions of enterprise is necessary to harness its transformative abilities. It seeks to provide firm managers with conceptual tools so that they can maximize long-term value for all stakeholders, not just short-term profits for shareholders. The purpose of this chapter has been to get a basic overview of stakeholder theory: first, by understanding the emergence of stakeholder framework as part of a broader shift away from purely mechanistic understandings of an enterprise's operations then, by seeing how this shift adopted a dichotomized model of human being that reinforces a form of Enlightenment-derived relational individualism. Are there ways in which postsecularism has challenged the framework of stakeholder theory as it has with contemporary American evangelical perceptions of enterprise? To that question, I turn.

---

61. Bucholz and Rosenthal, "Contemporary Conceptual Framework," 141.

6

How Can a Critical Engagement with Stakeholder Theory Help Contemporary American Evangelical Theology?

In its quest to establish the transformative parameters of capitalistic enterprise, stakeholder theory has provided a critical framework and integrative vocabulary for the moral dimensions of enterprise. It has challenged the dichotomization of an enterprise's financial and operational facets from its ethical and moral ones. For capitalistic enterprise to contribute to human flourishing in a transformative way, the stakeholder framework asserts that both sets must be factored into the exercise of managerial practical moral reason.

However, as stakeholder theory moves into a postsecular milieu, it faces less stable and predictable forces than it did before. The wave of corporate fraud scandals at the turn of the millennium, followed by the global financial crisis of 2007 to 2009, are clear evidence that managerial decision-making can affect a broad range of people and "corporate objectives can be easily disrupted by the actions of unexpected groups and individuals."[1]

When it emerged in the late twentieth century, stakeholder theory considered the moral features of enterprise by drawing on the categories of the individual and the social that have long defined western relational individualism. In this chapter, I show that postsecularism has exposed the shortcomings of stakeholder theory's reliance on relational individualism. Stakeholder theory argues that the sole pursuit of maximizing shareholder profits is a morally narrow purpose for capitalistic enterprise and does not take into consideration other stakeholder constituencies affected by its activities. Firms are morally improved if, instead, they pursue the maximization of long-term value (wellbeing) for all its stakeholders.

---

1. Parmar et al., "Stakeholder Theory," 403.

By appealing to a common good that transcends individual stakeholder interests, the stakeholder framework is appealing to a set of intrinsic relational goods that are socially embedded.[2] The realization of these intrinsic goods requires moral agents such as stakeholder managers to engage in discretionary ethical decision making that determines how conflicts in human interests are to be settled and mutual benefit optimized for people living together in groups.[3] For this, moral agents must factor in their inherent social embeddedness and relational interconnectedness with other moral agents, especially those situated in multinational firms with complex intercultural integration.

The problem for the stakeholder framework is that Enlightenment derived relational individualism minimizes contextuality, inhibiting moral deliberation and, therefore, the realization of common goods. Whether in the form of utilitarian or consequentialist approaches, individualist constructs characterize moral agents as free consumers unconstrained by external forces and rationally equipped to achieve self-validated ends.[4] In these instrumentalizing constructs, there is no compelling basis for pursuing intrinsic social goods such as justice, fairness, or mercy, that diminish when pursued for their utility.

Postsecularism has accentuated this problem: first, by extending the reach of capitalistic enterprise's instrumentality into previously unreached areas of human experience, which increase the burden of self-realization through economic exchange where human worth is reduced to utility. Second, economic globalization has created more diffuse and unstable organizations in which the high value of individualism remains, but in a more brutal form. Contemporary capitalist enterprises, ever intensifying in structural volatility and the pursuit of short-term performance, call out for employees who can operate with temporary connections and high degrees of career uncertainty.[5]

Excessive reliance on individualist categories isolates stakeholder constituents from historical contexts, which are central to being and meaning. According to Wicks et al., "Persons are fundamentally connected with each other in a web of relationships which are themselves integral to any proper understanding of 'the self.'"[6] As "creatures-in-process," human

---

2. Girardi and Petito, "Postsecular Reflections."
3. Hardin, *Morality*.
4. Quinn et al., "Pragmatic Business Ethics," 1429.
5. Sennett, *Culture of New Capitalism*.
6. Wicks et al., "Feminist Reinterpretation," 483.

identities are linked to social relations and historical contingencies.[7] Disproportionate individualistic focus can shed the social and relational dimensions, dehumanizing the stakeholder system. Without significant recontextualization, atomized stakeholders become static, vacuous concepts with no history and context.

To promote capitalistic enterprise's transformative contributions to common social good, stakeholder theory needs to strengthen its framework for a postsecular context. This requires drawing on alternative sources of intrinsicality that can help recontextualize stakeholder constituencies and restore fundamental human sociality so that practical moral deliberation can take place. Properly positioned, religion and spirituality comprise an abundant source of intrinsicality.

On the way to a postsecular revision of its own framework, this presents an opportunity for contemporary American evangelical theology. First, to validate the limits of capitalistic enterprise's contributions to human flourishing. Second, to demonstrate how practical theological methodology can enrich the stakeholder framework. As a source of intrinsicality, practical theology's concept of reflexivity can enhance managerial moral reflection and decision making.

I proceed by elaborating two points: first, the challenges to the stakeholder framework leveled by postsecularism and second, the contributions of practical theological methodology and corresponding implications for contemporary American evangelical theological perceptions of enterprise.

The Postsecular Challenge to Stakeholder Theory

In contending that postsecularism challenges stakeholder theory, I position myself within an alternative ethical stream in the stakeholder literature, generally referred to as virtue based approaches.[8] Rather than emphasize either an action's consequences (consequentialism) or the act itself (deontology), virtue ethics prioritizes character as fundamental to moral and ethical deliberation.[9] Rooted in Aristotle's concept of *eudaimonia,* modern virtue ethics surfaced mainly as a result of British analytical philosopher G. E. M. Anscombe's essay "Modern Moral Philosophy." She criticized the modern

---

7. Johnson, *Moral Imagination*, 33. See also Quinn et al., "Pragmatic Business Ethics," 1422.

8. For a helpful overview of virtue ethics, see Sanford, *Before Virtue.*

9. Donaldson and Preston, *Stakeholder Theory*, 9.

scholarly philosophical community for a preoccupation with law-focused concepts of duty and obligation.[10]

For virtue stakeholder approaches, MacIntyre has been the most influential articulator. A full analysis of MacIntyre and virtue ethics is beyond scope. I focus on his critique of relational individualism in the context of capitalistic enterprise to chart the postsecular challenge to the stakeholder framework. For MacIntyre, the deontology and utilitarian ethical systems of the Enlightenment "have failed to provide a meaningful definition of 'good.' Lacking such a definition, business managers have no internal standards by which they can morally evaluate their roles or acts."[11] His argument rests on two key concepts: practice and internal (intrinsic) good.[12] Both are necessary for the development of virtue. Practices are "complex, collaborative, socially organized, goal-oriented, sustained" activities.[13] Building on Aristotle, MacIntyre argued that practices are teologically directed toward some perceived good: either, external instrumental goods such as material wealth obtained for the purposes of use, or internal intrinsic goods obtained for the purpose of experience. External goods are "characteristically objects of competition in which there must be losers as well as winners."[14] Internal goods are only achieved in community through the practice itself. Virtue, then, is "an acquired human quality the possession and exercise of which tends to enable us to achieve those goods internal to practices and the lack of which prevents us from achieving any such goods."[15]

By putting the focus of ethics on the rightness of individual acts apart from the character of the actor, Enlightenment derived relational individualism shifted the traditional western focus on the character of the person and his/or her relationship to society.[16] The abstracting of ethical categories such as the "individual" and "rights" out of their inherent sociality and contextuality implicitly prioritizes the achievement of external goods over internal intrinsic goods. It also misconstrues the *telos* of human practice as self-determining, which amounts to a veneer of rationality. Both deontological-based

---

10. Hacker-Wright, "Virtue Ethics without Action."

11. Horvath, "Excellence vs. Effectiveness," 499. It is important to note that while MacIntyre believed "the tradition of the virtues is at variance with central features of the modern economic order" (MacIntyre, *After Virtue*, 254), he was "a critic of a certain type of business, rather than . . . of business per se" (Dobson, "Alasdair Macintyre's Aristotelian Business Ethics," 43).

12. Dobson, "Alasdair Macintyre's Aristotelian Business Ethics," 43.

13. Hicks and Stapleford, "Virtues of Scientific Practice," 449.

14. MacIntyre, *After Virtue*, 190–91.

15. MacIntyre, *After Virtue*, 191.

16. Horvath, "Exellence vs. Effectiveness," 507.

and utilitarian-based approaches are liable: the former by assuming that rational alone is sufficient to "motivate individuals in the face of emotional and/or social pressures to act contrary" to a sense of duty and the latter by reducing all normativity to individual preferences.[17]

When engaged in the pursuit of external goods in a competitive market economy, organizations are placing effectiveness and output at the ethical base. Moral actors such as managers within firms are compartmentalized into cost-benefit, utilitarian practices, and ethical decision making. This encourages a myopic focus on maximizing short-term corporate profits above all other considerations.[18]

Of course, stakeholder theory has critiqued this shareholder approach as morally insufficient, arguing that virtuous organizations should focus on maximizing long-term shared value for all their stakeholders. Here, we arrive at the problem MacIntyre's analysis raises for the stakeholder approach, a problem intensified by the phenomenon of postsecularism.

By appealing to a common good that transcends individual stakeholder interests, the stakeholder framework summons organizations to the achievement of intrinsic internal goods. However, this would require that the organization and its moral agents regularly engage in community-bound practices not solely focused on the instrumental maximizing of utility. The very idea of meaningful work "moves beyond the notion of work as merely a means to the ends of economic productivity and shareholder value creation."[19] It requires that they have shared collective values about how interdependent relationships are sustained and shared understandings about how the firm contributes to social wellbeing.[20] In other words, stakeholders are motivated by more than financial compensation and moral standards rise above the level of individual preference.

Postsecularism has intensified this dilemma by resurrecting Enlightenment relational individualism in the form of neoliberalism.[21] It can be defined as a "free market ideology based on individual liberty and limited government that connected human freedom to the actions of the rational, self-interested actor in the competitive marketplace."[22] By summarizing the

---

17. Horvath, "Excellence vs. Effectiveness," 507. MacIntyre called this emotivism, "The doctrine that all evaluative judgments and more specifically, all moral judgments are nothing but expressions of preference, expressions of attitude or feeling, insofar as they are moral or evaluative in character" (MacIntyre, *After Virtue*, 11–12).

18. MacIntyre, *After Virtue*, 357.

19. Michaelson et al., "Meaningful Work," 84.

20. Roberts, *Modern Firm*, 18.

21. See Possamai, *I-zation of Society*.

22. Jones, *Masters of the Universe*, 2.

vast complexities of human experience under market terminology, it has ushered in an "age of authenticity."[23] More than simply a reaffirmation of the individual and social categories that have dominated western modernization, it is a radical prioritization of the individual over the social in the pursuit of human flourishing.[24] As such,

> the goal of proper moral deliberation . . . is to extract ourselves from our immediate context, employ practical reason to find the correct ethical rule, and then use our will power in such a way as to act in accordance with this rule.[25]

However, this neglects a crucial component of moral deliberation in human agency: "the ability to take an evaluative stance toward one's own preferences and desires."[26] Ethical decision-making requires taking up a moral horizon in which qualitative and not just quantitative (i.e., cost-benefit) judgments are made. It is intersubjective: "we interpret who we are with a language and a set of values that we share with our community."[27] These contextual discriminations that recognize fundamental human relationality are not easily merged into an instrumentalist account.

The predominance of neoliberal approaches in postsecular capitalistic settings helps explain how "the bits and pieces of evidence that we possess about morality and honesty in the typical corporation is sufficient to give us pause."[28] The most comprehensive survey of the ethical culture in US workplaces showed that nearly 50 percent of workers reported observing ethical misconduct, while 30 percent admitted "feeling pressure to compromise their company's ethical standards because of deadlines, overly aggressive objectives, concerns about the company's survival and other factors."[29] Moreover, "employees in multinational companies in the private sector are more likely to observe misconduct and to feel pressure to compromise standards than employees of companies operating only in one country."[30]

Overly individualized conceptions of enterprise can also impose ill effects on the individual experience in enterprise.[31] For example, poorer

---

23. To use Taylor's term. See Taylor, *Secular Age*.
24. Taylor, *Secular Age*, 475; Quinn et al., "Honesty, Individualism," 1424.
25. Quinn et al., "Honesty, Individualism," 1424.
26. Quinn et al., "Honesty, Individualism," 1424. See also Taylor, *Sources of the Self*.
27. Quinn et al., "Honesty, Individualism," 1427.
28. Quinn et al., "Honesty, Individualism," 1425.
29. Verschoor, "Workplace Ethics," 14.
30. Verschoor, "Workplace Ethics," 19.
31. Dyck and Schroeder, "Management, Theology," 707.

interpersonal relationships, increased mental disorders, environmental and social injustices.[32] Summarizing the vast mental health studies that have been performed along these lines, Layton et al. pointed out that the destabilizing forces of rapid globalization and increasing income inequality are capable of producing "traumatogenic" environments in "which individual and group physical safety, social security, and symbolic capacities all are simultaneously" challenged.[33]

Surveying contemporary articulations of stakeholder theory, Wicks et al. identified the idea that the "corporation is an autonomous entity which is fundamentally separate from its environment" as a core assumption of traditional stakeholder thinking.[34] To highlight a firm or stakeholder's role in a value chain, this core assumption can be quite helpful, but if left unrestrained it takes the firm or stakeholder out of the nexus of relations to which it is ontologically bound.

There is undoubtedly a pointed conceptual purpose served by highlighting individual financial interests in a web of economic exchange. However, the challenge is to construe the social embeddings of a firm and its stakeholders with as much rigor as the financial. In the western capitalist contexts that permeate stakeholder theory, there is a tendency for market efficiency to become the dominant construct through which all else is understood, even mainline efforts such as "corporate social responsibility."

As Solomon cautioned, stakeholder arguments for the social responsibilities of business often begin with the assumption of the corporation as an autonomous, independent entity, which then needs to consider its obligation to the surrounding community. However, as with individuals, corporations are integrated with "the communities that created them, and the responsibilities that they bear are not products of argument or implicit contracts but are intrinsic to their very existence as social entities."[35]

The paucity of non-financial and non-market articulation of what is meant by "community" within contemporary stakeholder theory has, in due course, left significant dissimilarity of opinion about how genuine community should represent itself in stakeholder relationships.[36] Dunham et al. correspondingly lamented: "Community as a stakeholder has come to represent something of a default, a sort of error term containing all sorts of

---

32. See Burroughs and Rindfleisch, "Contemporary Conceptual Framework"; McCarty and Shrum, "Influence of Individualism."
33. Layton et al., "Psychoanalysis, Class, and Politics," 3.
34. Wicks et al., "Feminist Reinterpretation," 479.
35. Solomon, *Ethics and Excellence*, 83.
36. See Freeman, "Managing for Stakeholders."

interests and externalities that fail to find homes within customer, supplier, employee, or shareholder groups."[37]

The relational individualism of the stakeholder framework undercuts the development of robust community by reducing all relational activity to economic exchange. Bucholz and Rosenthal explain that in the stakeholder system:

> self-interested individuals and institutions that have separate wills and desires are constantly colliding. To minimize the collisions and reduce conflict, people and institutions may come together to establish some sort of a relationship to work out differences. But while peripheral ties may be established when antecedent individuals enter into a contract with one another or come together to more readily secure, their own individualistic goals, these bonds cannot root them in any ongoing endeavor which is more than the sum of their separate selves, separate wills, separate egoistic desires. . . . This tension between the individual and the community presents a great deal of difficulty in arriving at mutually satisfactory solutions to social problems.[38]

The Contributions of Practical Theological Methodology

Thus far, it has been established that postsecularism has exposed the limits to which the stakeholder framework's excessive reliance on relational individualism can facilitate critical moral deliberation and the exercise of practical moral reason in instrumentalizing contexts. To respond compellingly, stakeholder theory must move beyond its dependence on purely individualistic notions and develop a more well-rounded concept of a transcending "common good," or the collective interest shared by members of the community.[39] Atomic individualist frameworks need critical reflection as to whether they provide an "adequate foundation" for analyzing "the relational nature of the corporation and society."[40] To actively

---

37. Dunham et al., "Enhancing Stakeholder Practice," 38.

38. Bucholz and Rosenthal, "Contemporary Conceptual Framework," 138.

39. The "common good" concept within stakeholder theory received early treatment by Argandoña ("Stakeholder Theory and the Common Good"), but Girardi and Petito noted that it received very little response from academics, "possibly as a result of the argument being cast in fairly abstract philosophical terms" (Girardi and Petito, "Postsecular Reflections," 9).

40. Bucholz and Rosenthal, "Contemporary Conceptual Framework," 139.

sustain meaningful sociality in organizational settings, alternative sources of intrinsicality are necessary.

What remains is to show how this informs a postsecular renewal of the theme of transformation for contemporary American evangelical theology. Both stakeholder theory and contemporary American evangelical theology view capitalistic enterprise as potentially transformative for human flourishing. Both have been challenged to sustain this view in light of postsecularism, which has intensified individualist and materialist conceptions of human flourishing and obscured the social and relational dimensions. A critical engagement with stakeholder theory validates that for contemporary American evangelical theology to achieve a postsecular renewal, it must retrieve an intrinsic basis for human sociality that overcomes relational individualism. In so doing, it can fulfill the call of a public oriented theology and enrich the stakeholder framework, which is itself in need of critical sources of intrinsicality.

As described previously, one of the effects of postsecularism has been to open a space in the public dialogue for discussions about the spiritual and religious dimensions of enterprise. Biberman and Tischler suggested "one viable reason is that society is seeking spiritual solutions to better respond to tumultuous social and business changes and that global changes have brought a growing social, spiritual consciousness."[41] Remarking on this shift, Rynes et al. observed:

> A sharpened focus on care and compassion in organizations is consistent with a paradigm shift in the social sciences that emphasizes neurological, psychological, and sociological bases of human interrelating that have other-interest as opposed to self-interest at their core.[42]

A groundswell of interest in the nature of community in organizational studies like stakeholder theory is a recognition that "our understanding of the human phenomenon must reflect an adequate balance between the individual and the social dimensions."[43] By nature, humans are social, expressed in interdependent relationships that are more than just contracting. There is wide reaching support from both normative business ethicists and organizational theorists that moral deliberation in organizations has

---

41. Bucholz and Rosenthal, "Spirituality in Business," 106.

42. Rynes et al., "Care and Compassion," 505.

43. Grenz, "*Community* as a Theological Motif," 400. See also Helminiak, "Human Solidarity," 37.

a highly community-oriented nature and function.[44] Donaldson and Werhane, for example, stated:

> Business, like other social phenomena, is a set of *social* practices. Managers play a special role in society by virtue of their role in business organizations, and their role in these organizations requires that they cultivate the kind of organizational excellence appropriate to managers. Ethical excellence and social excellence are thus intertwined.[45]

Traditionally, religion and spirituality have been critical sources of intrinsicality for human sociality in the conceptualization of common transcending goods.[46] Commenting on the unique understandings of community shared by the three Abrahamic faiths (i.e., Judaism, Islam, and Christianity) that have import to stakeholder theory, Ray et al. note that a "key insight from the Abrahamic faith traditions is that the individual firm is, indeed, part of a wider community in every place where it operates."[47] Communitarian flourishing depends on the regular restoring and reconciling of relationships, which religious and spiritual traditions can help facilitate.

Conventional stakeholder management approaches have been undergirded by a secularized, individualist-materialist motif.[48] Virtue-based theological models enable a turn away from conventional approaches to "radical" alternative approaches grounded in more integrative moral points of views.[49] Weber, one of the earliest management theorists, criticized the extreme focus in management theory on "maximizing productivity, efficiency, and profitability and on beating the competition."[50] Weber argued that the individualist-materialist perspective that dominated this approach imprisoned workers in an "iron cage" and challenged management theorists "to describe a non-conventional ideal-type of management that is based on a moral point-of-view that—unlike conventional management theory and practice—does not place a primary emphasis on materialism and individualism."[51]

---

44. Hay and Menzies, "Model of Human Nature," 190.
45. Donaldson and Werhane, *Ethical Issues in Business*, 23.
46. Girardi and Petito, "Postsecular Reflections," 1.
47. Ray et al., "Reframing Normative Stakeholder Theory," 342.
48. Neubert and Dyck, "Sustainable Management Theory," 304.
49. Dyck and Schroeder, "Management, Theology," 705.
50. Dyck and Schroeder, "Management, Theology," 705.
51. Dyck and Schroeder, "Management, Theology," 706. See also Weber, *Protestant Ethic*, 180–83.

All expressions of organizational theory and management practice are already theological in the underlying anthropological presuppositions made.[52] As a discipline focused on the contextualized integration of theory and practice, practical theology is ideally suited to support radical alternative management approaches. To close this chapter, I want to mark out two enrichments to the stakeholder framework made by specifically practical theological methodology that also advances a postsecular renewal of the theme of transformation in contemporary American evangelical theology. Here, I am explicitly drawing on the transforming praxis and neo-Aristotelian trajectories within contemporary practical theology identified in chapter 1.

The first contribution that practical theological methodology can make is a reprioritization of human finitude that the stakeholder framework's relational individualism has minimized. The functional compartmentalizing of individuals and stakeholders destabilizes human relationality by not properly accounting for the vulnerabilities of human finitude. In contrast to the compartmentalizing scheme that has dominated western accounts, practical theology holds "in human life, there is only one realm of experience. We love hate, work, and play everywhere. They might be expressed differently, but same impulses move us in the home or in the office."[53] The emphasis and distinguishing characteristic is not the "segmentability" and atomization of the various dimensions of human experience, but rather their interconnectedness. By segmenting economic and consumptive dimensions, the stakeholder framework empties itself of the ability to identify and revise the ways in which consumer capitalistic enterprise can entrap allegedly autonomous consumers.

Drawing on Neo-Marxist and poststructural frameworks, the transforming praxis trajectory has drawn attention to the ways in which neoliberal capitalistic conceptions of human autonomy can dehumanize. Influential to this assessment were the critical social theory approaches of the Frankfurt school, which understood political, social, and economic forces as potentially oppressive and sustained through consciousness.[54] An early voice in the Frankfurt school, Adorno advanced Marx's general criticism of capitalism as dehumanizing, but not merely because all human phenomena were socially determined. Despite the profession of individual ideology, capitalistic consumer systems can thwart individual autonomy

---

52. See Miller, "Organizational Research as Practical Theology"; Pattison, *Faith of the Managers*; Biberman and Tischler, *Spirituality in Business*.

53. Nicholson, *Managing the Human Animal*, 2.

54. Held, *Introduction to Critical Theory*, 1–8.

with restrictive social, economic and, political power structures.[55] For Adorno and other critical social theorists, the Enlightenment idealized a vision of human social ordering wherein rationality would free individuals from the oppressive institutional structures (including religious dogma). Yet, when left unchecked in capitalistic systems that atomized producers and consumers, reason becomes instrumentalized and enables a new kind of oppression.[56] This oppression manifests subtly, for example in the "culture industry" of consumer capitalistic contexts.[57] Allegedly free consumers are atomized in a cycle of profit generation that obstructs the development of a critical consciousness and obscures the temporality and finitude of human experience.

In the mid-twentieth century, these critiques of capitalistic structures' dehumanizing tendencies were integrated with the growing liberation theology movements, which focused on fostering socially aware and contextually grounded praxis.[58] Together, they formed the basis of the transforming praxis trajectory in contemporary practical theology.[59] A central feature of this trajectory has been to challenge the compartmentalizing schemes of neoliberal relational individualism.

The increasingly globalized political, economic, and social environment indicate that human individuality and sociality is much more like a complex "living human web."[60] We might be able to distinguish difference environments within this living web, but the distinguishability of sub-environments does not betray the fact that the complex entirety involves interdependence and interconnectedness at all levels. Reality is not a collection of tightly demarcated categories and inherently stable closed system. There are rather inherently fragile "open systems," where all things "are composed of innumerable, interacting open systems with differential capacities of self-organization set on different scales of time, agency, creativity, viscosity, and speed."[61]

What is the difference between the two? If independent persons and stakeholders are fundamentally distinct from their social surroundings

---

55. See Jarvis, *Adorno*.

56. Adorno wrote, "In the most general sense of progressive thought, the Enlightenment has always aimed at liberating men from fear and establishing their sovereignty. Yet the fully enlightened earth radiates disaster triumphant" (Adorno and Horkheimer, *Dialectic of Enlightenment*, 23).

57. Adorno and Horkheimer, *Dialectic of Enlightenment*, 23.

58. Thiem, "Schmittian Shadows," 2–9.

59. See Osmer, "Empirical Theology"; Gayarre, "Challenges of Liberation Theology," 34–38.

60. Miller-McLemore, "Living Human Web."

61. Connolly, *Capitalism and Christianity*, 123.

and act as rational, self-interested consumers in a competitive marketplace, self-determined human flourishing takes place in an essentially stable environment. In such an environment, capitalistic enterprise becomes a value-free conduit through which natural-goods-seeking persons obtain *eudaimonia* primarily through individualized material consumption that operates largely separate from social relations. However, in a highly interconnected and fragile network, capitalist enterprise faces limits in its ability to facilitate human flourishing. Resourced communities are necessary that support the very vulnerabilities of human finitude exposed by postsecular capitalism's destabilizing effects.

This leads to a second contribution that practical theological methodology can make—its account of the importance of reflexivity for complex moral decision making. Reflexivity is "the ability to take an evaluative stance toward one's own preferences and desires."[62] Ethical decision making requires taking up intersubjective moral horizons that interrogate the behaviors and practices of the self, not merely in terms of consumer-oriented preferences, but also in the discerning of responsibilities.[63]

Drawing on MacIntyre, the neo-Aristotelian trajectory within contemporary practical theology has highlighted the importance of reflexively oriented assessments of moral practices. All practices are community bound and carry "epistemic weight."[64] Evaluating and assessing moral practices, especially in complex decision-making environments such as consumer capitalistic contexts, demands a broader view than provided by relational individualism. Practical theology's emphasis on the role and importance of perceptual lenses can help stakeholder theory reincorporate historical context into stakeholder constituencies, which overly individualist conceptualizing has tended to isolate. If "our conceptual scheme mediates even our most basic perceptual experience," then the human mind has a great deal of impact in shaping experience and in reasoning through it.[65] What has often been called a "worldview" in evangelical theology, is better identified in the cognitive sciences as a "mental model" or "sensemaking" function.[66] The point being that the human mind—including in acts of ethical reasoning—is unceasingly involved in the process of categorizing, reframing, filtering, and interpreting experience, data, and stimuli. Even scientists interpreting

---

62. Quinn et al., "Honesty, Individualism," 1424.

63. Klaasen, "Practical Theology," 2–5.

64. See Dykstra, "Reconceiving Practice."

65. Railton, "Moral Realism," 172.

66. See Sire, *Universe Next Door*; Senge, *Fifth Discipline*; Weick, *Sensemaking in Organizations*.

"hard data" are accessing that data through mental models, subjecting the data to interpretive and observational bias.[67]

Generally speaking, stakeholder theorists have been slow to acknowledge the role of perceptional lenses, which could partly explain the relatively sparse lack of reflection on excessive individualism as a mitigating conceptual limit.[68] Atomized and individualized, stakeholder entities easily lose the contextual bearings that are the very elements that ground them—and the more substantial theorizing itself—in reality, and not just theoretical apparatus. McVea and Freeman asserted that when generalizing stakeholder constituencies without reference to the unique human histories that comprise each one, uncritical stakeholder theory has so homogenized its own framework that it is difficult "for practitioners to incorporate the normative dimension within the everyday language of business decision making."[69]

Postsecular contexts have attached significant social and cultural—theologians would even say religious—value to the domain of vocation and has become increasingly complex in its network of relationships. If stakeholder theory is going to remain viable, it must have the inner discipline to subject its own perceptional lenses to reflexive self-critique and self-scrutiny.[70] This is an attribute that practical theology for some time has placed a high degree of emphasis on: "The orientation to multidimensional dynamics of social context and embodiment is one of the most salient features of the discipline," such that "the insights and reflections on the meaning of context and human experience are a conversation itself."[71] Among other things, this orientation has enabled the discipline of practical theology to balance the often-abused bifurcation between theory and practice.

As previously argued, a neglect of the role of historical context brought about by atomizing conceptualization within stakeholder theory makes it difficult for stakeholder theory to offer a compelling account of authentic community because all relational activity is reduced to economic exchange. By emphasizing the role of perceptual lenses as practical theology does, stakeholder theory has better material with which to foster genuine community within stakeholder constituencies. In stakeholder theory's scheme,

---

67. Sorensen et al., "Theology and Organization," 19. See also Mitroff and Denton, *Spiritual Audit*.
68. Fort, *Ethics and Governance*.
69. McVea and Freeman, "Names-and-Faces Approach," 63.
70. Werhane, *Moral Imagination*, 95.
71. Cahalan and Mikoski, *Opening the Field*, 12.

this heightens the responsibility of managers, who are seen as essentially having an adjudicative function.[72]

In line with its foundational emphases on the role of perceptual lenses and the relational nature of human beings, the discipline of practical theology stresses the balancing out of individualistic understandings of faith with corporate and social implications, particularly in view of postsecular impetuses to privatize religious expression. Applied to stakeholder theory, this signifies, "firms and their managers would be enjoined from simply pursuing self-interest for its own sake, but rather would be expected to take into account the needs of the communities in which they do business."[73] This is a critical warning for stakeholder theory to be aware as it formulates its understandings of the nature of profit-generating enterprise in an age that defies the individual and material often at the loss of the human.

Are there any specifically Christian theological perspectives that can be practically applied to the stakeholder framework for the purposes of guiding management decision-making? Dyck and Schroeder point to the Anabaptist tradition as a viable candidate for three primary reasons.[74] First, it comprises a moral point-of-view that has historically deemphasized individualism and materialism. Going back to its beginnings as a radical movement within the early Reformation period, this was expressed through the concept of *gelassenheit*. The term was used in Anabaptist communities to convey the necessity of yielding material and individual interests to God for the strengthening of relational bonds. Second, *gelassenheit* orientation produced a decidedly non-instrumental approach to stewarding power and positions of leadership within the community. Third, contemporary North American Anabaptist entrepreneurial efforts employing these values in small-scale businesses have experienced notable financial and organizational success.[75]

From the perspective of practicing the values of *gelassenheit* within stakeholding management, managers can: (a) identify shortcomings of the conventional structures and systems (compassion); (b) approach others in a friendly and community-building manner (submission); (c) invite others to identify where loosing and binding may be appropriate (discernment); and (d) experimentally implement practices consistent with a non-conventional moral point-of-view.[76]

72. Smith, *Normative Theory and Business Ethics*, 82.
73. Breitenberg, "To Tell the Truth," 63.
74. Dyck and Schroeder, "Management, Theology," 709–15.
75. See also Kraybill and Nolt, *Amish Enterprise*.
76. Dyck and Schroeder, "Management, Theology," 726.

Conclusion

The focus of this chapter has been a critical engagement with the stakeholder framework. I have argued that the dynamic growth of postsecular capitalism has exposed the shortcomings of stakeholder theory's reliance on relational individualism. The functional compartmentalization of human experience makes it difficult to capture fundamental human sociality, thus, exposes the limits of capitalistic enterprise's contributions to human flourishing. Contemporary American evangelical theology can fill the void with methodological resources drawn from a practically oriented theology.

For a postsecular revision of the theme of transformation, this clarifies the path forward. It shows that if contemporary American evangelical theology is going to viably integrate Christian faith with capitalistic enterprise for moral and spiritual transformation, it needs to retrieve an intrinsic basis for human sociality that overcomes relational individualism. Given, then, the applicability of the Anabaptist tradition of *gelassenheit* to the stakeholder framework as a radical moral point-of-view raises, might it also represent a specific source of retrieval? That is the focus of the remaining two chapters.

7

What Is the Anabaptist Concept of *Gelassenheit* and How Can It Renew the Theme of Transformation for a Postsecular Context?

The theme of transformation in contemporary American theology needs a postsecular renewal. In part one of this book, I showed why. In part two, I show how. The last two chapters focused on the first layer in this renewal, an interdisciplinary engagement with stakeholder theory that established the limits of capitalistic enterprise's contributions to human flourishing and the theological resources available to overcome relational individualism. In the final two chapters, I focus on the second layer.

Streaming into the American evangelical quest for integration of faith and work is a rich heritage in the Christian traditions of grappling with the instrumentalizing tendencies of wealth and enterprise in the face of the triangulating love of God. Mining this heritage is essential for the theme of transformation's postsecular renewal. Two figures—Augustine and Aquinas—loom in the triangular love tradition and have primarily been the focus of evangelical scholarship. However, there is a neglected third figure, the medieval German mystic Meister Eckhart. In the late fifteenth century, early south German Anabaptist communities appropriated Eckhart's practice of mystical *gelassenheit* ("detachment") to counter what they perceived as increasing individualism and materialism. They operationalized the theological concept of *gelassenheit* into a distinctive spirituality that emphasized the fostering of strong relational collectives.

Early Anabaptist spirituality represents an ideal source of retrieval for contemporary American evangelical theology. Like contemporary American evangelical theology, these Anabaptists were concerned to show how Christian faith could be transformative in instrumentalizing contexts. As with contemporary American evangelical theology, these Anabaptists were operating from the position of a political-social minority with limited cultural power. Finally, like contemporary American evangelical theology, these early Anabaptists placed a high value on the role of Scripture in shaping spiritual practice.

I make the case in three movements. First, I define in greater detail the ethic of triangulating love developed in the New Testament and the Christian traditions. Second, I overview Eckhart's mystical *gelassenheit* and its appropriation by early Anabaptist spirituality. Third, I identify the implications of this appropriation for contemporary American evangelical theology's theme of transformation.

What Is the Ethic of Triangulating Love Developed in the New Testament and Christian Tradition?

For two millennia, love has been a central theme in Christian theological ethics.[1] The diversity of offerings in the Christian traditions about the nature of divine and human loves reflects the scriptural diversity about what love is.[2] No single text lays out a single definition of love. In the New Testament, emphases vary across the source traditions (e.g., Johannine, Pauline). Attempts have been many to construct a distinctly Christian account of love around the *agape* word group[3], probably none more well-known or polarizing than Nygren, whose work on the topic has focused on developing categories of love by contrasting *agape* with *eros*.[4] While the hard distinctions he drew between word groups in the scriptural texts have been widely criticized, his categories remain influential in theological ethics.[5]

This is to be expected, of course, given the complex nature of Scripture as a collection of various writings, authors, intentions, and traditions. Running through the theological diversity is a unifying thread that divine love and human love stand in relationship to each other. One of the clearest places that this emerges is an account recorded in both the gospels of Matthew (22:34–40) and Mark (12:28–34).

---

1. Peckham, "Ethics of Love," 14. Among the many modern ethical theologies in the west that have prioritized the concept of love, prominent ones include Niebuhr, *Love and Justice*, and Tillich, *Love, Power, and Justice*.
2. Oord, *Nature of Love*.
3. ἀγαπάω, ἀγάπη, ἀγάπητos
4. See Nygren, *Agape and Eros*.
5. Carson, *Gagging of God*, 32. The linguistic ambiguity is captured itself in the phrase "the love of God" (τὴν ἀγάπην τοῦ θεοῦ). Whether τοῦ θεοῦ functions as a subjective or objective genitive often determines its meaning in scriptural texts.

While in the temple on the week of his Passion, Jesus was approached by a rabbi and asked what he considered the most important law to be.[6] His response was twofold. First, referencing the sacred *Shema* of Deuteronomy 6, Jesus said: "The most important one is . . . Hear, O Israel, the Lord our God the Lord is one. Love the Lord your God with all your heart and with all your soul and with all your mind and with all your strength." Second, referencing Leviticus 19, Jesus said: "love your neighbor as yourself. There is no commandment greater than these." Here, Jesus is upholding the ancient Jewish ethical tradition of grounding harmonious human relationships in an obedient and loving response to a redeeming God, who graciously and lovingly freed the people of Israel from their bondage to Egypt and now covenants with them.[7]

For the triangular scheme, the central feature of note is that human love is its purest when it gives without regard for receiving from another, but only out of an appreciative response to the God who loves. The Johannine corpus heavily stresses this: "Greater love has no one than this, that someone lay down his life for his friends" (John 15:13); "A new commandment I give to you, that you love (ἀγαπᾶτε) one another: just as I have loved you, you also are to love one another" (John 13:34). Here, "divine love, modeled in the incarnate one himself, is presented as the ground for truly Christian love."[8] In the Pauline corpus, the emphasis of triangular love is placed on God's love demonstrated in the death and resurrection of the Christ, which inspires human love for another (e.g., Rom 5:8; Eph 5:2).

There are two critical dimensions of love in the triangular scheme. First, love is active. In the New Testament, particularly in the gospels, to be a believer in Jesus is to be a disciple of Jesus, and the clearest mark of discipleship is mutual and obedient love (John 14:15, 24). Meaning, love for Jesus and God (Matt 22:37; John 8:42) and love for fellow humans (John 15:17), including even enemies (Luke 6:35; Matt 5:44). The New Testament abounds in exhortations to nascent Christian communities to ground human relationality in deeds of unconditional love that resist instrumentalizing another for personal gain. For instance, because "God's love has been poured into our hearts" (Rom

---

6. Mark refers to the scribe as γραμματεύς, but Matthew uses the less conventional νομικοr (expert of the law). Throughout the passage, Matthew's version shortens Mark's narrative, a common tendency. The Matthean community was likely embroiled in controversies with the Pharisees, which comes through in the focus that Matthew's version places on Jesus' rebuke of Pharisaic interpretation. It "predominately limited neighborly love to fellow Jews, proselytes, or aliens within their borders," but Matthew's "Jesus taught love beyond such borders" (Viljoen, "Double Love Commandment," 11).

7. Mittleman, *Short History of Jewish Ethics*, 8–9, 62–63.

8. Peckham, "Ethics of Love?," 16.

5:5), Christians are to "let love be genuine" (Rom 12:9) and "owe no one anything except to love one another" (Rom 13:8).

Evident in several of these passages is the second dimension of love: It is affective. The Gospels present Jesus as challenging (particularly with the Pharisees) the idea that obedient action has spiritual value regardless of the motives of the actor. A pure heart produces pure obedience (or "fruit" [Matt 7:15–20]). A corrupted heart produces partial external conformity that seeks self-enhancement (Mark 7:20–23). Jesus called the Pharisees "hypocrites" (ὑποκριταί) because their acts of partial obedience were "done for people to see" (Matt 23:5–7). The Pharisees instrumentalized human relations because "they loved the glory that comes from man more than the glory that comes from God" (John 12:43).

Understood together, the active and affective dimensions of love point to the triangulating effect that the love of God has in human relationality. The love of God expressed in Jesus—and the human response to God's love through faith in Jesus—checks against instrumentalizing tendencies by reorienting human relationality as a gracious response to a redeeming God, transforming the desires of the heart in the process so that they flow from a condition of non-possessive, triangulating love.

Two significant figures are typically identified in western Christian theology who develop the triangular theme. The first and earliest is Augustine. He distinguished between enjoyment (*frui*) and use (*uti*) in love: "You have made us for yourself, and our heart is restless until it rests in you."[9] Love is properly ordered (*ordo amoris*) when everything in creation is loved according to its proper relationship to God. Only when God is pursued as the ultimate enjoyment can the material world be truly enjoyed and intrinsically valued, which is to say properly used. Apart from this triangulating effect, humans are apt to inordinately abuse others for their own ends.[10]

Augustine was quick to point out that triangular love does not eliminate instrumentality entirely, but rather elevates it from an exclusive form to an inclusive form. The latter "includes the other in the sense of having the other enjoy the benefits produced by such action," but the former "excludes the other from their ends."[11] O'Connor continues:

> The neighbor in this life is always in some sense an object for us. . . . A kind of instrumental attitude, then, is present in all temporal relationships. In charity, however, we treat the neighbor with

---

9. Augustine, *Confessions*, 43.

10. Conversely, to live according to the *ordo amoris* enables humans to "participate in the very trinitarian life and mutual love of God" (Schlabach, "Ethics," 323).

11. O'Connor, "Uti/Frui Distinction in Augustine's Ethics," 50.

a regard for his eternal destiny and include him in the desired end, while in cupidity he is excluded from the desired end.[12]

Augustine saw human beings as having a teleological orientation that is heart-led and producing certain habits.[13] If one loves material things, one will be consumed by the perishable and remain in flux. If one wishes to change these loves and find God, he or she must be reoriented by the Spirit of God. This produces an intersubjective *eudemonism*: "A social vision of using and enjoying one another in God just as the persons of the Trinity use and enjoy one another in community of mutual love."[14]

Another figure frequently identified is Aquinas. He posited that God's charity reroutes human desire through himself by drawing it in as a response to God's gracious love for humans so that it may then reengage the created order as love for other humans.[15] Aquinas quoted Augustine's definition of charity as "the movement of the soul toward the enjoyment of God for his own sake."[16] Because the objective is God, it resists idolizing its immediate object, thus, is triangulating and non-possessive.

This is important for Aquinas because the human heart and disposition have a nearly infinite appetite for happiness or fulfillment that only God can satisfy. If humans target any created object or person directly, rather than by triangulation through the love of God, "we are in danger of either idolizing them or of turning away from them in boredom."[17] In either case, the object or person is instrumentalized. For Aquinas, the unchecked desire for individual material gain represents "bad infinity" that can leave a person "wandering from one particular created thing to another in a futile quest for fulfillment in this life."[18] Whereas, when our desires are triangulated or mediated through God, we can properly value other objects and persons intrinsically.[19]

---

12. O'Connor, "Uti/Frui Distinction in Augustine's Ethics," 59.
13. Augustine, *City of God*, 205.
14. Gregory, *Politics and the Order of Love*, 343.
15. Schockenhoff, "Theological Virtue of Charity," 251–52.
16. Aquinas, *Summa Theologica*, 2308.
17. Nieuwenhove, "Religious Dispoition," 691.
18. Aquinas, *Summa Theologica*, 1097.
19. For Aquinas, "friendship" is the term that comes nearest to describing human relationality that is non-instrumentalized. "That which is loved with the love of friendship is loved simply and for itself. . . . Because he wishes and does good by his friend, by caring and providing for him, for his sake" (Aquinas, *Summa Theologica*, 1095–98).

How Does the Anabaptist Tradition of *Gelassenheit* Develop the Theme of Triangular Love?

An overview of the central figures in the triangular love tradition helps to see how it contrasts with the instrumentality of postsecular consumerist spirituality. Clearly, it represents a helpful source of retrieval as contemporary American evangelical theology revises the theme of transformation to counter the instrumentalizing tendencies of consumerist spirituality. However, knowing that what is needed is a revision that manifests in spiritual practice, how can the triangular tradition be appropriated into a lived relational ethic?

Here, contemporary American evangelical theology is benefited by an analysis of a third figure in the triangular tradition, the German medieval mystic, Meister Eckhart. More than Augustine and Aquinas, Eckhart developed triangular love into a reflective spiritual practice.[20] Eckhart's practical theology, embodied in the concept of *gelassenheit* ("detachment"), was operationalized by a community of early Anabaptists in south Germany in the late sixteenth century. The degree to which economic power and instrumentality were influencing the community of faith was a significant concern for them in light of the New Testament vision of genuine love. I first overview Eckhart's concept of *gelassenheit* and then discuss how it was appropriated by early Anabaptist spirituality.

Eckhart's *Gelassenheit*

Eckhart was born in Germany sometime in the mid-twelfth century. Around the age of 18, Eckhart joined the Dominican order at nearby Erfurt, with his studies taking him to universities of Cologne and Paris. Beginning his work as Prior in Erfurt in 1294, Eckhart took up a Dominican chair of theology in Paris a couple of years later. He then returned to Germany and began a decade rise in Dominican leadership, being made a provincial for Saxony and eventually vicar-general for Bohemia. His various writings and talks during this period attracted enough attention that he was invited back to Paris for a second period as *magister* (an honor previously attained only by Thomas Aquinas).

By this time, Eckhart's reputation as a strong academic theologian was well-established.[21] However, his penchant for delivering expository

---

20. Nieuwenhove, "Religious Disposition," 689–90.

21. "With the death of Duns Scotus in 1308, Eckhart stood without a peer in Western Europe in his grasp of philosophical and theological traditions" (Linge, "Mysticism, Poverty, and Reason," 470).

spiritual messages in the vernacular eventually embroiled him in controversy with the Catholic hierarchy, which was in the beginning stages of the Inquisition. Many regions of France and Germany were in disarray as church government sought to resist the growing emergence of localized pious lay communities. Though generally supported by local Dominican authorities, Eckhart came under formal inquisitorial investigation by the archbishop of Cologne, Hermann von Virneburg, who eventually appealed to the Pope in Avignon.[22] The result of this was the issuing of a bull (*In agro dominico*) by Pope John XXII on March 27, 1329, that condemned portions of his teachings as heresy and some as suspect while refraining from calling Eckhart a heretic directly.[23]

What was the fundamental reason for Eckhart's controversial status? Earlier scholarship pinpointed the ongoing ecclesial dispute between the Franciscan and Dominican orders as central, but that has given way to the majority position that it was his mystical understanding of the presence of God in the individual soul that garnered the most opposition.[24]

Eckhart reasoned, God's presence in the individual soul meant that the human should strive for conformity to the divine will since God's will is necessarily all good: "A good man ought so to conform his will to the divine will that he should whatever God wills."[25] This end is attained by a posture of *gelassenheit*, an intentional detached non-willing or releasement that cuts the individual off from worldly will and allows for the fostering on an "empty spirit."[26] This is necessary because people can easily

---

22. Including an initial defense by Nicholas of Strasbough, the pope's ruling representative over the Dominican monasteries in Germany.

23. This ambiguity toward Eckhart as a figure, in some sense, has remained with the Catholic church. Aside from a few references in Johann Tauler's sermons, Eckhart's body of work was largely unread until the nineteenth century, when interest was revived with Franz Pfeiffer's publication of addition sermons in 1857 and H. S. Denifile's translation of his Latin works beginning in 1886. The Dominican order appealed for a full rehabilitation of Eckhart's orthodoxy in 1990s and the Vatican responded by saying that this was unnecessary because he was never specifically condemned as a heretic, only portions of his teachings. Commenting on the general tensions between mystics such as Eckhart and the Catholic Church, McGinn noted: "Such tensions are not merely accidental, the result of the bad will of heretics or the mistakes and incomprehension of authority figures, but that they also are partly the result of inherent issues, pressure points if you will, in the relation of mysticism and magisterium in the history of Christianity" (McGinn, "Tensions," 194).

24. McGinn, *Harvest of Mysticism*, 103.

25. Meister Eckhart, *Essential Sermons*, 79.

26. Meister Eckhart, *Essential Sermons*, 248. According to Eckhart: "I usually speak of detachment and say that a man should be empty of self and all things; and secondly, that he should be reconstructed in the simple good that God is; and thirdly, that he

lose sight of God as the Ultimate when they "place ultimate value on finite realities such as their children, spouses, possessions, social reputations, ethnic groups, or nations."[27]

How is *gelassenheit* accomplished? The triangulating role of God's love is essential.[28] When one yields to God's mysterious and often uncomfortable work of detachment (*geschiedenheit*),[29] one allows God to realign the affections of the heart and soul so that they can make their way back to God through "the way of the Cross," resembling Jesus' own life, death, and resurrection.[30]

A "metaphysics of flow" characterizes Eckhart's portrayal of the intersection of divine and human loves: the abundance of Trinitarian love boils over to fill the cosmos and detachment pulls one's soul upward through the power of love into union with God.[31] Human autonomy exercised within creation is only in appearance since no being possesses its own ontological foundation. A lived *gelassenheit* continually resists the instrumentalizing effects of material and individual indulgence and produces within the soul intrinsic values of love, mercy, and kindness to others. In this way, *gelassenheit* pushes back against the tendency to instrumentalize: "it designates the attitude of a human who no longer regards objects and events according to their usefulness, but who accepts them in their autonomy."[32]

---

should consider the great aristocracy which God has set up in the soul, such that by means of it man may wonderfully attain to God; and fourthly, of the purity of the divine nature" (Eckhart quoted in Braybrooke, *Beacons of Light*, 316–17).

27. Finger, "Anabaptist Social Spirituality," 94. Like Augustine, Eckhart held tightly together love and being—one becomes what one loves. In a triangulating scheme, Eckhart upholds an irreducible simplicity in love: "Correspondingly, the human being who loves perfectly ought to love equally and in the same way God in the neighbor and the self, and the neighbor and the self in God, because then she loves one and the same. Pure love of God, self, and neighbor are, hence, equivalent in Eckhart's thought. As a practical upshot of his capacious account of love, Eckhart intensifies the ethical demand to love your neighbor by refusing to sublate it to the love of God" (Radler, "Centrality of Love," 184).

28. When speaking of love, Eckhart used a variety of terms (*amor. dilectico. caritas* in Latin and *minne* and *liebe* in German) that reflect an expansive range of meanings and that, as Radler rightly noted, resist the dualisms often attributed to him. See Radler, "Centrality of Love."

29. Eckhart used both the *gelassenheit/gelassen/lassen* and *abegescheiden/Abegescheidenheit* word groups to communicate very similar ideas. Technically speaking, in Eckhart's thought *lassen* and *gelassen* denote the process while *abgescheidenheit* denotes the goal. See Forman, *Mystic as Theologian*, 241.

30. Meister Eckhart, *Essential Sermons*, 52–55.

31. Radler, "Centrality of Love," 178.

32. Schürmann, *Meister Eckhart*, 16.

For Eckhart and his early followers, spiritual poverty entailed a life of material poverty.[33] However, detachment was also a way of reengaging the material world in a healthier way, not withdrawing entirely. As a "mendicant rather than an enclosed monk, Eckhart was dedicated to a life of active service in preaching, teaching, and administration. Instead of glorifying the spirituality of the strictly contemplative orders, he enjoined his reader to discover God in all times and places, in all persons and things."[34]

Considering the times, Eckhart's mystical asceticism is significant. The late-thirteenth and early-fourteenth centuries were the beginning of a wave of socioeconomic expansion that would propel continental Europe into modernity. His "was one of the earliest and deepest responses to the religious problem created by the new wealth and relative abundance that was becoming available to a growing class of people."[35] This becomes all the clearer when looking at how Eckhart's *gelassenheit* was adopted by early Anabaptist spirituality.

Early Anabaptist Spirituality

The term "Anabaptist" (from the Greek ἀναβαπτισμός; literally, "one who baptizes again") is a broad description for various movements that emerged in Europe during the time of the Protestant Reformation in the sixteenth and seventeenth centuries. They are rooted in the "radical" wing of the Reformation era that not only critiqued and separated from the Catholic church in company with the "magisterial Reformation" movements represented by Luther, Calvin, and Zwingli, but also differed from the magisterial groups in their belief that baptism is a sacramental right that should be undergone only by professing believers.[36] Opposition to infant baptism put Anabaptists at odds with established state and local governments and elicited severe

---

33. Linge, "Mysticism, Poverty, and Reason," 467.
34. Kieckhefer, "Union with God," 225.
35. Linge, "Mysticism, Poverty, and Reason," 460.
36. Esterp, *Anabaptist Story*, 9–13, 179. See also Williams, *Radical Reformation*. The oldest Anabaptist confession on baptism (found in the Schleitheim Confession of 1527) stated: "Baptism shall be given to all those who have learned repentance and amendment of life, and who believe truly that their sins are taken away by Christ, and to all those who walk in the resurrection of Jesus Christ, and wish to be buried with Him in death, so that they may be resurrected with Him, and to all those who with this significance request it [baptism] of us and demand it for themselves. This excludes all infant baptism, the highest and chief abomination of the pope. In this you have the foundation and testimony of the apostles. This we wish to hold simply, yet firmly and with assurance" ("Schleitheim Confession," 247).

persecution from both Catholic and mainline Protestant quarters.[37] It also shaped a distinctive spirituality centered on *gelassenheit*.[38]

The ethic of *gelasseneheit* first emerged as a central theme in the early south German Anabaptist movement of the late 1500s and early 1600s, a movement that had close ties to the German Rhineland mystical spirituality. Appropriation of Rhineland mysticism into early Anabaptist spirituality was sparked by the German Peasants' War against noble overlords in Germany led by Thomas Müntzer. Just as God had purged his own soul of inordinate attachments, Müntzer claimed, so too was God going to purge the land of all the social inequalities that had been wrought at the hands of the wealthy on the backs of the laborers.[39]

The failure of Müntzer's revolt did not abate the spread of Rhineland mysticism, but it did profoundly shape the ethic of nonviolence that came to characterize the Anabaptist way.[40] If reform was going to happen, it must be a silent opposition to ecclesial and state establishment, even if in martyrdom. Over the next three decades, the mystical approach represented in *gelassenheit* took root through two prominent figures. The first is Hans Hut (c. 1490–1527), who became a central leader of the southern German Anabaptist movement after coming under the influence of Müntzer during the Peasant War and then being baptized by Hans Denck.

Hut emphasized the mysterious and challenging internal process of *gelassenheit* that defines the Christian way and to which all of nature points:

> Nothing comes to fruition without suffering. The grape must be crushed, the animal must be butchered and roasted, the grain must be ground and baked. Likewise, the human being must suffer in order to become a worthy instrument of the will of God.[41]

The second significant figure of Anabaptist Rhineland mysticism was Hans Denck (c.1495–1527). Born in Bavaria, Denck was perhaps the most intellectually gifted of the early Anabaptists, receiving a classical education and becoming a headmaster in Nuremberg before being influenced to join the Anabaptist movement by Müntzer.[42] Denck was a particularly vocal critic of established (Catholic and Lutheran) clergy, which in his view had lost

---

37. Chadwick, *Early Reformation*, 351–70. In the sixteenth century, likely "between 3,000 to 4,000 Anabaptist followers were burned at the stake, drowned in rivers, starved in prisons, or beheaded" (Kling, *Bible in History*, 163).
38. Murray, *Naked Anabaptist*, 171; Klaassen, "Gelassenheit and Creation," 23.
39. See Williams, *Spiritual and Anabaptist Writers*.
40. Bender, *Conrad Grebel*, 111.
41. Liechty, *Early Anabaptist Spirituality*, 63.
42. See Baumann, *Hans Denck*.

the way to true faith by becoming consumed with amassing political and economic gain. In his "Concerning True Love," Denck showed clear mystical influence and remarked on the centrality of the triangulating force of the pure love of God to resist instrumentality expressed in Jesus of Nazareth:

> Love is a spiritual power. The lover desires to be united with the beloved. Where love is fulfilled, the lover does not objectify the beloved. The lover forgets himself, without shame he yearns for his beloved. . . . When love is true and plays no favorites, it reaches out in desire to unite with all people (that is, without causing division and instability). . . . A person who loves God most truly and as much as possible can help his neighbor also to know and love God. Whoever wants to know true love can receive it no better than through Jesus Christ.[43]

Overall, the early Anabaptist spiritual practice of *gelassenheit* took the mystical influence of medieval predecessors—which understood *gelassenheit* primarily passive in nature—and added an active component:

> In medieval devotion, this word for self-surrender was invariably passive. It referred to the soul's submission before God. But in the radical reformation of Anabaptism, it came to mean both passive yieldedness and active unyieldedness.[44]

As the spiritual discipline of detachment was adopted into their community praxis, *gelassenheit* moved from a strictly spiritual disposition to a full-blown theological ethic for developing triangulating love expressed in *koinonia*. In the throes of persecution, the early Anabaptists came to believe that internal spiritual disposition and external obedience were not only linked in discipleship, but mutually nourishing—true transformation started in the soul and then moved outward.[45] Internal purification from lust and greed, for instance, could not but result in specific outward and social manifestations, such as baptism and church membership. Thus, the "uprooting of attachments to creaturely goods intrinsically led to sharing those goods with others."[46]

The early southern German appropriation of mystical *gelassenheit* served as the basis for development by second and third generation

---

43. Denck quoted in Liechty, *Early Anabaptist Spirituality*, 111–13.

44. Augsburger, *Dissident Discipleship*, 88.

45. According to Finger, "Jesus' earthly journey no longer functioned chiefly as a symbol for an inner mystical process. It also provided the pattern for pursuing this process in one's concrete daily walk" (Finger, "Anabaptist Social Spirituality," 5).

46. Finger, "Anabaptist Social Spirituality," 5.

Anabaptist leaders as Anabaptism spread beyond southern Germany. Menno Simons set the stage for the emphasis on *gelassenheit* within the Mennonite tradition with his devotional work *The Cross of Christ*. Among the Phillipite brethren in Moravia in the 1530s, Hans Haffner produced *Concerning the True Soldier of Christ* in which he proclaimed *gelassenheit* as the distinguishing mark of Christian community.[47]

It was the utilization of the concept among the Hutterite brethren, however, that gave the term its association with the divestiture of material goods and individual ambitions for the good of the broader community. Peter Reidemann (1506–1556), a Polish-born Hutterite, regarded as a secondary founder of the Anabaptist branch, distinguished *gelassenheit* as an expression of communal love that was triangulated in response to God's love in Christ.[48] He wrote:

> But brotherly love implies that we lay our lives down for each other, just as Christ did for all of us, and gave us an example to follow in his footsteps. So I should not live for myself alone, but live to serve my brothers—not seek my prosperity and betterment, but theirs, my whole life long; also, I should take care not to let my brother be grieved or weakened by my work or words.[49]

In the Article Book, the significant doctrinal tract of the Hutterites produced in the late 1540s in connection with Reidmann's *Account of Our Religion, Doctrine, and Faith*, Article Three is entirely devoted to the practice of *gelassenheit*. The surrendering of personal goods where material needs exist is case as a means of sustaining community bonds, "we should expect the Lord's work and Cross daily, as we have surrendered unto His discipline and have agreed to accept whatever He may send upon us with thanksgiving, and to bear it with patience."[50] In this regard, *gelassenheit* produced some of the most distinctive and visible socioeconomic features that defined the early Anabaptist communities: the formation of production and consumption roles, the renouncing of material excess, and the communal ownership of hard assets.

In all, the ethical core of triangulating love expressed in early Anabaptist spirituality through the posture of *gelassenheit* has at least three

---

47. Haffner wrote, "When we truly realize the love of God, we will be ready to give up for love's sake even what God has given us" (Haffner quoted in Friedmann, *Hutterite Studies*, 253).
48. See Funk, *Gelassenheit*.
49. Riedemann, *Love Is Like Fire*, 19.
50. Gelder, "Article Book," 462. See also Friedmann, "Introduction."

levels of resonance with classic evangelical theology.[51] First, early Anabaptist spirituality stressed the priority of the human relationship with God. In their criticism of the corruption of the clergy by political and economic power, early Anabaptist communities emphasized the commonality of spiritual practice and relationships. Accordingly, many early Anabaptists picked up a trade upon leaving the monastery. Anabaptists perceived that reigning religious authorities had terminally separated external conformity from internal moral quality.

Second, early Anabaptist spirituality stressed the priority of radical discipleship. As a means of sourcing and retaining power, the majority of Christian clergy focused on what one needs to do to secure salvation. For early Anabaptist communities, the question of how one becomes a follower of Christ in daily life dominated, with an emphasis on fostering obedience and love. Naturally, this led to a sense of living outside the worldly order, yet, submitting to political authority whenever possible. The radical component of this understanding of discipleship was often connected in the early Anabaptist spirituality to Jesus' *kenosis* (Phil 2:7) or self-emptying, which served as a model for *gelassenheit*.[52] Dyck suggested that early Anabaptist writers saw in mystical expressions of *gelassenheit* as found in Eckhart a pattern of enduring suffering and martyrdom by returning to a spiritual desert, much like the wilderness experience of early church leaders.[53] It is difficult to understate the effects that the reality of martyrdom had on Anabaptist understanding of discipleship and particularly the importance of pacifism.

Third, early Anabaptist spirituality stressed the corporate nature of the Christian life. The individual's relationship with God was activated by and experienced in the gathered assembly of believers, which represented the mysterious presence of the body of Christ. This union of believers was a primary source of sustaining and even growing the body through the waves of endured martyrdom and persecution.[54]

---

51. See Liechty, *Early Anabaptist Spirituality*, 9–11.
52. Detweiler, *Breaking the Fall*.
53. See Dyck, *Spiritual Life in Anabaptism*.
54. Liechty summarized Anabaptist spirituality well: "They taught nothing but love, faith, and the need of the bearing of the cross. They showed themselves humble, patient under much suffering; they break the bread with one another as an evidence of unity and love. They helped each other faithfully" (Liechty, *Early Anabaptist Spirituality*, 12).

What Are the Implications for the Theme of Transformation?

To close this chapter, I draw out the implications of Anabaptist spirituality's mystical *gelassenheit* for contemporary American evangelical theology's postsecular renewal of the theme of transformation. I demonstrate that it renews the hard-soft transformation spectrum with an alternative that moves beyond the reductive categories of the individual and the social.

In part one of the book, I described the theme of transformation as a dominant way contemporary American evangelical theology understands the relationship of Christian faith to capitalistic enterprise. Generally, it designates the call of Christians to transform enterprise by (a) positively influencing for-profit enterprise for the common good and (b) engaging in personal conversion where opportunity allows by sharing the gospel with others to spread the kingdom of God.

Within this general theme, I differentiated two varieties. Hard transformation KNC speaks about integrating faith and work from the standpoint of God's worldwide kingdom rule in all areas of life and emphasizes the Christian's responsibility to be involved in the transformation of enterprise for the common good. Soft transformation TKP speaks about integrating faith and work from the standpoint of God's unique kingdom rule through Christ (as opposed to his general kingdom rule over humanity) and emphasizes the Christian's responsibility to live faithfully in enterprise as part of the common/human kingdom, which may involve transformation as part of the redemptive kingdom.

When applied to this spectrum, mystical *gelassenheit*'s relational ethic of triangulating love offers a needed postsecular revision. The posture of *gelassenheit* forces contemporary American evangelical theology to ask: What should be the focus of Christian ethics in discussions about transformation in enterprise? The hard-soft spectrum—reflecting a dichotomized paradigm that construes the conceptual categories of the individual and social as fundamentally separable—presents two basic options: the general state of society (the social) or the inner life of the believer (the individual).

However, drawing on the example of the Anabaptist communities that employed *gelassenheit*, an alternate option is present: the common life of faith communities (or "the church"). The conviction that drove *gelassenheit* practice in early Anabaptism was that "inward sanctification . . . cannot occur apart from outward actions" in a communal context and "neither can lasting individual or social change emerge apart from inward participation in Jesus' life, death, and resurrection."[55]

Throughout its history, Anabaptism has been characterized by a tension between transformational and separatist poles.[56] On the one end, Anabaptist theology has fostered a "strong sense of the incarnational reality of the Gospel in culture" that has created a "transformational grammar."[57] On the other end, separatism has pushed back against transformationism through social separation from culture and moral deterioration in the community. A central concern of the early Anabaptists was the illegitimacy of institutionalized forms of ecclesiology.[58] There was a growing sense among Anabaptists that church and state should be terminally separated, thus, broadly speaking, there was an adoption of the TKP promulgated by Luther.[59]

While affirming Luther's critique of reigning Catholic theology that "the world social order could not be Christianized," among early Anabaptists, there was a certain "abandonment of non-Christian society to its own management and a concentration on the evangelism of individuals from that non-Christian society."[60] However, while "Luther believed Christians should participate in the secular kingdom if action needed to be taken. . . . Anabaptists supported a more separatist view" in which voluntarily formed, small-scale Christian communities functioned as a counter cultural witness.[61]

It was certainly true that the Anabaptists' opposition to the sacred rite of pedobaptism—which amounted to an undermining of the medieval social order in the eyes of many established local authorities (both Catholic and Protestant)—was the spark of dissent that set off a wave of Anabaptist persecution. However, for Zwingli, Calvin, and Luther, the essential heresy of Anabaptism was their resistance to the expansive authority of the nation-state. Anabaptists contended that a true two kingdom theology warranted significant separation from secular society, whereas critics perceived it as an

---

55. Finger, "Anabaptist Social Spirituality," 16.

56. Loewen, "Peace in the Mennonite Tradition, 106–12.

57. Loewen, "Peace in the Mennonite Tradition," 108. See also Harder, "Power and Authority," 90.

58. Stayer wrote, "The sixteenth-century Anabaptists began by attacking the authority of established power structures in church and rulership" (Stayer, "Anabaptist Revolt," 70).

59. This, of course, is a broad description of the relationship between Anabaptism and two kingdoms doctrine. For a more nuanced analysis that points out some the differences at the molecular level, see Bauman, "Theology of the 'Two Kingdoms.'"

60. Wenger, *Doctrines of the Mennonites*, 54–55.

61. Halteman, "Anabaptist Approaches to Economics," 2.

"inability to resolve within the Christian conscience the underlying antithesis between the kingdom of God and the kingdoms of this world."[62]

The dualistic application of two kingdoms theology by the early Anabaptist communities, in which the objective was to establish free and visible fellowships patterned after the earliest churches of the New Testament, involved a separation of the "true church" from the world as a means of transforming both.[63] *Gelassenheit* facilitated this transformation by placing the focus on "disestablishment" of the community of faith, from which other practices flowed, "They renounced warfare and use of the sword; they refused to conform to many civic mores, including swearing by the civil oath and bringing suit in courts of law."[64]

One of the New Testament models that early Anabaptists used was the faith community in Ephesus. A brief look shows why. The exhortation in Ephesians "to walk worthy of the calling to which you have been called" (4:1) is grounded by the author in the purpose of God to bring unity to all creation in Christ (1:3–14). How is this accomplished? Against the backdrop of political empire and military kingdom, the author of Ephesians located the mechanism of God's work in an altogether different kingdom, "the church that is his body," which will "fill all in all" (Eph 1:22–23).

Certainly striking to its original readers, this relatively meager conduit is further described in 2:11–22 as a grand temple with *both* Jews and Gentiles present because it is established on the Christ's ultimate act of triangulating love, the cross, which "reconciles us both to God in one body . . . thereby killing the hostility" (Eph 2:16–17). Nearly the entire second half of the letter becomes a mandate to fulfill the building of this body, again, not with individual or social exercises of economic power, but through the fostering of a triangulating ethic of love such that the common life of faith communities becomes a compelling force of social reordering. So, in prayer (3:14–21), in the distribution of gifts (4:1–15), in the settling of disputes (4:25–32), in moral obedience (5:1–21), and in household relationships (5:22–6:9), the guiding

---

62. Bauman, "Theology of the 'Two Kingdoms,'" 38–39.

63. Friedmann, *Theology of Anabaptism*, 36–56. Felix Mantz, an early Anabaptist leader in Zurich who was also one of the first martyrs, proclaimed that Christians should live in the "love, unity and community of all things, like the apostles in Acts 2, and necessarily avoid occupying any form of government rule" (Mantz quoted in Shenk, *Anabaptism and Mission*, 211).

64. Kyle, "Concept and Practice of Seperation," 33. Pacifism comprises another common characteristic of the Anabaptist tradition. See the widely cited study by Bender, "Pacifism." Approaching the subject, Stayer offered a wise caution: "Like much else in early Anabaptism, nonresistance seems to have been a series of ideas without a general consensus behind it in its Swiss origins, but it became a major focus of the movement in the Moravian emigration before 1535" (Stayer, "Anabaptist Revolt," 12).

ethic is triangulating love: "Be imitators of God . . . and walk in love, as Christ loved us and gave himself up for us" (5:1).

These texts indicate that the exercise of active and affective triangulating love within the community of faith—in response to Jesus' own act of sacrificial love—is the primary means for building up of the transformational kingdom of God. Here, we have a thick description of a distinctly Christ-oriented and intrinsic relational ethic.[65] Despite the tendency in contemporary American evangelical theology to connect the effort of transformation to the kingdom of God in broad terms, the New Testament narrows the vision to focus on ecclesial relationships.[66] The early mystical Anabaptist emphasis on the exercise of *gelassenheit* within faith communities is a way of saying that the goal is not "in the first instance to transform a culture but to form one."[67]

That the common life of faith communities should be the primary focus of the theme of transformational in light of the American postsecular consumerist spirituality is the case for three reasons. First, postsecular consumerist spirituality has arisen partly to fill the void that has been left by the post-Niebuhr decline of the structural influence of American evangelicalism on society, thus, the general effectiveness of the transformation option. Hauerwas and Willimon posited that Niebuhr's death and the transition soon after marked the proverbial end to the Christendom that had directly influenced western culture since the time of Constantine.[68]

For many in evangelicalism, Niebuhr's matrix presented in *Christ and Culture* represented great hope for the idea that the Christian faith can and should be involved in "transforming" culture, including enterprise:

> When Richard Niebuhr's book first appeared almost everyone in America rushed to locate himself among the "transformationalists." . . . It was as if the "typology" or clustering of Christian approaches to man's work in culture and history had suddenly collapsed in 1951, so universal was the conviction that, of course, the Christian always joins in the transformation of the world whenever it is proposed.[69]

65. Turner, *Christian Ethics and the Church*, 104.
66. See McKnight, *Kingdom Conspiracy*.
67. Turner, *Christian Ethics and the Church*, 155.
68. See Hauerwas and Willimon, *Resident Aliens*. "Christendom" can be understood as "the concept of western civilization as having a religious arm (the church) and a secular arm (civil government), both of which are united in their adherence to Christian faith, which is seen as the so-called soul of Europe or the west" (Carter, *Rethinking Christ and Culture*, 13).
69. Ramsey and Hallowell, *War and the Christian Conscience*, 112–13.

THE ANABAPTIST CONCEPT OF *GELASSENHEIT*

One of the reasons Hauerwas and Willimon said Niebuhr's death marked the beginning of the end for Christendom aspirations in America is because of the relative failures of American Christendom political efforts since Niebuhr's time. This was acknowledged by as influential a figure in American conservative evangelicalism as Carl Henry, who said,

> Despite all the media tumult over the Moral Majority and the high public visibility of its leader, its extensive solicitation of funds during a six-year political crusade—claiming to speak for six million households—has not achieved passage of a single major piece of legislation cherished by the conservative right.[70]

More recently, this point has been leveled by Hunter and Balmer, both of whom assess that American evangelical efforts to influence broader cultural currents through political and commercial power have severely weakened.[71] Mirroring much more closely the conditions of the early church as depicted in the New Testament, American evangelicalism now principally operates at the margins of influence from a position of social weakness, not strength. Such a position demands a way of living that demonstrates the distinctiveness of its offering—in the case of consumerist spirituality, how human relationships oriented around triangulating love look different from those grounded in instrumentality.

Early Anabaptist spirituality represents a promising postsecular alternative to the polarizing choices of hard-soft transformation, and it is not difficult to see why. The rise of Protestantism in the 1600s was primarily an effort at reforming the Christian church. The mainline Reformation of Calvin and Luther represented an effort to do so utilizing the means of political authority with a desire to preserve and, in some ways, restore the Christian state in the west.

The Anabaptist radical reformation was different—an attempt to "articulate and foster a Christian spirituality which was independent of the political establishment" and suspicious of possessions of economic power by the church community.[72] Whatever else it involved, the emergence of the Anabaptist tradition "represented a break with the inherited system of intermingled religious and political power."[73] For it, religious power "re-

---

70. Henry, *Confessions*, 394. See also McKnight, *Kingdom Conspiracy*, 214.
71. See Hunter, *To Change the World*; Balmer, *God in the White House*.
72. Liechty, *Early Anabaptist Spirituality*, xii.
73. Redekop and Redekop, *Power, Authority, and the Anabaptist Tradition*, vii.

sided in the local fellowship of believers, the *koinonia*, a totally voluntary banding-together of fellow believers."[74]

Second, rapid economic globalization has resulted in the loss of relational outposts that operate on a rich ethic of triangulating love. Returning to the point made in chapter 3, the instrumentalizing tendencies of postsecular consumer spirituality are part of a broader loss of intrinsicality in the modern industrialized west that has inhibited the appreciation of dimensions of human experience that are necessary for human relational flourishing but limited in their individual economic utility. Collectively, we are "less interested in equipping, and refining thought, more interested in creating and mastering technologies that will yield measurable enhancements of material well-being—for those who create and master them, at least."[75]

Following the vision of the New Testament, local communities of Christians marked by an ethical core of triangulating love could provide one of the few places that human identities could be forged in an intimate environment that embraces human finitude and vulnerabilities rather than attempts to take advantage of them. While consumerist spirituality proposes that even moral goods such as strong character can be acquired in a short period through privatized means, the triangular tradition's approach to human relationality holds that one's interior moral life can only be advanced "by living over a protracted period of time with others who adopt similar practices and have similar goals."[76]

Third, a focus on the common life of faith communities surmounts the reductive categories of the individual and the social underlying the hard-soft transformational spectrum. This neoliberal paradigm, which construes the human individual as an atomistic and rational actor fundamentally distinct from his or her social embedding, was shown in the previous chapter to be significantly undermined in its ability to capture the complex dimensions of human experience. It contributes to a new kind of suffering imposed from the burdens of self-making.

What is emerging from the increasing interconnectedness and volatility of the postsecular global economy is rather an intricate relational ecosystem in which human experience is socially embedded in every dimension. An emphasis on the embodied norms of faith communities in shaping both the individual and the social offers a fuller model for articulating

---

74. Redekop, "Power in the Anabaptist Community," in Redekop and Redekop, *Power, Authority, and the Anabaptist Tradition*, 185.

75. Robinson, *Givenness of Things*, 3.

76. Turner, *Christian Ethics and the Church*, 179.

transformational thinking that can counter third-order suffering with the cultivation of strong collectives.

What does a focus on expressing triangulating love in the common life of faith communities broadly entail? It entails the carrying out of Christian community practices in a triangulating way that counters the consumerist narratives—heavily underwritten by a loss of intrinsicality—that human flourishing is achieved and sustained by the ever-greater consumption of goods and services for individual and material gain.[77] The mystical strain of *gelassenheit* suggests that this requires profound detachment. Meaning, "identifying and letting go, often painfully, of ways they have become inordinately attached to values, behaviors, persons, and things . . . at equally deep levels by healthy, non-grasping, non-possessive ways of relating to all other creatures."[78]

This undoubtedly involves three attachments identified in the gospels as sources of hostile social division that "the love of God renders subordinate to one's devotion"[79] to the kingdom of God: (a) relational bonds,[80] in that one, incorporates a universal and mysterious body of fellow followers into the familial bonds of one's life, irrespective of race, gender, or ethnicity; (b) possessions, in that one relinquishes the claim over any material goods for the higher calling of stewarding God's provisions for the care and joy of others; and (c) status, in that one seeks approval on the basis of the extent to which he or she has become a servant of God rather than the extent to which others have become servants to him or her.

In these and any other sources of consumerist attachment, what were once primary sources of competitive and hostile social division become "aspects of life provided by God because God knows them to be necessary."[81]

---

77. According to Nieuwenhove: "When we are detached we are devoid of self-centeredness and possessiveness, and this allows us to reengage with the world in a proper manner without instrumentalizing it or subjecting it to our concerns. . . . Paradoxically, it is a kind of "goal" that cannot be pursued directly through our own efforts" (Nieuwenhove, "Religious Disposition," 693–94).

78. Finger, "Anabaptist Social Spirituality," 4–5. The threat of inordinate attachment is not limited to material things: "Quite often, desires for security, self-worth, even love and affection lead us to grasp after not only material goods, but also persons or social position or reputation or power, and to possess them" (Finger, "Anabaptist Social Spirituality," 7). We might even say that in a postsecular age, where entrepreneurial enhancement is the cultural expectation, inordinate attachment to ideals not things poses a greater liability.

79. Turner, *Christian Ethics and the Church*, 159–61.

80. Turner used the term *family*, but I prefer here the term *relational bonds* on the grounds that its connotation is broader and brings under investigation not just one immediate or secondary family but other primary and secondary intimate relationships.

81. Turner, *Christian Ethics and the Church*, 161.

Together, these re-orderings enable followers of Jesus to respond faithfully to the fundamental call to love God and love neighbor.

Conclusion

In this chapter, I have begun to establish that contemporary American evangelical theology could achieve a postsecular renewal of the theme of transformation by appropriating early Anabaptist spirituality's expression of mystical *gelassenheit*. I first defined in greater detail the ethic of triangulating love developed in the New Testament and the Christian tradition. I then overviewed Eckhart's mystical *gelassenheit* and its appropriation by early Anabaptist spirituality. To close, I drew out the implications of this appropriation for contemporary American evangelical theology's theme of transformation.

American evangelicalism stands today on the other side of capitalism's unprecedented economic development. An analysis of the vantage point of the 1500–1600s brings to bear a vital theological problem: that we understand how and why early Anabaptist spirituality's "religious response to material wealth was smothered by the kinds of accommodations western religious traditions have worked out in the modern period."[82] To that I turn.

---

82. Linge, "Mysticism, Poverty, and Reason," 477.

8

How Can a *Gelassenheit* Model Strengthen Evangelical Reflexivity?

In the final two chapters, I am showing how a critical appropriation by contemporary American evangelical theology of the Anabaptist theme of *gelasseneheit* enables a postsecular revision of the theme of transformation that counters the instrumentalizing excesses of postsecular consumerist spirituality. The fundamental insight of the early Anabaptist mystical spiritual practice of *gelassenheit* was that the fostering of genuine intrinsic love for God and others in one's soul manifesting in active discipleship of the ways of Jesus was possible only when the instrumentalizing tendencies of individual and material economic gain were regularly resisted by a reorienting devotion to God.

To close the last chapter, I showed how this insight renewed the hard-soft transformation spectrum with a focus on the common life of faith communities that moved past the reductive categories of the individual and the social. In what ways does that insight affect actual contemporary American evangelical theological practice and how might *gelassenheit* foster a cluster of spiritual activities undergirding reflexivity?

In the introduction, I stated that if it is successful, this book's central achievement would be the construction of a model for strengthening evangelical reflexivity that addresses the inevitable ambiguities of spiritual practice. A scripturally rooted vision of transformation focused on fostering strong relational collectives in faith communities is insufficient by itself. Like any other, the actual lived beliefs and practices of Christian faith communities do not easily integrate. Indeed, "they are mostly non-Christian practices—eating, meeting, greeting—done differently, born again, to an unpredictable effect."[1]

---

1. Tanner, "Theological Reflection," 230. See also Richter, "Religious Practices," 207.

This has been the critique leveled against a phrase of Hauerwas often repeated by evangelicals: "The first task of the church is not to make the world more just, but to make the world the world."[2] But how? Any appropriation of *gelassenheit* for evangelical faith communities needs to overcome the tendency to treat Christian practices as easily distinguishing the church from the world.[3] Attending to ambiguities of practice is to acknowledge that to some extent they are normal, not inherently a threat to faithful practice but potentially a means of growing in faith. Sometimes, they invite resolution, other times promotion, and still other times simply acceptance and affirmation. In no instance should their presence be denied, invalidated, or ignored. Accordingly, meaningfully attending requires not a specific skill set, but a posture of reflexivity, more like the strengthening of a muscle integral to the functioning of the body rather than a new prepackaged tool that the body can readily pick up.

For American evangelical theology in a postsecular consumerist context, this challenge is intensified by two factors. First, the topic at hand is inherently intangible and elusive. What is being targeted for reform here is the reorientation of an inner state of spirituality through the critical reforming of daily consumer habits that are deeply rooted but often concealed![4] Any constructive model for strengthening reflexivity must be capable of surfacing ambiguities to reflect upon them critically. Second, the tradition at hand (American evangelicalism) has historically favored individualistic and personal lenses over structural and abstract ones in moral reflection.[5]

Ironically, while American evangelicalism places the Bible as the central norm, "it is central not as theory, but as practice."[6] It rests on a deep commitment to experience, even though the transition from experience to new practice often skips critical reflection. Any constructive model for strengthening reflexivity must be able to bridge the two horizons of ancient scriptural texts and contemporary interpretive contexts.[7]

---

2. Hauerwas, *Hannah's Child*, 158.

3. Pitts, "Anabaptist Theologies," 323.

4. Finger notes: "We cannot attack the roots of these problems if the desires and patterns which produce them are rooted in ourselves. . . . Appeals to consume do not simply impinge on people from outside, as on a blank slate, leaving them fully free to respond. They are woven through nearly everything we experience. . . . If we seek to alter today's systems while we and their victims are still deeply structured by these creaturely attachments, we will, at best, produce some altered version of them" (Finger, *Anabaptist Social Spirituality*, 4).

5. Emerson and Smith, *Divided by Faith*; Jones, "Analysis."

6. Root, "Evangelical Practical Theology," 93.

7. For an overview of the concept to two horizons, see Thiselton, *Two Horizons*.

Yet, these intensifying factors are precisely why mystical *gelassenheit* offers a robust contribution for strengthening reflexivity. I will develop a constructive model that enables individuals and collectives embedded in postsecular consumerist contexts to interrogate ambiguities of practice as they imperfectly love God and neighbor. The model integrates Turpin's four stage process for reflexive faithful consumption with mystical *gelassenheit* and primarily focuses on the areas of familial bonds, possessions, and status.[8]

I proceed in four movements. First, I set up the model by analyzing how a *gelassenheit* epistemology can help contemporary American evangelical theology to reunite the cognitive and affective dimensions of theology necessary for engaging ambiguities of practice. Second, I explain the model. Third, I demonstrate how to use the model with two narrative examples, one drawn from Fulkerson's ethnographic congregational study and the other from personal experience.[9] Fourth, I briefly explore how *gelassenheit* can support reflexive orientation with other spiritual practices.

A *Gelassenheit* Epistemology for Faithful Practice

Gelassenheit strengthens contemporary American evangelical theological reflexivity by first revising the classic foundationalist epistemology that has inhibited it. In chapter 2, I demonstrated how contemporary American evangelical theology has been reliant on classic foundationalism in its attempt to secure an impenetrable foundation upon which it can build its theological edifice. This has downplayed the formative roles of perceptual lenses and worldviews in shaping theological belief and creaturely epistemic limits. In the case of perceptions of enterprise, this has amounted to the espousing of an allegiance to scriptural values (like the New Testament core of triangulating love), all the while in practice remaining complicit with the instrumentalizing tendencies of postsecular consumerist spirituality. By divorcing cognitive assent from affective engagement—"theology" from "ethics," as it were—its internal consistency and explanatory power are undermined.[10]

8. Turpin, *Branded*.
9. Fulkerson, *Places of Redemption*.
10. This point helps clarify the nature of my argument. The conviction of this book has been that the theme of transformation should not be entirely abandoned by contemporary American evangelical theology, but rather revised for a postsecular milieu. By pointing to the concept of *gelassenheit* as a source of contribution, my argument is not that *gelassenheit* is the only way to accomplish a postsecular revision of the theme of transformation. To make such an argument, it seems to me, would be epistemically

Classic foundationalist schemes discourage the self-interrogation necessary for strong reflexivity because theology is limited to abstracted beliefs and doctrines while phenomenal forms are treated as inessential.[11] A brief look at Heidegger's use of *gelassenheit* shows the shortcomings of such schemes. Heidegger emphasized that our relation to the world, including in theological reflection, is already a precognitive construal of the world.[12] Borrowing from and adapting Eckhart, Heidegger posited *gelassenheit* as a way that humans can cognitively engage their surrounding world while being affectively shaped in the process.[13] For Eckhart, this was crucial because the movement into the triangulating love of God is not just cognitive but also affective. It involves the "voluntary emptiness" of one's attempts to instrumentalize things and images for one's own purpose.[14] This requires a continual surrendering and detaching in mystery of one's mind, body, and soul to the love of God. Accordingly, for the early Anabaptists, *gelassenheit* represented the faith community's movement from lesser forms of love (merely cognitive) to higher forms (fully engaged).

Taken seriously, this inverts the traditional evangelical scheme and restores the organic connection between ethics and theology. It is also a challenge to consumerist spirituality, which separates the conscious pursuit of spiritual fulfillment through the acquisition of goods and services from the underlying distortions that such habit-shaping consumer liturgies enact on affective desires. The process of detachment found in *gelassenheit* works in the opposite direction, rewiring self-centered loves so that they align with objectives of properly theological edicts.

No doubt, some within American evangelicalism might want to resist any appropriation of *gelassenheit* because the theologies of Eckhart, early Anabaptist spirituality and Heidegger do not qualify as "evangelical." What I am calling for is a critical and not wholesale appropriation of such systems, but operating below the surface of this concern is a foundationalist framework that reaffirms the contributions of a *gelassenheit* epistemology.

---

unviable because it would require quantifying and then measuring abstract conceptual categories that do not easily lend themselves to such analysis. I argue that by employing the conceptual paradigm of *gelassenheit* gives contemporary evangelical theological perceptions of enterprise more internal coherence, thus, passing a primary criterion for truth and achieving greater clarity.

11. Smith, "Secular Liturgies," 162. See also Mahmood, "Secularism, Hermeneutics, and Empire."

12. Smith, "Secular Liturgies," 169.

13. Linge, "Mysticism, Poverty, and Reason," 483.

14. Schürmann, *Meister Eckhart*, 109.

To make one's appropriation of any moment in theological history contingent on doctrinal symmetry alone is to suggest that the connection between theology and ethics is a straight linear line between cognitive assent and affect obedience. However, the ambiguities of practice evidenced by the grip of postsecular consumerist spirituality tell a different story. Correctly aligning one's doctrinal scheme with the ethical core of the New Testament is not difficult. I suspect that most American evangelicals recognize the challenge that postsecular consumerist spirituality's excessive instrumentality poses to the genuine love of God and neighbor. The challenge is how to translate this doctrinal assent into a genuine spiritual desire that manifests in collective normed practices.

Because they are socially and contextually embedded, practices are malleable, not set forms.[15] Religious, theological practice presents two unique challenges.[16] For one, they linger at the limits of human agency by contemplating ultimate questions like how to confront death. Additionally, they require paradoxical transcendence of self and not just a change of self.[17]

In the Aristotelian tradition, where the goal of practice is the achievement of mastery, practice is commonly portrayed as "something individuals perform to achieve technical ends in the present moment guided by theoretical principles."[18] Contrastingly, Christian practices have a "peculiarity about them" in that the goal is not mastery but rather "the right use of gifts graciously bestowed by a loving God for the sake of the good that God intends."[19] Evangelical theology has tended to view the practice as "individualistic, technological, ahistorical, and abstract" from the standpoint of a completely integrated belief system.[20] However, humans often operate in a multiplicity of conflicting practices, such that "being a self whose faith may not be as tidy as we imagine."[21] This is a direct challenge to the (unfulfilled) promise of postsecular consumer spirituality: unlike "products of

---

15. MacIntyre, *After Virtue*, 218.

16. Hunter, "Future of Pastoral Theology," 68–69.

17. Bass et al., *Christian Practical Wisdom*, 190.

18. Dykstra, *Reconceiving Practice*, 35.

19. Dykstra, *Reconceiving Practice*, 35. See also Bloesch, *Freedom for Obedience*, 191.

20. Richter, "Religious Practices," 205.

21. See Turpin, *Branded*, 46. According to Hunter: "Rather than assuming that the presence of multiple belief systems indicates hypocrisy and potential idolatry, we could assume that the believer is merely in the process of converting from one set of beliefs to another.... Many of us judge negatively the conflicted parts of our self as incomplete rather than joining Barth in recognizing our conflict as an indication of the fullness of our engagement in transformation" (Hunter, "Future of Pastoral Theology," 67).

a consumer society, simply there for the taking," discipleship and the right use of gifts takes time and work and "one must be an insider, a practitioner oneself disciplined by the practice."[22]

Fundamentally, I am addressing a question that has been asked going back to the time of Jesus, when he commanded his followers to be "in" the world but not "of" the world" (John 17:14–19). The influence of market capitalism and its instrumentalizing effects is vast and virtually inescapable. The elimination of any and all forms of instrumentality is neither possible nor warranted, but what is necessary is the ability to surface where said instrumentalizing tendencies are bearing unintended consequences. Fitch did an excellent job of framing the dilemma for American evangelicals, and it is worth quoting him at length:

> This ("being in the world and not of it") has never been more important as society fragments into its multiple justices and communities. But this has also rarely been more difficult as late capitalism extends its dominion over all manifestations of North American life. Capitalism intrudes upon every living space . . . and imposes enormous . . . pressures on its inhabitants that impede this kind of community. So, our congregations must work incessantly, paying off larger credit card bills and mortgages on bigger homes. Capitalist competitiveness and consumerism, as well as liberal individualism, shape us into being wealth accumulators, consumers. . . . There is little time for our people to be the body. . . . When we do come together, we come shaped as we are out of capitalism as individuals protecting our interests. We do not come determined first by our citizenship in Christ. . . . As a result, many evangelicals take on the communal characteristics of capitalism in strange ways. . . . Our people walk and talk like capitalists. . . . It is a shame to be poor or unsuccessful in capitalism. We do not look upon each other with "unlimited liability" one toward another. We surprisingly get our identities more from our jobs than our life in a Christian community pursuing God's kingdom on earth. And we treat our money as our own. We live in fear that to give up our possessions will leave us alone and destitute when our time of need comes. Our embedded individualism hurts us as we hoard our money, keep private our personal finances, and die a slow death of the soul as we never learn how to truly live, rejoicing with those who rejoice, weeping with those who weep (Rom 12:15). All of this makes practicing the justice of Christ

---

22. Hunter, "Future of Pastoral Theology," 67. Also Bass et al., *Christian Practical Wisdom*, 189.

in the local church more difficult. . . . How do we eat, live, and have jobs in capitalism and yet not become driven by the emotions and desires of "consumeritis," career success and the protection of our financial security? . . . Community in capitalism is so difficult because consumerism is always making us ask, "Are we meeting your needs?" But we do not need another pseudo-community that gathers to support its members in each other's striving for self-fulfillment and career advancement. . . . Instead, God calls us in Christ to a righteousness of another kind. How do we live as community *in* but not *of* capitalism?[23]

The *Gelassenheit* Model Explained

The epistemological opening created by *gelassenheit* opens the way for the development of a model that strengthens contemporary American evangelical reflexivity. It begins with what Turpin called "faithful consuming" that supports a "healthy multiplicity of the self."[24] Turpin proposed a fourfold process: (a) awakening: becoming aware to the ways that one's lifestyle and choices respond to the seeming normalcy of consumerism so that their meaning systems can be interrogated; (b) repentance: acknowledging the deep embeddedness of the meaning systems within one's own beliefs and practices so that turning away from them necessitates a patient commitment and resources extending beyond any one individual in a community; (c) justification: the reimagining of alternative spiritual meaning systems that provide new sources of worship and enable deeper and stronger bonds for the community; (d) regeneration: the emergence of renewed strength for continued resistance and meaning-making within a realigned set of allegiances and symbols as faith is strengthened, belief affirmed, and love grown.

Rooting the process in the scriptural language of conversion helpfully captures both the cognitive and affective dimensions of faith. According to Turpin, "It is faith rather than mere insight that is changing . . . conversion involves transformation of the love that requires heart, soul, mind, and strength."[25] Humility is required because conversion of deeply rooted faith systems is gradual, often lifelong. It is not a linear movement through sequential stages but an iterative sorting of detours that mandates "the continual recognition of divided loyalties."[26]

23. Fitch, *Great Giveaway*, 182–83.
24. Turpin, *Branded*. See also Gergen, *Saturated Self*.
25. Turpin, *Branded*, 59.
26. Turpin, *Branded*, 59.

Turpin's approach is ideal for contemporary American evangelical theology for two reasons. First, in keeping with the revised theme of transformation outlined above, it emphasizes strengthening reflexivity for the potential threat that consumerist spirituality poses to the ability of faith communities to provide alternative witness to consumer cultures. Second, being based on Wesley's *via salutis* ("path of salvation"), it aligns with the evangelical priority placed on Scripture in theological reflection.[27]

Integrating a process for faithful consuming with a *gelassenheit* posture of mystical spirituality produces a model that accounts for a critical feature of reflexivity that Turpin largely ignores: detachment. For instrumentalizing tendencies to be resisted effectively and intrinsic love to be fostered, a turning away (detaching) from inordinate attachments and a turning to God is essential.

The model, then, is as follows:

Figure 1. A *gelassenheit* model for strengthening spiritual reflexivity.

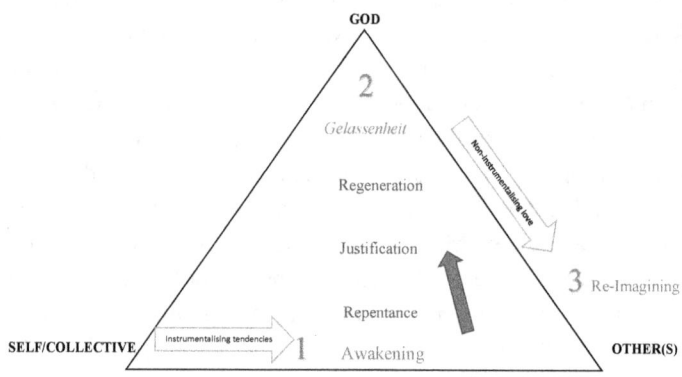

1. Stage one: Awakening

    The individual/collective, embedded in a consumer culture, experiences instrumentalizing tendencies in the form of enticements to utilize other(s) for individual and/or material gain.[28]

2. Stage two: *Gelassenheit*

---

27. See Wesley, *Sermons*; Collins, "Real Christianity."

28. The phrase "individual/collective" indicates that the model has application at both personal and collective levels in the context of faith communities. However, as is clear throughout the explanation and illustration of the model, an "individual" application of the model in no way implies that an individual can strengthen theological reflexivity without engaging his or her collective.

Either as part of a regular spiritual discipline routine or sudden event, the individual/collective is awakened to the instrumentalizing tendency, initiating the process of *gelassenheit* that involves progressing through the fourfold reflexive stages of "awakening-repentance-justification-regeneration" as the individual/collective detaches from the potential instrumentalizing source(s) and turns to God with inward surrender in response to God's gracious love, uniquely expressed in the incarnation and death and resurrection of Jesus.

3. Stage three: Reimagining

Having been reoriented by God's gracious love, the individual/collective's instrumentalizing tendencies are triangulated into expressions of active and affective triangulating love for the other(s).

As mentioned above, the model for strengthening contemporary American evangelical theological reflexivity in a postsecular consumerist context needs to account for two primary challenges in moral self-critique: the mysterious and intangible nature of the inner spiritual realities and the interpretive use of scriptural texts in shaping and reshaping those realities in contexts where individualistic and personal lenses are preferred over structural and abstract ones. Two core features of this model address these challenges.

The first significant feature of the model is that it is sacramental. While postsecular consumerist spirituality has intensified the challenge, religious traditions including Christianity have long struggled over how "to hold matter and spirit together without separating or identifying them."[29] The term *sacrament* originated in the Latin west with Tertullian, who used it to translate the Greek μυστήριον ("mystery"). From the earliest days in Christianity it generally referred "to the saving grace of God enacted in the rituals" of faith communities.[30] The concept has become a theological lightening rod, especially in regard to the Eucharist, but for the first millennium of the church the term was applied broadly as the visible form of invisible spiritual grace or a sign of a "sacred thing."

Applied to the task of cultivating a relational ethic of triangulating love for contemporary American evangelical theology, the sacramental dimension of the model is significant for two reasons. First, it reaffirms the importance of resisting a strict dichotomy between a purely spiritual form of love (the love of God and others) and a purely natural/material form of love

---

29. Rempel, "Sacraments in the Radical Reformation," 299. See also Milbank et al., *Radical Orthodoxy*.

30. Potts, *Cormac McCarthy*, 11.

(the love of self). As Browning suggested, Christian tradition's triangulating scheme of love counters this "dialectical" division with a "sacramental" ordering that acknowledges "all human relationships, like all people, as created good, potentially transformed by grace, and bearing a sacred meaning," however mysterious.[31]

Second, it highlights the role that narratives and story play in harmonizing theological belief with liturgical practice.[32] Part of the genius of narrative is its ability to simultaneously reveal and conceal. The mystery is inherent to storytelling because stories are not meant to examine, scientifically report objectively, or itemize exhaustively. Sacrament "helps us by way of mystery to enter into God's story, and may invite us to know God and ourselves in transformative ways."[33] Thus, liturgical practice emerges from certain narrative imaginations of the surrounding world that picture what we think life is about, what constitutes the "good life."[34] Imagination is both constructive and receptive and mental and physical.[35]

A second core feature of the model is the thickly relational hermeneutic cultivated by its sacramentality. The sacramental nature of the model has significant implications for contemporary American evangelical theology's notable emphasis on the importance of reading and interpreting Scripture in theological practice. Candler noted that before the late Middle Ages, when Thomistic theology's "grammar of representation" began to flatten the influence of sacramental theology, a "grammar of participation" was the dominant premodern theological, literary procedure.[36] It entailed an often-oral engagement with the scriptural texts as a way of sparking imaginative and meditative liturgical ritual.

For contemporary American evangelical theology, which is deeply rooted in personalist histories, the temptation is to approach this model

---

31. Browning, *Fundamental Practical Theology*, 172.

32. Commenting on the role of stories in the evolution of human meaning-making, Smith wrote, "We not only continue to be animals who make stories but also who animals who are made by our stories." Smith, *Moral, Believing Animals*, 64.

33. Ferguson, "Anabaptist Liturgy," 249. According to Potts: "For theology, meanwhile, this creative use of the sacramental tradition should remind theologians that the sacraments are as important for what they present as what they intend to represent. From a theological perspective, the historical danger of eucharistic theology has typically been a failure of dialectic, too weak a stomach for paradox. When theology has failed richly enough to account for the sacraments, its mistake has typically been to look too far beyond or behind the given signs of bread and wine" (Potts, *Cormac McCarthy*, 15).

34. Smith, *You Are What You Love*, 32.

35. Green, *1 Peter*, 26; Bryant, *Faith and the Play of Imagination*, 5.

36. Candler, *Theology, Rhetoric, Manuduction*.

from the standpoint of individual pietism that portrays the reordering of love as primarily a matter of "reading one's Bible."[37] However, the move from scriptural text to embodied practice cannot be accomplished apart from relational communities. Interpretation requires a "community competent to understand, and that means a community whose ethos, worldview, and sacred symbols . . . can be tuned" to the way particular texts "worked in the time past."[38]

The model promotes an evangelical reflexivity that is *Christopraxis* and not *Biblepraxis*.[39] A central focus on the continuing ministry of Jesus Christ in the world, thus, God in Jesus Christ as a subject of action, not merely a source of knowledge. Given that "practices do not merely flow out from particular convictions but shape and form the Christian imagination," the Scriptures have the "productive power of re-describing reality in a way that can engage and lead our imaginations."[40] The mystical *gelassenheit* of early Anabaptist spirituality nourishes the model with a way "to relocate and reimagine [the church's] role from the margins of society" in the face of materialistic and political empire.[41]

Having defined two core features of the model, I now turn to an explanation of its three main stages:

1. Stage one: Awakening

   Awakening is an image used throughout Scripture to evoke an initial state lacking awareness suddenly becoming aware (Eph 5:14; Isa 51:17). To awaken to postsecular consumerist spirituality "is to process and to pay attention to the ways in which our lifestyle and choices respond" to the seeming normalcy of instrumentalizing tendencies. Space is then opened to begin interrogating the meaning system of relational instrumentality to see how it conflicts with the New Testament ethical core of triangulating love for God and neighbor.[42]

   The discipline of paying attention is rare in consumer cultures that bombard persons with dehumanizing and commoditizing advertisements. It "will increase the possibility of attending to smaller, alternative narratives of meaning that one finds to be more adequately

---

37. Pannenberg offered one of the most well-known critiques of this historical lineage in evangelicalism. See Pannenberg, *Christian Spirituality*.

38. Meeks, "Hermeneutics of Social Embodiment," 192–93. See also Taylor, *Secular Age*, 171.

39. Anderson, *Shape of Practical Theology*.

40. Buschart and Eilers, *Theology of Retrieval*, 222.

41. Wilson-Hartgrove, *New Monasticism*, 85.

42. Turpin, *Branded*, 84.

integrated with faith perspectives."[43] The realization is that an individual or collective's partaking of instrumentalizing love no longer makes adequate sense of the praxis of faith, either in the general experience of dissatisfaction or an extraordinary experience.

This opens the community to critical reflection by beginning to question the ways that the prevailing meaning system of instrumentalizing love might be challenged and reordered by a Christ-like response to the gracious love of God preeminently displayed in the death and resurrection of Jesus.[44] While awakening is a crucial part of the process of ongoing conversion in strengthening reflexivity, in and of itself, it does not produce reformation and can even lead to denial or repression.

2. Stage two: *Gelassenheit*

- *Repentance*: Ongoing conversion along the spectrum of triangulating love moves from a call to awakening to the practice of repentance, a term that has a rich theological history but has been negatively affected by western individualism. After the initial discovery of the inadequacy of an instrumentalizing tendency to sustain relational harmony, a developing awareness of our implication in the consumer system can follow. Repentance is more difficult and most effective when it surfaces "our closely guarded and cleverly concealed 'programs for happiness'" that would prove to be very disruptive if changed.[45] Sacramental detachment from some of the consumerist habits we find essential to our lives "might begin to sensitize us, both to the conditions of hunger and want in which most of the world's inhabitants live and to our common conditioning as a society to expect and require consumer goods."[46]

- *Justification*: Only calling the prevailing instrumentalizing meaning systems into question and repenting from them can leave faith communities "stranded without an organizing system of meaning, or without the ritual support of the practices of their earlier belief

---

43. Turpin, *Branded*, 170.

44. Few contemporary theological movements have been as effective at raising critical awareness than the liberation tradition. Working this broad tradition into an educational pedagogy, Freire emphasized, "developing critical consciousness," or the ability of person's "to perceive critically the themes of their time, and thus to intervene in reality" with a "social and political responsibility and prepared to avoid the danger of massification" (Freire, *Pedagogy*, 7). See also Turpin, *Branded*, 87.

45. Mahan, *Forgetting Ourselves on Purpose*, 97.

46. Miles, *Practicing Christianity*, 103.

system."[47] Justification moves a community toward a renewed sense of wholeness and safety by replacing the old images of postsecular consumerist spirituality with "new images of beauty and goodness" and new objects of "worship' to sustain a changed lifestyle. This is the process of falling in love."[48] It also highlights the critical role that narratives play in shaping and reshaping theological imagination.

- *Regeneration:* Following justification, the process of regeneration provides new life for continued resistance to instrumentalizing tendencies and continued meaning making within the new set of allegiances and symbols to triangulating love as faith is strengthened, belief affirmed, and love grown.

3. Stage three: Reimagining

Constituting the gradual restoration of the image of God, reimagining is regeneration through small pedagogical communities of discipleship. They provide critical formation and support for the continued work of individual/collective transformation within the faith community and collaborative action for the transformation of the broader culture through displays of triangulating love that signify strong collectives.

These small, realistic communities of shared imaginations are designed to tolerate the ambiguities of practice that continue to occur and it is necessary to sustain alternative imaginations of triangulating love in the face of a lack of broader victory of such beautiful visions over the dominant instrumentality of consumerist cultures. Such communities derive joy and celebration, not from present victory, but from the development of resilience that has hope in future victory. According to Welch, "Rather than a hope for eventual victory, for a world without injustice or serious conflict," there can be a more modest hope, "a hope for resilience and for company along the way. . . . Seemingly lowered expectations for social change provide staying power and effectiveness."[49]

---

47. Turpin, *Branded*, 137.

48. Turpin, *Branded*, 137.

49. Welch, *Sweet Dreams*, xvi. In part, the need for modest hope can be understood as a way of normalizing the unfulfilled and unrealistic idealism operating within consumerism. Smail wrote: "The modern consumer is in this way a pleasure-seeking idealist, dislocated from a real world, a real body, and a real society. We must believe, among other things, that the earth's resources are infinite, that mind will triumph over matter and that there's no limit to what you can achieve if you really try" (Smail, *Power, Interest, Psychology*, 55).

Either as individuals or collectives, the reimaging stage of the model involves a turning back toward the other(s) in community with a renewed sense of the beauty and worth of triangulating love for sustaining relational unity. Several characteristics are necessary for such efforts to flourish and translate into long-term change[50]:

- Circles of grace extend radical acceptance in the face of human frailty and grant power to move forward on toward salvation.[51]
- Confessional honesty is "the practice of revealing failures to one another and to ourselves in order to find the grace to address them" so that self-deception can be avoided in the process of ongoing conversion and space can be opened for mutual subjection and accountability among the members.[52]
- Rhythmic pattern of common life is meeting regularly over extended periods of time to create steady celebration and remembrance that integrate with liturgical practices "to foster individual identity formation even as they assist in generating group identity" and "provide embodied experience of new faith and imagination, social relationships, and patterns of service."[53]
- Worship and immersion in new images that embody the new objects of faith, "not the passive witnessing of images central to the new meaning system to which participants are hoping for conversion" but rather "the community vividly embodies the images that are central to the new life of imagination that the community hopes to engender, creating a passionate encounter and evoking an adoring attitude toward them," offered not as dogma but as gifts that create opportunities for non-consumptive celebration.[54]
- Encouragement for corporate self-critique is the continued affirmation within the community that strengthening theological reflexivity remains its most important value and necessitates an openness to discoveries of brokenness and finitude.

---

50. Turpin, *Branded*, 119–21.

51. This is not a blanket acceptance of all states and behaviors but "careful balance of recognition that it matters deeply what we do and a sense that we will never be able to perfectly live into the vocations to which we are called" (Smail, *Power, Interest, Psychology*, 196).

52. Turpin, *Branded*, 203.

53. Turpin, *Branded*, 207.

54. Turpin, *Branded*, 209. See also Borgmann, *Power Failure*.

The *Gelassenheit* Model in Action

Having explained the primary features of the *gelassenheit* model and elaborated on its three stages, what remains is to illustrate how the model accomplishes its purpose of strengthening contemporary American evangelical theology reflexivity. To repeat, the model focuses on three primary categories of attachments identified in the Gospels that are subject to the distortions of instrumentality resulting in hostile social division: (a) relational bonds: a universal and mysterious body of fellow followers into the familial bonds of one's life, irrespective of race, gender, or ethnicity; (b) possessions: the relinquishing of claims over any material goods for the higher calling of stewarding God's provisions for the care and joy of others; and (c) status: the seeking of approval on the basis of the extent to which one has become a servant of God rather than the extent to which others have become servants to others.

In keeping with the nature of the model itself, it is primarily through small narrative stories addressing pivotal questions that liturgical habits are formed and reformed, not abstract theological meta-narratives packaged in universal solutions.[55] The identification of three primary categories is merely a heuristic mechanism and not a simplification of the many spheres and forms in which ambiguities of practice can emerge. Indeed, effective postsecular spiritual care should move beyond simplistic self-management techniques.[56]

I proceed, then, by analyzing two narratives through the model's scheme to surface and critically reflect upon pivotal questions about potential sources of ambiguities of practice. This analysis is not intended to be exhaustive but rather illustrative. The first is drawn from a congregational study, and one drawn from my own personal experience. To maximize the relevance to contemporary American evangelical theology, the two narratives, and the analysis are centered on one shortcoming of the traditional theme of transformation identified in chapter 3: colonialist and imperialist undertones.

There, I established that the transformationalist theme within contemporary evangelical theology has roots in western imperialism and colonialism in which civilization, whiteness, and Christianity were often associated with economic progress and development. This meant that as western Europeans and American explorers colonized the continent of Africa and portions of North America, they spoke of "transforming" the indigenous

---

55. See Darragh, "Practice of Practical Theology."
56. Rogers-Vaughn, *Caring for Souls*.

people groups in terms of a divinely commissioned project of civilizing out their paganism and "coloredness."

In these early transformationalist efforts, preaching the gospel to the groups of indigenous people, converting them to Christianity, and civilizing them to western modes of culture and economic practice were all one and the same. Contemporary American evangelical articulations of the theme of transformation rarely acknowledge these colonialist and imperialist undercurrents.

In the most exhaustive study of its kind, Emerson and Smith demonstrated that while well-intended white conservative American evangelicals have become increasingly involved in broad efforts to "transform" those in poverty through economic development programs (often at the congregational level); these efforts have primarily deepened racial divides because of a lack of due awareness to the social-structural forces that contribute to poverty.[57]

Given the role of self/collective awareness, I apply the *gelassenheit* model to the example of colonialist and imperialist undertones to show how it can enhance theological reflexivity by drawing attention to practices emerging from instrumentalizing tendencies in need of reorientation. My method was to evaluate two narratives through the model's three-stage scheme to identify for contemporary American evangelical theology pivotal questions raised by potential ambiguities of practice in the areas of relational bonds, possessions, and/or status. With each narrative, I first establish the setting, then employ the model's analysis, and finally identify pivotal questions for further reflection.

Narrative One: Fulkerson's Congregational Study

Practical theologian Fulkerson's *Places of Redemption* is an exploration of the contradiction between widely affirmed beliefs in American Christianity about racial inclusiveness and equal opportunity and the fact that most local churches remain racially homogeneous and do not include people with disabilities. To understand the problem better, Fulkerson explored through a participant-observer ethnographic congregational study the practices of an interracial and disability-friendly United Methodist church called Good Samaritan located in a suburb of Durham, North Carolina. While an analysis of the complete gamut of Fulkerson's study is beyond our purposes here, an examination of the highlights of Good Samaritan's "conversion story"

---

57. Emerson and Smith, *Divided by Faith*.

through the scheme of the model of mystical *gelassenheit* clearly illustrates its three stages and core features.

Stage one was awareness. The critical moment of awareness for Good Samaritan congregation came in July 1998, when the ten remaining members of the dying white congregation—situated in a racially transitional neighborhood near Durham—met for a Bible study in the home of its pastor, Dan Weaver. The subject of the study that evening was the account about Philip and the Ethiopian eunuch in Acts 8 in which Philip, a disciple of Jesus, encounters a culturally different political leader and engages him in an intimate conversation about the Hebrew scriptures that results in the eunuch's conversion. The group was captivated by the Bible story, particularly its vivid descriptions of the Christian gospel and the interaction between different cultures. They immediately became aware of the insufficiency of their understanding and approach to living out the Christian gospel as insulated, middle-class white Americans located in a racially transitional context. The group decided to reimagine the purpose of their church in light of its own cultural surroundings and intentionally seek people who were different. This initially involved focusing on racial (white and black) and social (rich and poor) divisions.

Stage two was *gelassenheit*. Repentance refers to having become aware of the insufficiency of their current spiritual meaning systems and aware that they were operating on an inadequate conception of scriptural love, the group was motivated to turn away from their current meaning system and seek an alternative. Justification refers to deciding not merely to turn away from old meaning systems but to pursue alternative ones, the group was energized to reevaluate the purposes of their church and its underlying instrumental approach, which had previously sought unchallenged homogeneity and comfort. The group resolved to intentionally seek people who were different, initially focusing on racial (white and black) and social (rich and poor) divisions that were tearing at the relational fabric of the surrounding community. Regeneration refers to a renewed sense of purpose and hope, the congregation decided to rename its church to "Good Samaritan" as a symbol and marker of its new life and focus. Within a short period of having broadened its relationships with more people from racially and economically diverse backgrounds, it also decided to intentionally pursue relationship building with people of physical and mental disabilities after seeing a group of students playing football and discovering that their organization (called New Hope) had previously visited other churches in the area but had felt unwelcomed. Good Samaritan quickly implemented bi-monthly Thursday evening worship services designed specifically for people with disabilities.

Stage three was reimagining. As the Good Samaritan congregation grew, it maintained a focus on cultivating small, highly relational collectives that supported the ongoing internal and external transformation of the faith community. Most of the congregation remained fairly uneducated in theological dogma, but a continual pattern of reading the Scriptures and then talking reflectively about their meaning and application to their own lives helped strengthen relational unity in the congregation, even as the ambiguities of practice in many ways only intensified as the community became more diverse.

Emerging from this congregational narrative are some pivotal questions that contemporary American evangelical faith communities could dwell upon to surface and reflect on ambiguities of practice that could potentially source relational division in their own context:

- *Relational Bonds*: What changes in socialization habits would an average suburban evangelical community need to make to build more socioeconomically diverse relational bonds? If the Good Samaritan United Methodist congregation eventually dissolved because of the strains placed on its community by its diverse makeup, would that undermine the validity of their re-envisioned purpose as church?
- *Possessions:* Would it be wise for an evangelical community to purposely downsize its physical building to create more financial margin in its budget to support outreach to the poor? What are the most significant tangible assets that American evangelical families could divest themselves of to contribute to less homogenous congregations?
- *Status:* How might Good Samaritan's story be different if they had decided to verify their convictions emerging from their group Bible study in Acts 8 with two other similar evangelical churches in the surrounding area? In what ways can their accommodations to serve the disability community serve as a model for other American evangelical congregations to follow?

Narrative Two: A Personal Experience

A second narrative illustration of the *gelassenheit* model comes from my own experience as a white Christian participating in a largely white evangelical conservative congregation in an upper-middle-class American city. The setting of this case study was a discussion that took place within the "small group" that myself and my family attended for the previous two years at this congregation. Because of the nature of the growth of the small group, it had become too large to be feasibly carried forward as a single group. Thus, the leader of the small group proposed that the group permanently divide into smaller units.

At the meeting to discuss the procedures for dividing the group, the leader praised the group for our apparent success at "transforming" our community with the "Gospel" as evidenced by the fact that we had grown large enough in size to need to segment. In presenting a method for dividing, the leader proposed that the best way would be to arrange ourselves geographically so that we could focus our groups' efforts on "loving our neighbors" as Scripture commands.

At the time, I responded favorably to the proposal and generally agreed with the reasoning. However, later, I was reading a commentary on 1 Corinthians that prompted me to reflect on the reason for my immediate affirmation. The author of the commentary noted that when contrasted with the highly stratified common meal in the ancient world, where "it was sociologically natural for the host to invite those of his/her own class to eat" in the dining room and the rest to eat in the courtyard, the taking of the Lord's Supper by multiple social classes within the Corinthian congregation amounts to a radical alternative.[58] The *gelassenheit* model offers a way to process this disruptive experience in a manner that strengthens theological reflexivity for the fostering of triangulating love.

Stage one is awakening. My experience reading about the Lord's supper in Corinth served as an awakening event that suddenly made me realize that underneath my affirmation of the decision to divide our small group around geographical lines was a meaning system that sought to surround myself and my family with people of similar socioeconomic status, since I lived in a mostly white middle-class geographic area. I now begin to reflect critically on how my prevailing meaning system (that I would be better off maintaining my current homogenous group status) was challenged by the experience of the early Corinthian community.

Stage two is *gelassenheit*. Repentance was in response to this surfacing of my closely guarded and cleverly concealed programs for happiness. I began an inward devotional turn to God that acknowledged my shortcomings and asked for forgiveness for my instrumentalizing of the situation to fit my own individual and material happiness apart from its effect on any broader community. This act of repentance opened me to reflect on ways that I might detach from my allegiance to and faith in the comforts of homogenous socioeconomic groups and reengage the love of God expressed through the

---

58. Fee, *First Epistle to the Corinthians*, 533–34.

Christ-event, which the Lord's supper commemorates. This took on the form of a personal symbolic recapitulation of the Eucharist liturgy.

Justification refers to imagining the gathering of a multi-ethnic and diverse socioeconomic group in first-century Corinth to celebrate the love of God expressed in the death and resurrection of Jesus produced in me new images of beauty and goodness that replaced the old images of what constituted good community that had previously been shaping my beliefs below the surface: images that were filled with people of the same race and social-class as myself.

Regeneration is being reminded that the commemoration of the Lord's Supper is a celebration of regenerating life that only God can provide. I began to reflect on how our small group might better resemble small pedagogical communities of discipleship that provide formative support and collaborative action as we seek to pursue more genuinely diverse fellowship in our broader community.

Stage three is reimagining. Reoriented in the process of *gelassenheit*, my instrumentalizing tendencies in the situation regard how my small group segments have been triangulated by a critical reflection on the love of God. I now have a more genuine desire to express triangulating love in my faith community that is actively and affective in tune with the New Testament vision of a fellowship that radically crosses socioeconomic lines. As a result, I have asked our small group to reconsider how we can segment in a way that encourages and challenges us to proactively pursue socioeconomic diversity, especially in the form of identifying and addressing the structural reasons why lower-class non-white people are virtually nonexistent in our fellowship.

Emerging from this personal narrative are some pivotal questions that contemporary American evangelical faith communities could dwell upon to surface and reflect on ambiguities of practice that could potentially source relational division in their own context.

- *Relational Bonds*: What is the difference between legitimate and illegitimate concerns for immediate family well-being in discerning one's participation in a local evangelical congregation? Is it okay for evangelical churches to only reflect the demographic makeup of their context or should they seek to go beyond that standard?
- *Possessions*: What types of changes in household giving patterns would be necessary for contemporary American evangelicals to contribute to the lessening of income inequality, which is a primary source of congregational homogeneity?

- *Status*: How might a more racially diverse small group might enhance and/or impair my own sense of personal value?

Gelassenheit Spiritual Practices

The purpose of this chapter was to apply the insights of *gelassenheit* to construct a model for strengthening evangelical reflexivity that nourishes spiritual practices. Having defined and explained the model, I want to close by exploring and developing *gelassenheit* as a revitalizer of ancient Christian spiritual practices in immersive consumerist contexts. A common conception of Christian spiritual practices is that they confront consumerist ideology by lessening the desire to consume, to move one away from material things (which ultimately do not satisfy) and toward an immaterial God (which ultimately satisfies). Through a practical theological lens, this assessment is insufficient on two fronts. First, desire is fundamental to human beings and, as Augustine remarked, our desires are in constant need of renewal. Second, because we are temporally bound, spirituality involves a complex interplay between the material and immaterial. Lessening the desire to consume, then, is not the fundamental issue. Everyone must consume to live.

Consumerism itself is a spiritual disposition in that it is a way of looking at the world that shapes desire. While often associated with greed or an inordinate attachment to material things, consumerism is in fact

> characterized by detachment from production, producers, and products. Consumerism is a restless spirit that is never content with any particular material thing. In this sense, consumerism has some affinities with Christian asceticism, which counsels a certain detachment from material things. The difference is that, in consumerism, detachment continually moves us from one product to another, whereas in Christian life, asceticism is a means to a greater attachment to God and to other people.[59]

Incessant detachment would seem to correspond to the increasingly fragmenting and isolating effects of postsecular consumerist spirituality discussed throughout this thesis.

The question, then, is how can embodied Christian spiritual practices orient consumptive desires toward the right *telos*? Cavanaugh frames it as a choice between consumeristic spirituality based in scarcity expressed in privatization and eucharistic spirituality based in abundance expressed in

---

59. Cavanaugh, *Being Consumed*, 7.

sharing.[60] Consumer markets assume resource scarcity. No one has enough, so there is trade: to get something, one must relinquish something else. Goods are not held in common, and consumption of goods is essentially a private experience. In contrast, Christian eucharistic consumption does not begin with scarcity, but abundance: "Jesus said to them, 'I am the bread of life. Whoever comes to me will never be hungry'" (John 6:35). Insatiable human desire is absorbed by the abundance of God's grace in the gift of the body and blood of Christ, which are not scarce commodities. They are inseparable from the *kenosis*, the self-emptying, of the cross. The consumer of the body and blood of Christ does not remain detached from what he or she consumes but becomes part of a larger body.

This is a helpful contrast, but more needs to be said. Whether ancient or modern, a distinguishing characteristic of Christian spiritual practices and disciplines has been to "promote virtues paradoxical to contemporary sensibilities": freedom via restraint, stability rather than mobility, receiving rather than seizing, and attachment rather than detachment.[61] Never has this been more difficult or urgent to achieve. Why? Because the increasingly digital nature of consumption blurs the line between material acts of consumption and the desires fueling them. Before the proliferation of internet technologies, physical spaces such as malls and shopping centers were where "consumerism roared and swelled, but inevitably, remained contained."[62] The era of digital retailing has dramatically changed this, embedding consumption into daily life. "Recent technologies have enabled the role of the *customer* to be fused with the newer role of the *user* who inhabits an entire system rather than a specific transaction."[63] Retailers are focused on reducing purchase friction and removing as many barriers to consumption as possible. For example, Amazon has built an entire digital ecosystem with the consumer/user at the very center. A user can instantly access millions of goods and services through his or her Amazon smartphone application, receive free 24-hour delivery with his or her Prime account, and even make purchases through his or her voice-controlled Alexa unit or small Dash buttons strategically located throughout their homes.

Here, *gelassenheit* can make a significant contribution. Any cluster of spiritual activities that hopes to combat the excesses of (increasingly digital) consumption must thread together external expression and internal disposition in a way that discerningly reorients consumptive desires toward a

60. Cavanaugh, *Being Consumed*, 135–38.
61. Richter, "Religious Practices," 209.
62. Bogost, "When Malls Saved the Suburbs," 2.
63. Austin, "Constant Consumer," 3.

eucharistic *telos* of abundance. Because of its emphasis on facilitating healthy detachment from material things to reattach more healthily, *gelassenheit* posturing has the capacity to fortify a number of traditional spiritual practices for a postsecular consumerist context. I close by exploring this thought through three ancient Christian practices: prayer, giving, and Sabbath.

Prayer

In contemporary spiritual practice, prayer is commonly associated with "asking for." Indeed, petitionary prayer (whether for oneself or others) is referenced throughout the Scriptures (e.g., 2 Chr 6:21; James 4:2; Ps 28:2; Luke 11:3). However, for much of Christian history (across Orthodox, Catholic, and Protestant traditions), contemplative prayer has been understood as a means of aligning desire and inner disposition around God.

Contemplative prayer can refer to a range of prayer practices (e.g., monastic prayer, centering prayer, the Jesus prayer, *lectio divina*) focused on the receptive dimensions of prayer as a means of experiencing the presence of God. Generally, the practices involve passive postures and extend periods of silence. The Greek *theoria* and Latin equivalent *contemplation*, which translate "contemplation" have an important history in ancient spirituality and primarily designated "looking at" something (with the eyes or the mind). Louth writes:

> The word *theoria* is derived from a verb meaning to look, or to see: for the Greeks, knowing was a kind of seeing, a sort of intellectual seeing. Contemplation is, then, knowledge, knowledge of reality itself, as opposed to knowing how: the kind of know-how involved in getting things done. To this contrast between the active life and contemplation there corresponds a distinction in our understanding of what it is to be human between reason conceived as puzzling things out, solving problems, calculating and making decisions—referred to by the Greek words *phronesis* and *dianoia*, or in Latin by *ratio*—and reason conceived as receptive of truth, beholding, looking—referred to by the Greek words *theoria* or *sophia* (wisdom) or *nous* (intellect), or in Latin *intellectus*. Augustine expressed this distinction by using *scientia* for the kind of knowledge attained by *ratio*, and *sapientia*, wisdom, for the kind of knowledge received by *intellectus*. Human intelligence operates at two levels: a basic level

concerned with doing things, and another level concerned with simply beholding, contemplating, knowing reality.[64]

Both the Hebrew and New Testament Scriptures reference forms of contemplative prayer intended to draw one beyond a realm of knowledge and words, for example, calls to "seek God's face" (1 Chr 16:11; 2 Chr 7:14; Ps 24:6; Hos 5:15) and to be still and quiet the soul (Ps 131). Prayer is often connected to a life lived in the immediacy of God's will (John 5:19; 12:49–50), accomplished through a surrendering to God (Isa 45; Rom 12:1), aided by the Spirit (Rom 8:26–27) and modeled after the love of Christ expressed through his incarnation and passion (Phil 2). In the Gospels, Jesus prioritized the spiritual practice of prayer (Matt 7:7), connecting it to the need to avoid the busyness of life (Luke 10:42).

Not until around the sixth century were contemplative prayer practices associated with mystical and ascetic approaches to spirituality, as they are now.[65] For Eckhart, the purpose of prayer was to bring oneself into union with God by surrendering one's thoughts and desires and opening the heart. The contemplative, silent prayer practices of *gelassenheit* were central. Detachment "purifies the soul and cleanses the conscience and kindles the heart and awakens the spirit and stimulates our longing and shows us where God is."[66] Contrary to modern conceptions of "lone mystics seeking highly individualized and subjective experiences," Eckhart understood contemplative prayer practice as a relationally grounded, non-dualistic integration of spirit and body that disabled the instrumentalizing of others and, therefore, enabled more robust community.[67] Those possessed with unhealthy attachments are unable to accept what is and are deprived of the freedom to wait upon God's presence. As participation in the Eucharist demonstrates, God's presence often comes to us in the mystery of silence practiced on display in ritual community worship.

Gelassenheit amounts to a way of "letting things be" and here we see the import of a *gelassenheit* prayer posture for consumerist contexts.[68] Contemplative prayer helps push back against the eschatology of acquisition operative in consumerism in which the "gradual, immanent progress toward abundance that the market, driven by our consumption, is always about to—but never actually does—bring about."[69] Instead, silent

64. Louth, "Theology, Contemplation, and the University," 66.
65. See Johnson, *Inner Eye of Love*.
66. Meister Eckhart, *Essential Sermons*, 292.
67. Turner, *Darkness of God*, 185.
68. Linge, "Mysticism, Poverty, and Reason," 483.
69. Cavanaugh, *Being Consumed*, 136.

contemplation of and participation in the Eucharist reshapes our desires with the reality that God has already acted in abundance and incorporated us into a body of plenty.

Interestingly, the practices of excessive consumption have been associated with a number of narcissistic behaviors and can impede "altruistic self-other relations."[70] On the contrary, a range of scientific studies have long affirmed the social and personal health benefits that come along with prayer. Benson, a Harvard cardiologist and pioneer in mind/body medicine, demonstrated that prayer could produce a "relaxation response" that decreases the body's metabolism and blood pressure and slows the heart rate.[71] A National Institutes of Health study found that over the long term, individuals who prayed daily were shown to be 40 percent less likely to have high blood pressure than those without. There has also been a demonstrated link between prayer and relational awareness. Newberg did a study of Franciscan nuns in contemplative prayer and found a decreased activity in the parts of the brain associated with a sense of self and increased level of dopamine associated with states of well-being and joy.[72] Moreover, the positive effects of particularly contemplative forms of prayer appear to be more than just the result of enhanced focus and concentration. Pargement tested two groups of migraine sufferers. Both groups meditated for twenty minutes; one using a spiritual affirmation (like "God is good. God is peace. God is love") and the other a nonspiritual mantra ("Grass is green. Sand is soft.") The first group experienced fewer headaches and more tolerance of pain.[73]

More recently, "mindfulness" has enjoyed a surge in popularity, especially in workplace contexts. It refers to a psychological state of awareness and a mode of processing information that emphasizes reflexivity: "Being aware of the 'reflective self' engaged in mentalizing, and the practice of fully experiencing the rising and falling of mental states with acceptance and without attachment and judgment."[74] Its range of benefits includes self-control, objectivity, improved concentration, and emotional intelligence, and the ability to relate to others and one's self with kindness, acceptance, and compassion.

---

70. See McDonald, Wearing, and Ponting, "Narcissim and Neo-Liberalism."
71. Benson, *Relaxation Response*.
72. Newberg, *Words Can Change*.
73. Pargement, *Psychology of Religion*.
74. Davis and Hayes, "Benefits of Mindfulness," 198.

Giving

Building on contemplative prayer, a second spiritual practice that *gelassenheit* posture can revive is giving. Contained in the scriptural concept of abundance in the Eucharist is a warning against over-spiritualizing its call to generous giving. Cavanaugh wrote:

> In the Eucharist, Christ is gift, giver, and recipient. We are neither merely active nor passive, but we participate in the divine vine life so that we are fed and simultaneously become food for others. Our temptation is to spiritualize all this talk of union, to make our connection to the hungry a mystical act of imaginative sympathy. We can thus imagine that we are already in communion with those who lack food, whether or not we meet their needs. Matthew is having none of this: he places the obligation to feed the hungry in the context of eschatological judgment. Paul, too, places neglect of the hungry in the context of judgment. At the eucharistic celebration in Corinth, which included a common meal, those who eat while others go hungry "show contempt for the church of God and humiliate those who have nothing" (1 Cor 11:22). Those who thus—in an "unworthy manner"—partake of the body and blood of Christ "eat and drink judgment against themselves" (11:27, 29). Those of us who partake in the Eucharist while ignoring the hungry may be eating and drinking our own damnation.[75]

While consumer capitalism has significantly advanced material well-being, it has not equally enhanced the practice of giving in American Christianity. On average, American Christians give 2.5 percent of their income to churches, and less than 20 percent of congregations tithe.[76] Overall, religious giving is down about 50 percent since 1990. Paradoxically, it is the poorer who tend to be more generous. Those with a salary of less than $20,000 are 8 times more likely to give than someone who makes $75,000. Of families that make more than $75,000, only 1 percent give away at least 10 percent of their income.[77]

In contrast, for the early Anabaptists, *gelassenheit* meant "the forsaking of all concern for personal property, thus, leading almost naturally to a complete community of goods."[78] According to Urry, "The early Anabaptists read the Bible not just as a guide to proper Christian conduct, but also to

---

75. Cavanaugh, *Being Consumed*, 125–26.
76. Nonprofits Source, "Ultimate List."
77. Nonprofits Source, "Ultimate List."
78. Friedmann, *Hutterite Studies*, 86.

identify appropriate forms of social community."[79] Ulrich Stadler, a leader of the nascent Anabaptist movement in the 1520s, wrote, "To have all things in common, a free, untrammeled, yielding, willing heart in Christ is needed. Whosoever is thus inwardly free and resigned (*gelassen*) in the Lord is also ready to surrender all temporal possessions."[80]

Sabbath

A final spiritual practice revived by a *gelassenheit* posture is Sabbath. Often associated with negative rules and restrictions "as a day of obligation (for Catholics) or a day without play (in memories of strict Protestant childhoods)," its scriptural bearing is located in themes "of creation, exodus, and resurrection will be essential if we are to discover the gifts it offers."[81] Genesis 2:3 contains the first reference to Sabbath: "Then God blessed the seventh day and sanctified it because in it He rested from all His work which God had created and made." The root meaning of the Hebrew words "Sabbath" and "rest" is "to cease." After having spent six days in his creative work, God ceased from his labors. Israel is instructed as part of the covenant to observe their own Sabbath rest in Exodus 20:8–11 and Deuteronomy 5:3, 12, the former passage emphasizing it as a command of "remembering" and the latter as "observing." Together, they capture the most fundamental stories and beliefs of the Hebrew scriptures, "creation and exodus, humanity in God's image and a people liberated from captivity. One emphasizes holiness, the other social justice. Sabbath crystallizes the Torah's portrait of who God is and what human beings are most fully meant to be."[82]

Jesus' position on the Sabbath was ambivalent. Sabbath regulation was a key struggle between Jesus and the Jewish religious leaders (e.g., Luke 6:1–11; Mark 2:23–33; Matt 12:1–146). While there is no record of him explicitly calling for the end of the Sabbath, he controversially declared himself its authority: "The Sabbath was made for man, not man for the Sabbath. So, the Son of Man is Lord even of the Sabbath" (Mark 2:27–28). Elsewhere, he would indicate that he is Israel's ultimate Sabbath rest:

> Come to me, all you who are weary and burdened, and I will give you rest. Take my yoke upon you and learn from me, for I am

---

79. Urry, "Wealth and Poverty," 36.
80. Friedmann, *Hutterite Studies*, 61.
81. Bass, *Receiving the Day*, 75.
82. Bass, *Receiving the Day*, 75.

gentle and humble in heart, and you will find rest for your souls. For my yoke is easy and my burden is light. (Matt 11:28–30)

The writer to the Hebrews exhorts his readers to "enter in" to the Sabbath rest provided by Christ (Heb 4).

Luther's associate Karlstadt differentiated between an external and spiritual Sabbath. The former was observed once per week, but the latter was to be an ongoing internal disposition that acknowledged that we are always to cease from our work apart from God and let God work through us. He called this *gelassenheit*.[83] Indeed, "sabbath marks the cessation of creative activity by implementing the divine *gelassenheit* or 'letting go' of creation."[84]

Gelassenheit, therefore, speaks of a need for Sabbath to take root in the interior of a person as much as it manifests in external observance. This speaks quite aptly to the needs of today's consumer capitalistic context, where the fundamental struggle is one of restlessness. According to Kessler, "both employers and clients expect that everything should be done *immediately*.[85] Mobile technology has exacerbated the situation by creating an expectation that we ought to be available at any place and at any time. The worldwide average for sleep was 8 hours in 1942, compared to 6.8 hours today. More than one-third of American adults are not getting enough sleep on a regular basis according to a study in the Centers for Disease Control and Prevention's *Morbidity and Mortality Weekly Report*. Sleep deprived people feel lonelier and less eager to engage with others, suggesting that it is "no coincidence that the past few decades have seen a marked increase in loneliness and an equally dramatic decrease in sleep duration."[86]

According to Bass, consumer capitalistic forces are

> nibbling away at the freedom of the day. Joining the assembly of Christians for the celebration of Word and Sacrament will remind us that Sabbath keeping is not about taking a day off but about being recalled to our knowledge of and gratitude for God's activity in creating the world, giving liberty to captives, and overcoming the powers of death. . . . Refraining from work on a regular basis is a way of setting limits on behavior that is perilous for both human welfare and the welfare of earth itself. Overworked Americans need rest, and they need to be reminded that they do not cause the grain to grow and that their greatest fulfillment does not come through the acquisition of

---

83. Rupp, "Andrew Karlstadt."
84. Brown, *Ethos of the Cosmos*, 36.
85. Brown, *Ethos of the Cosmos*, 386.
86. Moulin and Chung, "Technology Trumping Sleep," 300.

material things. Moreover, the planet needs a rest from human plucking and burning and buying and selling. Perhaps, as Sabbath keepers, we will come to live and know these truths more fully, and thus to bring their wisdom to the common solution of humanity's problems.[87]

Conclusion

The purpose of this chapter has been to show mystical *gelassenheit's* postsecular renewal of the theme of transformation and actual contemporary American evangelical practice. I developed a constructive model that enables individuals and collectives embedded in postsecular consumerist contexts to interrogate ambiguities of practice as they imperfectly love God and neighbor. I first set up the model by analyzing how a *gelassenheit* epistemology helps contemporary American evangelical theology reunite the cognitive and affective dimensions of theology necessary for engaging ambiguities of practice. Then, I explained the model as an integration of Turpin's fourfold process of faithful consuming with mystical *gelassenheit*. Third, I demonstrated how to use the model with two narrative examples, one drawn from Fulkerson's ethnographic congregational study and the other from personal experience. Finally, I showed how a *gelassenheit* posture could resource ancient Christian spiritual practices for consumerists contexts.

87. Bass, *Receiving the Day*, 84–85.

Conclusion

This book began with a simple but weighty consideration: Contemporary American evangelical theology's quest to integrate Christian faith and capitalistic enterprise through the theme of transformation is being challenged by postsecularism. The theme of transformationism has expressed the evangelical notion that capitalistic enterprise is morally and spiritually transformative in providing Christians a unique platform to harness prosperity for the common good and spread the gospel for the advancement of the kingdom of God.

Traditionally stated, the theme of transformation portrays Christian faith as harnessing the good of Western consumer market capitalism without being affected by its excesses. This reflects the sociopolitical conditions of the twentieth century when it was formed. Evangelical Christianity still exercises significant influence in American public life, and market capitalism's growth is relatively stable and predictable.

Postsecularism altered these conditions. Consumer capitalism's rapid growth has weakened American evangelicalism influence as institutionalized forms of Protestant Christianity have declined. It has also intensified individualist-materialist conceptions of spirituality that ground human relationships in self-interested market exchange. This contrasts with a prominent ethical thread in the Christian Scriptures that grounds human relationality in the triangulating force of God's intrinsic love, which checks the human tendency to instrumentalize for individual and material gain.

How can contemporary American evangelical theology reconstruct the theme of transformation for a postsecular context that counters the excesses of consumerist spirituality? Approaching this question, I located myself in the discipline of practical theology; especially, the empirical-analytical current that intends to make conceptual, theoretical categories operational to the lived realities of faith communities for the purposes of constructive theological ethics. My contention was that a postsecular revision resistant to consumerist spirituality would not amount to an anti-consumerist spirituality, but rather a reflexive spirituality. That is, contemporary American evangelical theology needs a spirituality that regularly interrogates its own practice.

A strong spiritual reflexivity enables evangelical faith communities to engage critically the ambiguities that inevitably emerge from immersive instrumentalizing contexts. For those within the evangelical tradition professionally engaged in capitalistic enterprise (like myself), this is vital. Abandoning consumerist contexts is rarely an option; sustaining and growing faithful practice in their midst is the goal.

Drawing on the interdisciplinary nature of practical theology, I identified two values that informed my method for strengthening evangelical reflexivity. First, was the contextuality of all Christian belief and practice. For contemporary American evangelical theology, a postsecular revision of the theme of transformation involves a reflexive retrieval of the rich Christian traditions that have grappled with the triangulating force of God's love against instrumentalizing tendencies. Specifically, I located the early Anabaptist appropriation of German mystic Meister Eckhart's practice of *gelassenheit* as a prime source of retrieval.

Second, were the public dimensions of Christian moral reflection. For contemporary American evangelical theology, a postsecular revision of the theme of transformation involves a reflexive engagement with disciplines beyond its own that are also contemplating the moral and spiritual dimensions of capitalistic enterprise. Specifically, I located stakeholder theory in the field of business management as a prime source. It has emerged as the dominant heuristic for understanding the transformative role of enterprise in contributing to human flourishing. However, it too has come under pressure to sustain its heuristic against the polarizing effects of consumer capitalism's postsecular growth.

Utilizing interdisciplinary and constructive practical theology, a model was developed for strengthening theological reflexivity in contemporary American evangelical perceptions of enterprise that articulates a transformationalist vision resistant to the instrumentalizing tendencies of postsecular consumerist spirituality. This model addresses two dimensions of theological reflexivity. First, is a conceptual inconsistency in the common articulation of the theme of transformation by restoring a scripturally faithful relational ethic of triangulating love. Second, are the ambiguities of practice that invariably emerge for individuals and faith communities trying to live out such an ethic by facilitating critical reflection in the areas of relational bonds, possessions, and status that translates into concrete embodied practices.

To close, I would like to reflect on several points of contribution that I believe emerge from this study, along with some of its limitations and areas for future exploration.

Contributions

The first contribution is a viable and reproducible example of constructive, practical theology that challenges the silos of the traditional theological encyclopedia. Since the eighteenth century, it has been standard in western Christian theology to divide the discipline of theology into four subdisciplines: exegetical/biblical, systematic, historical, and practical. Focused on the intersection of theory and practice, the branch of practical theology has seen vital growth in the last quarter century, especially in efforts to challenge the traditional encyclopedia and foster cross-discipline activity. However, one area that this has not occurred in is constructive theology, which has emerged mainly in systematic theology as a method for relating traditional Christian doctrines to contemporary questions of faith and ethics. This is striking given that questions of faith and ethics are at the heart of practical theology's concern for integrating theory and practice.

Working from the analytical-empirical current in practical theology, I have produced a constructive model for the strengthening of theological reflexivity. In so doing, I have also provided a reproducible blueprint for how practical theology can carry out its noble challenging of the silos of traditional theological encyclopedia with constructive theological reflection that pulls from all four forms: historical, systematic, biblical/exegetical, and practical. This blueprint generates and applies practical theological frameworks sensitive to both theoretical and empirical concerns with the goal of contributing to a more effective harmonizing of "belief" and "practice."

Second, is an exercise in evangelical practical theology that utilizes practical theological methodologies without compromising evangelicalism's traditional emphasis on the Christian Scriptures and the kerygma. As robust as the growth of contemporary practical theology has been, American evangelicalism has had very little representation within it. For its part, American evangelicalism has been suspicious of practical theology's emphasis on practice and experience in the formation of theological doctrine, viewing this emphasis as potentially undermining the hermeneutical priority of the Bible. For its part, practical theology has been suspicious of American evangelicalism's lack of critical self-reflection, viewing it as disconnected from the lived realities of faithful practice.

CONCLUSION

By utilizing practical theological methodology to strengthen reflexivity within contemporary American evangelical theology, I have pointed a viable way forward for future efforts in evangelical practical theology. My research addresses concerns on both sides. American evangelicalism now has an example of how practical theological frameworks can be utilized not just to honor but also advance its traditional emphasis on Scripture and kerygma. Practical theology now has an example of how American evangelicalism's respect for the hermeneutical priority of Scripture can contribute to faithful practice. The way forward was demonstrated not just in the form of theological abstraction but, more importantly, concrete embodied practices. These provide a means for faith communities to lean into the complexities of growing in faith in consumerist contexts, primarily in the form of pivotal questions that validate complexities rather than minimize them.

Third, is scholarly research on the contemporary American evangelical theological theme of transformation. The theme of transformation is one of the primary conceptual apparatuses by which both contemporary American evangelical theologians and laypersons understand the effort to integrate religious faith and professional work. Yet, its expressions in evangelical theologies and lay evangelical faith communities have never been critically compared. My research has countered this by contributing full-orbed, mixed-method research on the theme of transformation. This has come in three robust layers. First, was a conceptual analysis of the current state of transformationalist thinking in contemporary American evangelical theology as a spectrum with hard and soft varieties at the poles. Second, was a historical-theological analysis of the roots of this spectrum, tracing its development back through twentieth-century and pre-twentieth-century figures. Lastly, was a comparison of the conceptual spectrum to two rounds of focus group research with contemporary American evangelicals that saw representation from both hard and soft varieties.

Fourth, is a demonstration of how traditional Anabaptist theological values can be summoned to offer a robust transformationalist vision for small-scale engagement. Since its inception in the "radical" wing of the Reformation movements of continental Europe, Anabaptist theology has balanced tension between separationist and transformationist poles that were distinctly apparent in its engagement with enterprise. The earliest Anabaptist communities were mainly separationist in their approach and maintained (with a few exceptions) a limited engagement with enterprise that was almost exclusively agricultural.

With the establishment of Anabaptist communities in North America, this approach continued mostly unchecked. However, beginning in the twentieth-century, moderating voices emerged within the Anabaptist tradition that called for greater engagement in enterprise, even to the extent of seeking to "transform" secular practices in the context of small communities. This book fills a gap in contemporary American Anabaptist theology by demonstrating how traditional Anabaptist theological convictions can be summoned to offer a robust transformationalist vision for small-scale engagement.

A fifth contribution is an exposition of the relatively neglected triangulating theology of love found in Eckhart's concept of *gelassenheit* that connects its utilization in early Anabaptist mysticism to contemporary postsecular spirituality. Some of the earliest Anabaptist communities to emerge in the Reformation were in South Germany, and they are often categorized with the Rhineland mystic spirituality movement because of the appropriation of Meister Eckhart's emphasis on God's love by figures such as Thomas Müntzer and Hans Denk. Eckhart's theology of love is clearly expressed in the concept of *gelasseneheit*, representing one of the most significant but under-researched articulations of triangulating love in the Christian traditions. This book contributes to closing this gap by providing an analysis of Eckhart's scheme in its utilization by early Anabaptist spirituality to demonstrate its unique relevance and applicability to contemporary efforts to resist the instrumentalizing tendencies of postsecular consumerist spirituality.

A seventh area of contribution is a resourcing of the moral framework of stakeholder theory with a robust theological account of intrinsicality. Stakeholder theory has quickly emerged as the dominant heuristic in the field of business ethics for understanding the relationship of capitalistic enterprises with their broader constituencies. It calls for a shift away from prioritizing shareholder profit as the focus of an enterprise's value to its ability to profitably serve all its stakeholders. This shift has opened the door for meaningful challenges to the individualist and materialist excesses of capitalistic enterprise. While scholarly discussions in stakeholder theory have involved several interdisciplinary collaborators including sociology, psychology, and philosophy, theology has been largely absent.

This book contributes to this void by first bringing the two fields into comparative dialogue on the topic of the individualist and materialists excesses of postsecular consumerist spirituality. Then, showing how a practical theological framework can resource stakeholder theory's own moral framework with a robust account of intrinsicality.

Developing intrinsic goods such as character and compassion in organizational settings have become of greater focus as cultural and social understandings of organizations have shifted. Whereas the scientific era of management pictured organizations as fined-tuned machines operating on control and efficiency, greater awareness of social complexities within organizational life has altered this picture to one of human organisms that require normativity and consensus.

Out of this paradigm, normative stakeholder theory emerged with a conceptual framework that has a striking resemblance to the moral framework supporting *gelassenheit*. Rather than grounding the purpose of a firm in the maximization of shareholder self-interest, stakeholder theory grounds the purpose of the firm in the well-being of its community of stakeholders. What stakeholder theory lacks in and of itself—apart from philosophical or theological resources—is a convincing moral imperative for such a shift in understanding. *Gelassenheit's* ethic of triangulating love can provide a robust defense of the ability to triangulate love to advance relational health in organizational settings in ways that self-interested utility cannot.

A final contribution is a comparison of stakeholder theory and postsecular theory's shared conceptual framework that points to the need for a revising of the individual and social categories. As with stakeholder theory, likewise, postsecular theory in the discipline of the sociology of religion has emerged as a dominant heuristic for understanding the implications of capitalistic enterprise for its field, displacing an entrenched one. It has overturned secularization theory's long-held consensus that the economic and social modernization of western society would displace religions to contend that religious expression has not entirely dissipated but rather shifted. Thus far, there has been a little critical comparison of the two theories even though they have both developed against the backdrop of the rapid growth of consumer capitalism. This book contributes to the closing of this gap by showing how both theories have been pressed to their explanatory limits because of their dependence on a homo-duplex framework.

Limitations and Areas for Future Research

All research studies face limitations that can affect or influence the interpretation of findings. One of the core values informing my approach to this topic has been brevity. Too much scholarly theological research has been made inaccessible to faith communities because it is not presented in concise and clear forms, practical theology included. The nature of my topic demanded that I pull from a broad range of scholarly fields, but with assertions relevant to the realities of everyday faith communities. During my research, however, certain limitations were encountered, and areas of future research emerged that are important to highlight.

The first limitation relates to the research methodology. In critically analyzing the theme of transformation in contemporary American evangelical theology, I chose a blended research approach that combined conceptual analysis with focus groups and case studies. The qualitative components did provide tremendous texture, but the scope of applicability was narrow, and I ended up excluding that material from the final manuscript. An opportunity for future research would be a larger scale mixed methods study of contemporary American evangelical beliefs about transformation that could supplement qualitative research with quantitative survey research. This would enable large conclusions to be drawn about the population.

A second limitation also relating to research methodology was my position as an "insider" to the research subject. In my introduction, I described my own theological framework as outside of traditional evangelicalism, but I also stated that my upbringing and schooling had primarily been in evangelical environments. Throughout the research process, I was careful to use as neutral language as possible in describing evangelical concepts and norms. I also sought out critical evaluation of my research from informed evangelicals and non-evangelicals to balance the perspective. However, no amount of contextualization could change my position as an insider and the effects that this might have on the analysis. An opportunity for future research would be for a non-insider to assess the theme of transformation using similar methodology to see how his or her conclusions compared to my own.

A third limitation relates to the use of the Anabaptist tradition of *gelassenheit* for the source of critical historical analysis. While the fifteenth- and sixteenth-century south German Anabaptist movement provided many parallels to contemporary American evangelical theology's interaction with a consumerist society, it was also greatly distanced by time. This limited the ability to draw direct connections between a postindustrial sociohistorical context and a preindustrial one. An area for future research would be the building of a model of reflexivity using a more current faith community as a point of triangulation to determine if that model provides any additional sources for reflexivity.

Bibliography

Ackoff, Russell. *A Concept of Corporate Planning*. New York: John Wiley, 1970.
Adorno, Theodor, and Max Horkheimer. *Dialectic of Enlightenment*. Stanford: Stanford University Press, 2002.
Albanese, Catherine L. *Nature Religion in America*. Chicago: University of Chicago Press, 1992.
Alexander, Bruce K. *The Globalization of Addiction: A Study in Poverty of the Spirit*. Oxford: Oxford University Press, 2008.
Allan, Kenneth. *Explorations in Classical Sociological Theory: Seeing the Social World*. New York: Sage, 2005.
Allen, Paul. *Theological Method: A Guide for the Perplexed*. London: T&T Clark, 2012.
Alston, William P. *The Reliability of Sense Perception*. Ithaca: Cornell University Press, 1993.
Althaus-Reid, Marcella. *Indecent Theology*. New York: Routledge, 2006.
Anderson, Ray. *The Shape of Practical Theology*. Downers Grove, IL: InterVarsity, 2001.
Anscombe, G. E. "Modern Moral Philosophy." *Philosophy* 33 (1958) 1–19.
Ansoff, Igor. *Corporate Strategy: An Analytic Approach to Business Policy for Growth and Expansion*. New York: McGraw-Hill, 1965.
Antoun, Richard. *Understanding Fundamentalism: Christian, Islamic, and Jewish Movements*. Lanham, MD: Rowman & Littlefield, 2008.
Aquinas, Thomas. *Summa Theologica*. New York: Benzinger, 1980.
Argandoña, Antonio. "The Stakeholder Theory and the Common Good." *Journal of Business Ethics* 17 (1998) 1093–1102.
Arnold, Denis G., et al., eds. *Ethical Theory and Business*. Boston: Pearson Education, 2012.
Asad, Talal. *Genealogies of Religion: Discipline and Reasons for Power in Christianity and Islam*. Baltimore: Johns Hopkins University Press, 1993.
Atherton, John. *Transfiguring Capitalism: An Enquiry into Religion and Global Change*. London: SCM, 2008.
Audi, R. *Epistemology: A Contemporary Introduction to the Theory of Knowledge*. New York: Routledge, 2003.
Augsburger, David. *Dissident Discipleship*. Grand Rapids: Brazos, 2006.
Augustine. *City of God*. New York: Penguin, 2012.
———. *Confessions*. New York: Penguin, 1961.

Austin, Drew. "The Constant Consumer: Amazon's Mission Is to Make Customer Identity More Primary Than Citizenship." *Real Life*, September 10, 2018. Online. https://reallifemag.com/the-constant-consumer.

Badcock, Gary. *The Way of Life*. Grand Rapids: Eerdmans, 1998.

Bainbridge, W. S. "Sacred Algorithms: Exchange Theory of Religious Claims." In *Defining Religion: Investigating the Boundaries Between the Sacred and the Secular*, edited by Arthur L. Greil and David G. Bromley, 2–39. Boston: JAI, 2003.

Baird, Robert. "Late Secularism." *Social Text* 18 (2000) 123–36.

Balmer, Randall. *God in the White House*. New York: Harper, 2001.

Balthasar, Hans Urs von. *Theodrama*. San Francisco, Ignatius, 1998.

Barna, George, and David Kinnaman. *Churchless: Understanding Today's Unchurched and How to Connect with Them*. Carol Stream, IL: Tyndale, 2006.

Barrera, Albino. *Economic Compulsion and Christian Ethics*. New York: Cambridge, 2005.

Barrett, David, et al. *World Christian Encyclopedia*. 2 vols. New York: Oxford University Press, 2002.

Barton, S. C. "New Testament Interpretation as Performance." *Scottish Journal of Theology* 52 (1999) 179–208.

Bass, Diana Butler. *Christianity After Religion: The End of Church and the Birth of a New Spiritual Awakening*. New York: Harper, 2012.

Bass, Dorothy. *Receiving the Day*. San Francisco: Jossey-Bass, 2000.

Bass, Dorothy, et al. *Christian Practical Wisdom: What It Is, Why It Matters*. Grand Rapids: Eerdmans, 2016.

Baum, Gregory. "The Impact of Marxist Ideas on Christian Theology." In *The Twentieth Century: A Theological Overview*, edited by Gregory Baum, 173–85. Maryknoll, NY: Orbis, 1999.

Bauman, Clarence. *The Spiritual Legacy of Hans Denck: Interpretation and Translation of Key Texts*. Leiden: Brill, 1991.

———. "The Theology of the 'Two Kingdoms': A Comparison of Luther and the Anabaptists." *Mennonite Quarterly Review* 38 (1964) 37–41.

Baumeister, R. F., and M. R. Leary. "The Need to Belong: Desire for Interpersonal Attachments as a Fundamental Human Motivation." *Psychological Bulletin* 117 (1995) 497–529.

Bean, Lydia. *The Politics of Evangelical Identity*. Princeton: Princeton University Press, 2014.

Beaudoin, Tom. "Postmodern Practical Theology." In *Opening the Field of Practical Theology: An Introduction*, edited by Kathleen A. Cahalan and Gordon S. Mikoski, 183–202. Lanham, MD: Rowman & Littlefield, 2014.

Bebbington, David. *Evangelicalism in Modern Britain*. London: Unwin Hyman, 1989.

Beckford, James A., and N. J. Demerath. "Introduction." In *The Sage Handbook of the Sociology of Religion*, edited by James A. Beckford and N. J. Demerath, 1–16. London: Sage, 2007.

Beckley, Harlan. *Passion for Justice*. Louisville: Westminster, 1992.

Bender, Courtney. "Things in Their Entanglements." In *The Post-Secular in Question*, edited by Philip S. Gorski et al., 43–76. New York: New York University Press, 2012.

Bender, H. S. *Conrad Grebel: The Founder of the Swiss Brethren*. 1950. Reprint, Eugene, OR: Wipf & Stock, 1998.

———. "The Pacifism of the Sixteenth Century Anabaptists." *Church History* 24 (1955) 119–31.
Bennett, Zoe, et al. *Invitation to Research in Practical Theology*. New York: Routledge, 2018.
Benson, Herbert. *The Relaxation Response*. New York: HarperCollins, 1976.
Berg, J. A. van den, and R. R. Ganzevoort. "The Art of Creating Futures." *Acta Theologica* 34 (2014) 166–85.
Berger, Peer. *The Desecularization of the World: Resurgent Religion and World Politics*. Grand Rapids: Eerdmans, 1999.
———. *Sacred Canopy: Elements of a Sociological Theory of Religion*. Garden City, NY: Doubleday, 1967.
Bertens, Hans. *The Idea of the Postmodern: A History*. New York: Routledge, 1995.
Bevans, Stephen. *Models of Contextual Theology*. Maryknoll, NY: Orbis, 2002.
Beyer, Peter. "Sensing Religion, Observing Religion, Reconstructing Religion: Contingency and Pluralization in Post-Westphalian Context." *Social Compass* 63 (2016) 234–50.
Bhaskar, Roy. *From Science to Emancipation: Journeys toward Meta-Reality*. London: Sage, 2002.
Biberman, Jerry, and Len Tischler. *Spirituality in Business: Theory, Practice, and Future Directions*. New York: Palgrave Macmillan, 2008.
Biggar, Nigel. *Behaving in Public: How to Do Christian Ethics*. Grand Rapids: Eerdmans, 2011.
Bloesch, Donald. *Essentials of Evangelical Theology*. Peabody, MA: Hendrickson, 2005.
———. *Freedom for Obedience: Evangelical Ethics in Contemporary Times*. San Francisco: Harper & Row, 1987.
Blomberg, Craig. *Can We Still Believe the Bible? An Evangelical Engagement with Contemporary Questions*. Grand Rapids: Brazos, 2014.
Bloom, Harold. *The American Religion: The Emergence of the Post-Christian Nation*. New York: Simon & Schuster, 1992.
Bogost, Ian. "When Malls Saved the Suburbs from Despair." *The Atlantic*, February 17, 2018. Online. https://www.theatlantic.com/technology/archive/2018/02/when-malls-saved-cities-from-capitalism/553610.
Borgmann, Albert. *Power Failure: Christianity in the Culture of Technology*. Grand Rapids: Brazos, 2003.
Bourdieu, Pierre. *Outline of a Theory of Practice*. Cambridge: Cambridge University Press, 1997.
Bowie, Norman, ed. *The Blackwell Guide to Business Ethics*. Oxford: Blackwell, 2002.
———. *Business Ethics: A Kantian Perspective*. Cambridge: Cambridge University Press, 2017.
Bratt, James. *Abraham Kuyper: Modern Calvinist, Christian Democrat*. Grand Rapids: Eerdmans, 2013.
———. *Dutch Calvinism in Modern America*. Grand Rapids: Eerdmans, 1984.
———. "Sphere Sovereignty among Abraham Kuyper's Other Political Theories." In *The Kuyperian Center Review: Politics, Religion, and Sphere Sovereignty*, edited by Gordon Graham, 34–49. Grand Rapids: Eerdmans, 2010.
Braybrooke, Marcus. *Beacons of Light*. New York: O Books, 2009.
Breitenberg, E. H. "To Tell the Truth: Will the Real Public Theology Please Stand Up?" *Journal of the Society of Christian Ethics* 23 (2003) 55–96.

Brenner, P. S. "Identity Importance and the Overreporting of Religious Service Attendance: Multiple Imputation of Religious Attendance Using American Time Use Study and the General Social Survey." *Journal for the Scientific Study of Religion* 50 (2011) 103–15.
Bridoux, Flore, and J. W. Stoelhorst. "Microfoundations for Stakeholder Theory: Managing Stakeholders with Heterogeneous Motives." *Strategic Management Journal* 35 (2014) 107–25.
Briggs, Richard. "The Bible before Us." In *New Perspectives for Evangelical Theology*, edited by Tom Greggs, 14–28. New York: Routledge, 2010.
Broughton, Janet. *Descartes's Method of Doubt*. Princeton: Princeton University Press, 2002.
Brown, R. M. *For a Christian America: A History of the Religious Right*. Amherst: Prometheus, 2002.
Brown, William. *The Ethos of the Cosmos*. Grand Rapids: Eerdmans, 1999.
Browning, Don. *A Fundamental Practical Theology: Descriptive and Strategic Proposals*. Minneapolis: Fortress, 1995.
———. "Science and Religion on the Nature of Love." In *Altruism and Altruistic Love*, edited by Stephen Post et al., 335–45. New York: Oxford, 2002.
Bruce, F. F. *The New Testament Documents: Are They Reliable?* Grand Rapids: Eerdmans, 1974.
Bryant, David. *Faith and the Play of Imagination*. Macon, GA: Mercer University Press, 1989.
Bucholz, Rogene, and Sandra Rosenthal. "Toward a Contemporary Conceptual Framework for Stakeholder Theory." *Journal of Business Ethics* 58 (2005) 137–48.
Burns, J. H. "Happiness and Utility: Jeremy Bentham's Equation." *Utilitas* (2005) 46–61.
Burroughs, James, and Aric Rindfleisch. "Materialism and Well-Being: A Conflicting Values Perspective." *Journal of Consumer Research* 29 (2002) 348–70.
Buschart, David, and Kent Eilers. *Theology as Retrieval*. Downers Grove, IL: InterVarsity Academic, 2015.
Bussau, David, and Russell Mask. *Christian Microenterprise Development: An Introduction*. Carlisle, UK: Regnum, 2003.
Cadge, Wendy, et al. "Religion and Spirituality: A Barrier and a Bridge in the Everyday Professional Work of Pediatric Physicians." *Social Problems* 56 (2009) 702–21.
Cahalan, Kathleen A., and Gordon S. Mikoski. *Opening the Field of Practical Theology: An Introduction*. New York: Rowman & Littlefield, 2014.
Cahall, Perry. "The Proper Order of Conjugal Love: The Relevance of St. Augustine's Insights." *Logos: A Journal of Catholic Thought and Culture* 8 (2005) 117–28.
Calhoun, R. L. "Work and Vocation in Christian History." In *Work and Vocation*, edited by James Nelson, 82–115. New York: Harper, 1954.
Candler, Peter. *Theology, Rhetoric, Manuduction, or, Reading Scripture Together on the Path to God*. Grand Rapids: Eerdmans, 2006.
Canning, Roy. "Reflecting on the Reflective Practitioner: Muddled Thinking and Poor Educational Practices." Paper for UCET Conference, Birmingham, November 2008. Online. https://www.semanticscholar.org/paper/Reflecting-on-the-Reflective-Practitioner%3A-muddled-Canning/0cbf2311c6642be98571e8037d7d94988d8c5073.
Caputo, John. *Hoping Against Hope*. Minneapolis: Fortress, 2015.
Carson, D. A. *Christ and Culture Revisited*. Grand Rapids: Eerdmans, 2008.

———. *The Gagging of God: Christianity Confronts Pluralism*. Grand Rapids: Eerdmans, 1996.
Carter, Craig. *Re-Thinking Christ and Culture: A Post-Christendom Perspective*. Grand Rapids: Brazos, 2007.
Casanova, José. *Public Religions in the Modern World*. Chicago: University of Chicago Press, 1996.
Cavanaugh, William. *Being Consumed: Economics and Christian Desire*. Grand Rapids: Eerdmans, 2008.
Chadwick, Owen. *The Early Reformation on the Continent*. Oxford: Oxford University Press, 2001.
Chamberlain, G. L. "Protestant and Catholic Meanings of Vocation: Is Business a True Vocation?" In *Rethinking the Purpose of Business: Interdisciplinary Essays on the Meaning of Business from the Catholic Social Tradition*, edited by Michael Naughton and Steven Rumpza, 33–49. St. Paul: University of St. Thomas, 2002.
Chan, Simon. "Spiritual Practices." In *The Oxford Handbook of Evangelical Theology*, edited by Gerald McDermott, 247–61. Oxford: Oxford University Press, 2010.
Chaves, Mark. *American Religion: Contemporary Trends*. Princeton: Princeton University Press, 2011.
Cheit, Earl F., ed. *The Business Establishment*. New York: Wiley, 1964.
Child, James, and Alexei Marcoux. "Freeman and Evan: Stakeholder Theory in the Original Position." *Business Ethics Quarterly* 9 (1999) 207–23.
Christiano, Kevin J., et al. *Sociology of Religion: Contemporary Developments*. Lanham, MD: Rowman & Littlefield, 2015.
Churchman, C. West. *The Systems Approach*. New York: Dell, 1968.
Clark, David K. *To Know and Love God: Method for Theology*. Wheaton: Crossway, 2010.
Clegg, Steve. "The Moral Philosophy of Management: Book Review." *Academy of Management Review* 21 (1996) 867–71.
Clement, Ronald. "The Lessons from Stakeholder Theory from US Business Leaders." *Business Horizons* 48 (2005) 255–64.
Cobb, A. D. "Acknowledged Dependence and the Virtues of Perinatal Hospice." *The Journal of Medicine and Philosophy* 41 (2015) 25–40.
Collins, Kenneth. "Real Christianity as Integrating Theme in Wesley's Soteriology: The Critique of a Modern Myth." *The Asbury Theological Journal* 51 (1996) 1–30.
Connolly, William. *Capitalism and Christianity, American Style*. Durham: Duke University Press, 2012.
Crapanzano, Vincent. *Serving the Word: Literalism in American from the Pulpit to the Bench*. New York: New Press, 2000.
Crisp, Oliver. "Faith and Experience." In *The Oxford Handbook of Evangelical Theology*, edited by Gerald McDermott, 68–80. London: Oxford University Press, 2010.
Crook, Zeba. "On the Treatment of Miracles in New Testament Scholarship." *Studies in Religion* 40 (2011) 461–78.
Cunningham, David. *Christian Ethics: The End of the Law*. New York: Routledge, 2008.
Curry, D. C. "Where Have All the Niebuhrs Gone? Evangelicals and the Marginalization of Religious Influence in American Public Life." *A Journal of Church and State* 36 (1994) 97–114.
Dallmayr, Fred. "Review: Adorno and Heidegger." *Diacritics* 19 (1989) 82–100.

Darragh, Neil. "The Practice of Practical Theology: Key Decisions and Abiding Hazards in Doing Practical Theology." *Australian Ejournal of Theology* 9 (2007) 1–13.

Davis, Bret. *Heidegger and the Will: On the Way to Gelassenheit*. Evanston: Northwestern University Press, 2007.

Davis, Daphne, and Jeffrey Hayes. "What Are the Benefits of Mindfulness? A Practice Review of Psychotherapy-Related Research." *Psychotherapy* 48 (2011) 198–208.

De George, Richard T. *Business Ethics*. New York: Pearson, 2009.

De La Torre, Miguel. "Ethics." In *The Wiley Blackwell Companion to Practical Theology*, edited by Bonnie Miller-McLemore, 337–46. London: Blackwell, 2011.

Demerath, N. J. "Secularization and Sacralization Deconstructed and Reconstructed." In *The Sage Handbook of the Sociology of Religion*, edited by James Beckford and N. J. Demerath, 57–80. London: Sage, 2007.

DesJardins, Joseph. *An Introduction to Business Ethics*. New York: McGraw-Hill, 2003.

Detweiler, Robert. *Breaking the Fall: Religious Reading of Contemporary Fiction*. Louisville: Westminster John Knox, 1995.

Dias, Candice, and Justin Beaumont. "Postsecularism or Late Secularism? Faith Creating Place in the US." In *Exploring the Postsecular: The Religious, the Political and the Urban*, edited by Arie Molendijk et al., 267–79. Boston: Brill, 2010.

Diefenthaler, Jon. *The Paradox of Church and World*. Minneapolis: Fortress, 2015.

Dienhart, John. *Business, Institutions, and Ethics*. Oxford: Oxford University Press, 1999.

Dill, William. "Public Participation in Long Range Planning: Strategic Management in a Kibitzer's World." *Long Range Planning* 8 (1975) 57–63.

Dingemans, D. J. "Practical Theology in the Academy: A Contemporary Overview." *The Journal of Religion* 76 (1996) 82–96.

Dobson, John. "Alasdair MacIntyre's Aristotelian Business Ethics: A Critique." *Journal of Business Ethics* 86 (2009) 43–50.

Donaldson, Thomas, and Lee Preston. "The Stakeholder Theory of the Corporation: Concepts, Evidence, and Implications." *Academy of Management Review* 20 (1995) 65–91.

Donaldson, Thomas, and Paul Werhane. *Ethical Issues in Business: A Philosophical Approach*. Atlanta: Pearson, 2007.

Dooyeweerd, Herman. *A New Critique of Theoretical Thought*. Philadelphia: Presbyterian and Reformed, 1953.

Dove, E. S., et al. "Beyond Individualism: Is There a Place for Relational Autonomy in Clinical Practice and Research?" *Clinical Ethics* 12 (2017) 150–65.

Drucker, Peter. *Management: Tasks, Responsibilities, Practices*. New York: Harper & Row, 1974.

Duffy, Ryan, and Brian Dik. "Research on Calling: What We Have Learned and Where Are We Going?" *Journal of Vocational Behavior* 83 (2013) 428–36.

Dunham, Laura, et al. "Enhancing Stakeholder Practice: A Particularized Exploration of Community." *Business Ethics Quarterly* 16 (2006) 23–42.

Dunn, James D. G. *Jesus Remembered*. Grand Rapids: Eerdmans, 2003.

Durkheim, Emile. "The Dualism of Human Nature and its Social Conditions." In *Essays on Sociology and Philosophy*, edited by K. H. Wolff, 325–39. New York: Harper & Row, 1960.

———. *The Elementary Forms of the Religious Life*. New York: Free Press, 1965.

Dyck, Bruno, and David Schroeder. "Management, Theology and Moral Points of View: Towards an Alternative to the Conventional Materialist-Individualist Ideal-Type of Management." *Journal of Management Studies* 42 (2005) 705–35.

Dyck, Cornelius, ed. *Spiritual Life in Anabaptism*. Scottdale, PA: Herald, 1995.

Dykstra, Craig. "Reconceiving Practice." In *Shifting Boundaries: Contextual Approaches to the Structure of Theological Education*, edited by Barbara Wheeler and Edward Farley, 35–66. Louisville: Westminster John Knox, 1991.

Eckersley, Richard. "Culture, Spirituality, Religion, and Health: Looking at the Big Picture." *Medical Journal of Australia* 186 (2007) s54–s56.

Edgell, M. D. "Both for Profit and Not: Biblical Views of Organizational Hybridization." *Journal of Biblical Integration in Business* 15 (2012) 7–10.

Ehrenreich, Barbara. *A History of Collective Joy*. New York: Holt, 2006.

Ehrman, Bart. *Misquoting Jesus*. New York: HarperOne, 2005.

Einstein, Mara. *Brands of Faith: Marketing Religion in a Commercial Age*. New York: Routledge, 2007.

Elfstrom, Gerard. *Moral Issues and Multinational Corporations*. New York: Macmillan, 1991.

Ellingson, Stephen. "The New Spirituality from the Social Science Perspective." *Dialog* 40 (2011) 257–63.

Elliott, Anthony, and Charles Lemert. *The New Individualism: The Emotional Costs of Globalization*. New York: Routledge, 2006.

Emerson, Michael, and Christian Smith. *Divided by Faith: Evangelical Religion and the Problem of Race in America*. Oxford: Oxford University Press, 2002.

Enns, Peter. *The Sin of Certainty*. New York: HarperOne, 2016.

Esterp, William. *The Anabaptist Story: An Introduction to Sixteenth-Century Anabaptism*. Grand Rapids: Eerdmans, 1975.

Evan, William M., and R. Edward Freeman. "A Stakeholder Theory of the Modern Corporation: Kantian Capitalism." In *An Introduction to Business Ethics*, edited by G. D. Chryssides and J. H. Kaler, 254–66. London: Chapman and Hall, 1993.

Evans, Christopher. *The Kingdom Is Always but Coming: A Life of Walter Rauschenbusch*. Grand Rapids: Eerdmans, 2004.

Farley, Edward. *Deep Symbols*. New York: T&T Clark, 1996.

Fee, Gordon. *The First Epistle to the Corinthians*. Grand Rapids: Eerdmans, 1987.

Feinberg, Paul. "Inerrancy and Infallibility of the Bible." In *Evangelical Dictionary of Theology*, edited by Walter Elwell, 294–319. Grand Rapids: Baker, 2001.

Ferguson, Michelle. "Anabaptist Liturgy: Sacramental Theology." *Direction* 36 (2007) 247–57.

Finger, Thomas. "A Sixteenth-Century Anabaptist Social Spirituality." *The Conrad Grebel Review* 22 (2004) 93–104.

Fitch, David. *The Great Giveaway*. Grand Rapids: Baker, 2005.

Fitzgerald, Timothy. *The Ideology of Religious Studies*. New York: Oxford University Press, 2000.

Flanagan, Kieran. *Sociology in Theology: Reflexivity in Belief*. New York: Palgrave Macmillan, 2007.

Fombrun, Charles, and Mark Shanley. "What's in a Name? Reputation Building and Corporate Strategy." *Academy of Management Journal* 33 (1990) 233–58.

Forman, Robert. *Meister Eckhart: Mystic as Theologian*. Rockport, MA: Element, 1991.

Forrester, Duncan. *Forrester on Christian Ethics and Practical Theology*. Burlington, VT: Ashgate, 2010.

———. *Theological Fragments*. London: T&T Clark, 2005.

Fort, Timothy. *Ethics and Governance: Business as Mediating Institution*. Oxford: Oxford University Press, 2001.

Fox, Richard. *Reinhold Niebuhr*. San Francisco: Harper & Row, 1985.

———. "Richard Niebuhr's Divided Kingdom." *American Quarterly* 42 (1990) 93–101.

Frederick, Robert. *A Companion to Business Ethics*. New York: John Wiley, 2008.

Freeman, R. Edward. "Managing for Stakeholders." In *Ethical Theory and Business*, edited by Tom L. Beauchamp and Norman E. Bowie, 56–83. Englewood Cliffs, NJ: Prentice-Hall, 2008.

———. *Strategic Management: A Stakeholder Approach*. Cambridge: Cambridge University Press, 1984.

Freeman, R. Edward, and D. L. Reed. "Stockholders and Stakeholders: A New Perspective in Corporate Governance." *California Management Review* 25 (1983) 88–106.

Freeman, R. Edward, et al. *Stakeholder Theory: The State of the Art*. Cambridge: Cambridge University Press, 2010.

Freire, Paulo. *Pedagogy of the Oppressed*. New York: Continuum, 2000.

Friedman, Milton. "The Social Responsibility of Business Is to Increase Its Profits." *New York Times Magazine*, September 13, 1970. Online. https://www.nytimes.com/1970/09/13/archives/article-15-no-title.html.

Friedmann, Robert. *Hutterite Studies: Essays by Robert Friedman*. Goshen: Mennonite Historical Society, 1961.

———. "Introduction to 'Article Three of the Great Article' Book: A Notable Hutterite Document Concerning True Surrender and Christian Community of Goods." *Mennonite Quarterly Review* 3 (1957) 22–62.

———. *The Theology of Anabaptism*. 1973. Reprint, Eugene, OR: Wipf & Stock, 1998.

Fulkerson, Mary McClintock. *Places of Redemption*. New York: Oxford University Press, 2010.

Fuller, Robert. *Spiritual but Not Religious: Understanding Unchurched America*. Oxford: Oxford University Press, 2001.

Funk, Deborah. "Gelassenheit: The Union of Self-Surrender and Radical Obedience." MA thesis, Canadian Mennonite University, 2012.

Furani, Khaled. "Is There a Postsecular?" *Journal of the American Academy of Religion* 83 (2015) 1–26.

Garcia-Ruiz, Pablo, and Carlos Rodriguez-Lluesma. "Consumption Practices: A Virtue Ethics Approach." *Business Ethics Quarterly* 24 (2014) 509–31.

Gauthier, Francois, et al. "Introduction: Religion in Market Society." In *Religion in the Neoliberal Age: Political Economy and Modes of Governance*, edited by Francois Gauthier and Tuomas Martikainen, 1–20. New York: Routledge, 2013.

Gayarre, J. L. "The Challenges of Liberation Theology to Neoliberal Economic Policies." *Social Justice* 21 (1994) 34–45.

Gelder, Hendrik van. "Article Book." In *The Mennonite Encyclopedia: A Comprehensive Reference Work on the Anabaptist-Mennonite Movement*, edited by Cornelius Dyck, 123–26. Chicago: Mennonite Brethren, 1955.

Gergen, Kenneth. *The Saturated Self: Dilemmas of Identity in Contemporary Life*. New York: Basic, 1991.

Giacalone, R. A., and C. L. Jurkiewicz. *Handbook of Workplace Spirituality and Organizational Performance*. New York: Routledge, 2015.
Gillett, David. *Trust and Obey: Explorations in Evangelical Spirituality*. London: Darton, Longman & Todd, 1993.
Giordan, Giuseppe, and Enzo Pace. *Mapping Religion and Spirituality in a Postsecular World*. Leiden: Brill, 2012.
Girardi, Gherardo, and Fabio Petito. "Postsecular Reflections on the Value of the Stakeholder Approach in Business." *Globalization for the Common Good Initiative Journal* (2014) 1–14.
Glover, Richard. "Paying Attention to God: Liturgy in Consumer Culture." *Ethos: Evangelical Alliance Centre for Christianity & Society*, April 4, 2016. Online. http://www.ethos.org.au/site/Ethos/filesystem/documents/In-depth/Consumerism_as_Spirituality_Glover.pdf.
Goheen, Michael, and Craig Bartholomew. *Living at the Crossroads*. Grand Rapids: Baker Academic, 2008.
Goossen, Richard, and R. Paul Stevens. *Entrepreneurial Leadership*. Downers Grove, IL: InterVarsity, 2013.
Gorski, Philip S., et al., eds. *The Post-Secular in Question*. New York: New York University Press, 2012.
Grab, Wilhelm. "Practical Theology as Theology of Religion." *International Journal of Practical Theology* 9 (2005) 181–96.
Grabill, Stephen. "Observations on the Theology of Work and Economics." *Journal of Markets and Morality* 15 (2012) 203–6.
Graham, Elaine. *Between a Rock and a Hard Place: Public Theology in a Post-Secular Age*. London: SCM, 2013.
———. "Between a Rock and a Hard Place: Public Theology in a Post-Secular Age." *Practical Theology* 7 (2014) 235–51.
———. *Transforming Practice*. 1996. Reprint, Eugene, OR: Wipf & Stock, 2002.
———. "The 'Virtuous Cycle': Religion and the Practices of Happiness." In *The Practices of Happiness: Political Economy, Religion and Wellbeing*, edited by John Atheron, 224–34. New York: Routledge, 2011.
Graham, Elaine, et al. *Theological Reflection: Methods*. London: SCM, 2005.
Grammich, Clifford, et al. "US Religion Census: Religious Congregations and Membership Study, 2010." *Association of Religion Data Archives*, February 10, 2019. Online. http://www.thearda.com/Archive/Files/Descriptions/RCMSMT10.asp.
Graves, Samuel, and Sandra Waddock. "Institutional Owners and Corporate Social Performance." *Academy of Management Journal* 37 (1994) 1035–46.
Green, Joel. *1 Peter*. Grand Rapids: Eerdmans, 2007.
Greggs, Tom. *New Perspectives for Evangelical Theology*. New York: Routledge, 2010.
Gregory, Eric. *Politics and the Order of Love*. Chicago: University of Chicago Press, 2008.
Greil, Arthur L., and David G. Bromley, eds. *Defining Religion: Investigating the Boundaries between the Sacred and the Secular*. Boston: JAI, 2003.
Grem, Darren. *The Blessings of Business: How Corporations Shaped Conservative Christianity*. New York: Oxford University Press, 2016.
Grenz, Stanley. "*Community* as a Theological Motif for Evangelical Theology." *In die Skriflig* 28 (1994) 395–411.

———. *A Primer on Postmodernism*. Grand Rapids: Eerdmans, 1996.

———. *Renewing the Center: Evangelical Theology in a Post-Theological Era*. Grand Rapids: Baker, 2000.

Groothuis, Douglas. *Truth Decay*. Downers Grove, IL: InterVarsity, 2000.

Gustafson, Andrew. "In Defense of a Utilitarian Business Ethic." *Business and Society Review* 118 (2013) 325–60.

Gutiérrez, Gustavo. *On Job: God-Talk and the Suffering of the Innocent*. Maryknoll, NY: Orbis, 1973.

———. *A Theology of Liberation*. Maryknoll, NY: Orbis, 1969.

Habermas, Jurgen. "Notes on a Post-Secular Society." *New Perspectives Quarterly* (2008) 17–29.

Hacker-Wright, John. "Virtue Ethics without Right Action: Anscombe, Foot, and Contemporary Virtue Ethics." *Value Inquiry* 44 (2010) 209–24.

Haight, Roger. "The Mission of the Church in the Theology of the Social Gospel." *Theological Studies* 49 (1988) 477–98.

Halteman, James. "Anabaptist Approaches to Economics." In *The Oxford Handbook on Christianity and Economics*, edited by Paul Oslington, 245–62. Oxford: Oxford University Press, 2014.

Hammond, S. R. "'God Is My Partner': An Evangelical Business Man Confronts Depression and War." *Church History* 80 (2011) 498–519.

Harder, Lydia. "Power and Authority in Mennonite Theological Development." In *Power, Authority, and the Anabaptist Tradition*, edited by Benjamin W. Redekop and Calvin W. Redekop, 73–94. Baltimore: Johns Hopkins University Press, 2001.

Hardin, Russell. *Morality within the Limits of Reason*. Chicago: University of Chicago Press, 1988.

Hardy, Lee. *The Fabric of This World*. Grand Rapids: Eerdmans, 1990.

Harrison, Jeffrey S., and Caron H. St. John. "Managing and Partnering with External Stakeholders." *Academy of Management Executive* 10 (1996) 46–60.

Harrison, Peter. *"Religion" and the Religions in the English Enlightenment*. Cambridge: Cambridge University Press, 1990.

Hart, D. G. *The Lost Soul of American Protestantism*. Lanham, MD: Rowman & Littlefield, 2004.

Hartman, Edwin. *Organizational Ethics and the Good Life*. Oxford: Oxford University Press, 1996.

Hartz, Louis. *The Liberal Tradition in America*. New York: Harcourt, Brace, 1955.

Hauerwas, Stanley. *Hannah's Child: A Theologian's Memoir*. Grand Rapids: Eerdmans, 2010.

Hauerwas, Stanley, and William Willimon. *Resident Aliens: Life in the Christian Colony*. Nashville: Abingdon, 1989.

Hawk, Daniel, and Richard Twiss. "From Good: 'The Only Good Indian Is a Dead Indian'; To Better: 'Kill the Indian and Save the Man'; To Best: 'Old Things Pass Away and All Things Become White.' An American Hermenutic of Colonization." In *Evangelical Postcolonial Conversations*, edited by Kay Higuera Smith et al., 47–60. Downers Grove, IL: InterVarsity, 2014.

Hay, Donald, and Gordon Menzies. "Is the Model of Human Nature in Economics Fundamentally Flawed? Seeking a Better Model of Economic Behavior." In *Theology and Economics*, edited by Jeremy Kidwell and Sean Doherty, 88–99. New York: Palgrave Macmillan, 2015.

Haynes, Stephen. *Noah's Curse: The Biblical Justification of American Slavery*. New York: Oxford University Press, 2002.
Hays, Richard B. *Echoes of Scripture in the Letters of Paul*. New Haven: Yale University Press, 1989.
Heelas, Paul, and Linda Woodhead. *The Spiritual Revolution: Why Religion Is Giving Way to Spirituality*. London: Wiley-Blackwell, 2005.
Heitink, Gerben. *Practical Theology: History, Theory, Action Domains*. Grand Rapids: Eerdmans, 1999.
Held, David. *Introduction to Critical Theory*. Cambridge: Polity, 1980.
Helminiak, Daniel. "Human Solidarity and Collective Union in Christ." *Anglican Theological Review* 70 (1988) 1–37.
Henry, Carl F. H. *Confessions*. Madison: Word, 1989.
———. "Fortunes of the Christian World View." *Trinity Journal* 19 (1998) 63–176.
———. *God, Revelation, and Authority*. Waco, TX: Word, 1979.
Hershberger, Guy. *War, Peace, Nonresistance*. Scottdale: Herald, 1986.
Heslam, Peter. *Creating a Christian Worldview: Kuyper's Lectures on Calvinism*. Grand Rapids: Eerdmans, 1998.
Hicks, D. J., and Tom Stapleford. "The Virtues of Scientific Practice: MacIntyre, Virtue Ethics, and the Historiography of Science." *Isis* 107 (2007) 449–72.
Holmes, Stephen. "British (and European) Evangelical Theologies." In *The Cambridge Companion to Evangelical Theology*, edited by Timothy Larsen and Daniel Treier, 241–58. Cambridge: Cambridge University Press, 2007.
Horvath, C. M. "Excellence v. Effectiveness: MacIntyre's Critique of Business." *Business Ethics Quarterly* 5 (1995) 499–532.
Houwer, Jan de, and Dirk Hermans. "Do Feelings Have a Mind of Their Own?" In *Cognition and Emotion: Reviews of Current Research and Theories*, edited by Jan de Houwer and Dirk Hermans, 38–65. New York: Psychology, 2010.
Hsieh, Nien-he. "The Normative Study of Business Organizations: A Rawlsian Approach." In *Normative Theory and Business Ethics*, edited by Jeffery Smith, 93–117. Lanham, MD: Rowman & Littlefield, 2008.
Hudson, W. Donaldson. *Wittgenstein and Religious Belief*. New York: St. Martin's, 1975.
Hunter, J. D. "The Culture War and the Secular/Sacred Divide: The Problem of Pluralism and Weak Hegemony." *Social Research* 76 (2009) 1307–22.
———. *Culture Wars: The Struggle to Control the Family, Art, Education, Law, and Politics in America*. New York: Basic, 1992.
———. *Evangelicalism: The Coming Generation*. Chicago: University of Chicago Press, 1987.
———. *To Change the World: The Irony, Tragedy, and Possibility of Christianity in the Late Modern World*. Oxford: Oxford University Press, 2010.
Hunter, R. J. "The Future of Pastoral Theology." *Pastoral Psychology* 29 (1980) 58–69.
Huntington, Samuel. *Who Are We? The Challenges to America's National Identity*. New York: Simon & Schuster, 2005.
Husted, B. W., and D. B. Allen. "Toward a Model of Cross-Cultural Business Ethics: The Impact of Individualism and Collectivism on the Ethical Decision-Making Process." *Journal of Business Ethics* 82 (2008) 293–305.
Huyssteen, J. Wentzel van. *The Shaping of Rationality: Towards Interdisciplinarity in Theology and Science*. Grand Rapids: Eerdmans, 1999.

———. "What Makes Us Human? The Interdisciplinary Challenge to Theological Anthropology and Christology." *Toronto Journal of Theology* 26 (2010) 143–60.
Iannaccone, Lawrence R. "Religious Markets and the Economics of Religion." *Social Compass* 39 (1992) 123–31.
Janssen, Jacques, and Theo Verheggen. "The Double Center of Gravity in Durkheim's Symbol Theory: Bringing the Symbolism of the Body Back In." *Sociological Theory* 15 (1997) 294–306.
Jarvis, Simon. *Adorno: A Critical Introduction*. Cambridge: Polity, 1998.
Jenkins, Philip. *The Next Christendom*. Oxford: Oxford University Press, 2011.
Johnson, Mark. *Moral Imagination: Implications of Cognitive Service for Ethics*. Chicago: University of Chicago Press, 1993.
Johnson, William. *The Inner Eye of Love*. New York: HarperCollins, 1997.
Johnstone, R. L. *Religion in Society: A Sociology of Religion*. New York: Routledge, 2007.
Jones, D. W. "An Analysis of the Relationship between Fowlerian Stage Development and Self-Assessed Maturity in Christian Faithfulness among Evangelical Christians." PhD diss., Southern Baptist Theological Seminary, 2003.
Jones, Daniel. *Masters of the Universe: Hayek, Friedman, and the Birth of Neoliberal Politics*. Princeton: Princeton University Press, 2013.
Jones, Serene, and Paul Lakeland, eds. *Constructive Theology: A Contemporary Approach to Classical Themes*. Minneapolis: Fortress, 2005.
Jones, T. M., and A. C. Wicks. "Convergent Stakeholder Theory." *Academy of Management Review* 24 (2009) 206–21.
Juzwik, Mary. "American Evangelical Biblicism as Literate Practice: A Critical Review." *Reading Research Quarterly* 49 (2014) 335–49.
Kant, Immanuel. *Grounding for the Metaphysics of Morals*. Translated by James Ellington. Indianapolis: Hackett, 1993.
Keene, Timothy. "Kuyper and Dooyeweerd: Sphere Sovereignty and Modal Aspects." *Transformation* 33 (2016) 65–79.
Keller, Tim. *Every Good Endeavor: Connecting Your Work to God's Work*. New York: Penguin, 2012.
Kelley, Dean. *Why Conservative Churches Are Growing*. New York: Harper & Row, 1972.
Kessler, Volker. "The Sabbath as a Remedy for Human Restlessness." *In die Skriflig* 46 (2012) 46–52.
Kidwell, Jeremy. "The Righteousness of Industrialism? Analyzing the Legacy behind 'The Present Moment' in Christian Technological Ethics." In *The Present Moment*, edited by Markus Bockmuehl and David Lincicum, 89–97. Oxford: Oxford University Research Archives, 2011.
Kieckhefer, Richard. "Meister Eckhart's Conception of Union eith God." *Harvard Theological Review* 71 (1978) 203–25.
Kim, David, David McCalman, and Dan Fisher. "The Secular/Sacred Divide and the Christian Worldview." *Journal of Business Ethics* 109 (2012) 203–8.
Klaasen, John. "Practical Theology: A Critically Engaged Practical Reason Approach of Practice, Theory, Practice and Theory." *HTS Teologiese Studies* 70 (2014) 1–6.
Klaassen, Walter. "Gelassenheit and Creation." *Conrad Grebel Review* 9 (1991) 23–35.
———. "Love: New Testament and Early Jewish Literature." In vol. 4 of *The Anchor Bible Dictionary*, edited by David Freedman, 209–22. New York: Doubleday, 1992.
Klein, William W., et al. *Introduction to Biblical Interpretation*. Rev. ed. Grand Rapids: Zondervan, 2004.

Kling, David. *The Bible in History: How the Texts Have Shaped the Times*. Oxford: Oxford University Press, 2004.
Kluver, Jesse, et al. "Behavioral Ethics for Homo Economicus, Homo Heuristicus, and Homo Duplex." *Organizational Behavior and Human Decision Processes* 123 (2014) 150–58.
Knoll, Mark. *Between Faith and Criticism: Evangelicals, Scholarship, and the Bible in America*. San Francisco: Harper & Row, 1986.
———. *In the Beginning Was the Word: The Bible in American Public Life, 1492–1783*. New York: Oxford University Press, 2012.
———. "What Is 'Evangelical'?" In *The Oxford Handbook of Evangelical Theology*, edited by Gerald McDermott, 19–34. New York: Oxford University Press, 2013.
Knott, Kim. *The Location of Religion*. London: Equinox, 2005.
Kraybill, Donald, and Steven Nolt. *Amish Enterprise: From Plows to Profits*. Baltimore: Johns Hopkins University Press, 1995.
Kuyper, Abraham. *Lectures on Calvinism*. Peabody: Hendrickson, 2008.
———. "Sphere Sovereignty." In *Abraham Kuyper: A Centennial Reader*, edited by James Bratt, 14–25. Grand Rapids: Eerdmans, 1998.
Kyle, Richard. "The Concept and Practice of Separation from the World in Mennonite Brethren History." *Direction* 13 (1984) 33–43.
Labberton, Mark, ed. *Still Evangelical?* Downers Grove, IL: InterVarsity, 2018.
Latimer, Joanna. "All-Consuming Passions: Materials and Subjectivity in the Age of Enhancement." In *The Consumption of Mass*, edited by Nick Lee and Rolland Munro, 158–73. Oxford: Blackwell, 2001.
Lee, Chang Kyoo. "Practical Theology as a Theological Discipline: Origins, Developments, and the Future." *Korean Journal of Christian Studies* 75 (2011) 293–313.
Leezenberg, Michiel. "How Ethnocentric Is the Concept of the Postsecular?" In *Exploring the Postsecular: The Religious, the Political, and the Urban*, edited by Arie Molendijk et al., 91–112. Boston: Brill, 2010.
Lewis, Gordon, and Bruce Demarest. *Integrative Theology*. Grand Rapids: Zondervan, 1996.
Liechty, Daniel, ed. *Early Anabaptist Spirituality: Selected Writings*. New York: Paulist, 1994.
Linge, David. "Mysticism, Poverty, and Reason in the Thought of Meister Eckhart." *Journal of the American Academy of Religion* 46 (1978) 465–88.
Littler, Craig. "Understanding Taylorism." *The British Journal of Sociology* 29 (1978) 185–202.
Loewen, Howard John. "Peace in the Mennonite Tradition: Toward a Theological Understanding of a Regulative Concept." In *Baptism, Peace, and the State in the Reformed and Mennonite Traditions*, edited by Ross T. Bender and Alan P. F. Sell, 87–122. Waterloo, ON: Wilfrid Laurier University Press, 1991.
Logan, Dana. "Commerce, Consumerism, and Christianity in America." *Oxford Research Encyclopedia of Religion*, December 2017. Online. https://oxfordre.com/religion/view/10.1093/acrefore/9780199340378.001.0001/acrefore-9780199340378-e-414.
Long, D. Stephen. "Can (Analytic) Philosophers Tell Theologians the Truth? Richard Rorty and Methodological Nominalism." In *Rorty and the Religious*, edited by Jacob Goodson and Brad Elliott Stone, 23–45. Eugene, OR: Cascade, 2012.

Louth, Andrew. "Theology, Contemplation, and the University." *Studia Theologica* 17 (2004) 69–79.
Luckmann, Thomas. *The Invisible Religion*. New York: Macmillan, 1967.
———. "Shrinking Transcendence, Expanding Religion?" *Sociological Analysis* 50 (1990) 127–38.
Luke, Timothy. "Civil Religion and Secularization: Ideological Revitalization in Post-Revolutionary Communist Systems." *Sociological Forum* 2 (1987) 108–34.
Lunn, Andrew. "Theological Reflection and Reflexivity: Theology on the Waves of Social Change." *Practical Theology* 154 (2016) 22–31.
Lyotard, Jean-Francois. *The Postmodern Condition: A Report on Knowledge*. Translated by Geoff Bennington and Brian Massumi. Minneapolis: University of Minnesota Press, 1984.
MacIntyre, Alasdair. *After Virtue*. Notre Dame: University of Notre Dame Press, 1984.
———. *Dependent Rational Animals: Why Human Beings Need the Virtues*. Chicago: Open Court, 1999.
———. "Utilitarianism and Cost-Benefit Analysis: An Essay on the Relevance of Moral Philosophy to Bureaucratic Theory." In *Values in the Electric Power Industry*, edited by Kenneth Sayre, 217–37. Notre Dame: University of Notre Dame Press, 1977.
———. "Why Are the Problems of Business Ethics Insoluble?" In *Moral Responsibility and the Professions*, edited by Bernard Baumrin and Benjamin Freedman, 350–59. New York: Haven, 1982.
Madsen, Richard. "What Is Religion?" In *The Post-Secular in Question*, edited by Philip S. Gorski et al., 23–42. New York: New York University Press, 2012.
Mahan, Brian. *Forgetting Ourselves on Purpose*. San Francisco: John Wiley, 2010.
Mahmood, Saba. "Secularism, Hermeneutics, Empire: The Politics of Islamic Reformation." *Public Culture* 18 (2006) 323–47.
Marie, Megan. "Selling Christianity: Megachurches, Megatheory, Markets, and Class at the Turn of the Twenty-First Century." *Works and Days* 23 (2005) 175–96.
Marsden, George. "Christianity and Cultures: Transforming Niebuhr's Categories." *Insights* 115 (1999) 4–15.
———. *Understanding Fundamentalism and Evangelicalism*. Grand Rapids: Eerdmans, 1991.
Martin, Stephanie. "Evangelical Economic Rhetoric: The Great Recession, the Free Market, and the Language of Personal Responsibility." PhD diss., UC San Diego, 2013.
Mbiti, John. *African Religions and Philosophy*. London: Heinemann, 1990.
McCallum, Richard. "Micro Public Spheres and the Sociology of Religion: An Evangelical Illustration." *Journal of Contemporary Religion* 26 (2011) 173–87.
McCarthy, Thomas. *Race, Empire, and the Idea of Human Development*. Cambridge: Cambridge University Press, 2009.
McCarty, John, and L. J. Shrum. "The Influence of Individualism, Collectivism, and Locus of Control on Environmental Beliefs and Behavior." *Journal of Public Policy & Marketing* 20 (2001) 93–104.
McCloskey, Deirdre. *Bourgeois Equality*. Chicago: University of Chicago Press, 2016.
McClure, John. *Partial Faiths*. Athens: University of Georgia Press, 2007.
McCutcheon, Russell T. *Manufacturing Religion: The Discourse on Sui Generis Religion and the Politics of Nostalgia*. New York: Oxford University Press, 2003.

McDonald, Matthew, et al. "Narcissism and Neo-Liberalism: Work, Leisure, and Alienation in an Era of Consumption." *Loisir et Société / Society and Leisure* 30 (2007) 489–510.

McGilchrist, Iain. *The Master and His Emissary*. New Haven: Yale University Press, 2009.

McGinn, Bernard. "Evil-Sounding, Rash, and Suspect of Heresy: Tensions between Mysticism and Magisterium in the History of the Church." *Catholic Historical Review* 90 (2004) 193–212.

———. *The Harvest of Mysticism*. New York: Crossroad, 2005.

McGrath, Alister. "Evangelical Theological Method: The State of the Art." In *Evangelical Futures: A Conversation on Theological Method*, edited by John G. Stackhouse Jr., 6–19. Grand Rapids: Baker, 2010.

———. *T. F. Torrance: An Intellectual Biography*. Edinburgh: T&T Clark, 1999.

McGuire, Meredith. *Lived Religion: Faith and Practice in Everyday Life*. Oxford: New York: Oxford University Press, 2008.

McIlhenny, Ryan. "A Third-Way Reformed Approach to Christ and Culture: Appropriating Kuyperian Neo-Calvinism and the Two-Kingdoms Perspective." *Mid-America Journal of Theology* 20 (2009) 75–94.

McIntosh, Daniel N. "Religion-as-Schema, with Implications for the Relation between Religion and Coping." *International Journal for the Psychology of Religion* 5 (1995) 1–16.

McKnight, Scott. *Kingdom Conspiracy*. Grand Rapids: Brazos, 2014.

McLennan, Gregor. "The Postsecular Turn." *Theory, Culture, and Society* 27 (2010) 3–20.

McVea, John F., and R. Edward Freeman. "A Names-and-Faces Approach to Stakeholder Management: How Focusing on Stakeholders as Individuals Can Bring Ethics and Entrepreneurial Strategy Together." *Journal of Management Inquiry* 14 (2005) 57–69.

Meeks, Wayne. *In Search of the Early Christians: Selected Essays*. Edited by Allen R. Hilton and H. Gregory Snyder. New Haven: Yale University Press, 2002.

Meister Eckhart. *The Essential Sermons, Commentaries, Treatises and Defense*. Translated by Edmund Colledge and Bernard McGinn. New York: Paulist, 1981.

Merrick, Teri. "Tracing the Metanarrative of Colonialism and Its Legacy." In *Evangelical Postcolonial Conversations*, edited by Kay Higuera Smith et al., 107–20. Downers Grove, IL: InterVarsity, 2014.

Michaelson, Christopher, et al. "Meaningful Work: Connecting Business Ethics and Organizational Studies." *Journal of Business Ethics* 121 (2014) 77–90.

Milbank, John. *The Word Made Strange: Theology, Language, Culture*. Oxford: Blackwell, 1997.

Milbank, John, et al., eds. *Radical Orthodoxy: A New Theology*. New York: Routledge, 1999.

Miles, Margaret. *Practicing Christianity: Critical Perspectives for an Embodied Spirituality*. New York: Crossroad, 1998.

Mill, J. S. *Utilitarianism*. Oxford: Oxford University Press, 1998.

Miller, David. *God at Work: The History and Promise of the Faith at Work Movement*. New York: Oxford University Press, 2007.

Miller, Kent. "Organizational Research as Practical Theology." *Organizational Research Methods* 18 (2015) 276–99.

Miller, Steven. *The Age of Evangelicalism: America's Born-Again Years*. Oxford: Oxford University Press, 2014.

Miller, Vincent. *Consumer Religion: Christian Faith and Practice in a Consumer Culture*. New York: Continuum, 2003.

Miller-McLemore, Bonnie. "The Living Human Web: Pastoral Theology at the Turn of the Century." In *Through the Eyes of Women*, edited by Jeanne Moessner, 9–26. Minnesota: Augsburg Fortress, 1996.

———. "Practical Theology." In vol. 3 of *Encyclopedia of Religion in America*, edited by Charles Lippy and Peter Williams, 1739–43. Washington, DC: Congressional Quarterly, 2010.

Mises, Ludwig von. *Theory and History: An Interpretation of Economic and Social Evolution*. Auburn: Ludwig Von Mises Institute, 2007.

Mitroff, Ian, and Elizabeth Denton. *A Spiritual Audit of Corporate America: A Hard Look at Spirituality, Religion, and Values in the Workplace*. San Francisco: Jossey-Bass, 1999.

Mittleman, Alan L. *A Short History of Jewish Ethics*. Malden, MA: Wiley-Blackwell, 2012.

Moore, R. Laurence. *Selling God: American Religion in the Marketplace of Culture*. Oxford: Oxford University Press, 1994.

———. *Touchdown Jesus: The Making of Sacred and Secular in American History*. Louisville: Westminster John Knox, 2003.

Moreland, J. P. *Kingdom Triangle: Recover the Christian Mind, Renovate the Soul, Restore the Spirit's Power*. Grand Rapids: Zondervan, 2007.

Moreland, J. P., and Gary Deweese. "The Premature Report of Foundationalism's Divide." In *Reclaiming the Center: Confronting Evangelical Accommodation in Postmodern Times*, edited by Millard J. Erickson et al., 81–108. Wheaton: Crossway, 2004.

Moser, Paul K., ed. *The Oxford Handbook of Epistemology*. New York: Oxford University Press, 2005.

Moulin, Kerry, and Chia-Jung Chung. "Technology Trumping Sleep: Impact of Electronic Media and Sleep in Late Adolescent Students." *Journal of Education and Learning* 6 (2016) 294–321.

Muller, Julian. "Postfoundational Practical Theology for a Time of Transition." *HTS Teologiese Studies* 67 (2011) 1–5.

Murray, Stuart. *The Naked Anabaptist: The Bare Essentials of a Radical Faith*. Waterloo, ON: Herald, 2010.

Naselli, Andrew. "D. A. Carson's Theological Method." *Scottish Bulletin of Evangelical Theology* 29 (2011) 245–74.

Naugle, David. *Worldview: The History of a Concept*. Grand Rapids: Eerdmans, 2002.

Naveh, Eyal. "Dialectical Redemption: Reinhold Niebuhr, Martin Luther King, Jr., and the Kingdom of God in America." *Journal of Religious Thought* 48 (1992) 57–63.

Nesmith, Bruce. *The New Republican Coalition: The Reagan Campaigns and White Evangelicals*. New York: P. Lang, 1994.

Neubert, Mitchell J., and Bruno Dyck. "Developing Sustainable Management Theory: Goal-Setting Theory Based in Virtue." *Management Decision* 54 (2016) 304–20.

Newberg, Andrew. *Words Can Change Your Brain*. London: Penguin, 2014.

Nicholson, Nigel. *Managing the Human Animal*. London: Thomas, 2000.

Niebuhr, H. Richard. *Christ and Culture*. New York: Harper & Row, 1951.

———. *The Kingdom of God in America*. Middletown, CT: Wesleyan Paperback, 1988.

———. *Love and Justice: Selections from the Shorter Writings of Reinhold Niebuhr*. Edited by D. B. Robertson. Louisville: Westminster John Knox, 1992.

———. *The Responsible Self*. Louisville: John Knox, 1962.

Nieuwenhove, Rik van. "The Religious Disposition as a Critical Resource to Resist Instrumentalisation." *Heythrop Journal* 50 (2009) 689–96.

Nonprofits Source. "The Ultimate List of Charitable Giving Statistics for 2018." Online. https://nonprofitssource.com/online-giving-statistics.

Noonan, Jeff. "MacIntyre, Virtue and the Critique of Capitalist Modernity." *Journal of Critical Realism* 13 (2014) 189–203.

Norris, Pippa, and Ronald Inglehart. *Sacred and Secular: Religion and Politics Worldwide*. Cambridge: Cambridge University Press, 2012.

Novak, Michael. *Business as a Calling*. New York: Free Press, 2013.

Nygren, Anders. *Agape and Eros*. Chicago: University of Chicago Press, 1982.

O'Connor, William. "The Uti/Frui Distinction in Augustine's Ethics." *Augustinian Studies* 14 (1983) 45–62.

O'Donovan, Oliver. *The Ways of Judgment*. Grand Rapids: Eerdmans, 2005.

Olson, Elizabeth, et al. "Retheorizing the Postsecular Present: Embodiment, Spatial Transcendence, and Challenges to Authenticity among Young Christians in Glasgow, Scotland." *Annals of the Association of American Geographers* 103 (2013) 1421–36.

Oord, Thomas J. *The Nature of Love: A Theology*. St Louis: Chalice, 2010.

Orsi, Robert. *Between Heaven and Earth: The Religious Worlds People Make and the Scholars Who Study Them*. Princeton: Princeton University Press, 2005.

Osmer, Richard Robert. "Empirical Practical Theology." In *Opening the Field of Practical Theology: An Introduction*, edited by Kathleen A. Cahalan and Gordon S. Mikoski, 61–78. Lanham, MD: Rowman & Littlefield, 2014.

———. *Practical Theology: An Introduction*. Grand Rapids: Eerdsman, 2008.

———. *The Teaching Ministry of Congregations*. Louisville: Westminster John Knox, 2005.

Paine, Lynn. "Managing for Organizational Integrity." *Harvard Business Review* 72 (1994) 106–17.

Pannenberg, Wolfhart. *Christian Spirituality*. Philadelphia: Westminster, 1983.

Parchami, Ali. *Hegemonic Peace and Empire: The Pax Romana, Britannica, and Americana*. New York: Routledge, 2009.

Pargement, Kenneth. *The Psychology of Religion and Coping*. New York: Guilford, 1987.

Parigi, Paolo, and Warner Henson. "Social Isolation in America." *Annual Review of Sociology* 40 (2014) 153–71.

Park, Jerry, and Samuel Reimer. "Revisiting the Social Sources of American Christianity, 1972–1998." *Journal for the Scientific Study of Religion* 41 (2002) 733–46.

Parmar, B. L., et al. "Stakeholder Theory: The State of the Art." *The Academy of Management Annals* 3 (2010) 403–45.

Pattison, Stephen. *The Challenge of Practical Theology*. London: Jessica Kingsley, 2007.

———. *Faith of the Managers: When Management Becomes Religion*. London: Bloomsbury, 1997.

———. "Religion, Spirituality, and Health Care: Confusions, Tensions, Opportunities." *Health Care Analysis* 21 (2013) 193–207.

———. *Saving Face*. New York: Routledge, 2016.

———. "Spirituality and Spiritual Care Made Simple: A Suggestive, Normative, and Essentialist Approach." *Practical Theology* 3 (2010) 351–66.
Peckham, John. "Ethics of Love? Morality and the Meaning of Divine Love." *Andrews University Seminary Student Journal* 2 (2016) 1–16.
Penzel, Klaus. "Some Thoughts on Schleiermacher and Practical Theology Today." *Perkins Journal* 35 (1985) 1–7.
Perez, Carlota. *Technological Revolutions and Financial Capital: The Dynamics of Bubbles and Golden Ages*. Cheltenham, UK: Edward Elgar, 2003.
Pfeffer, Jeffrey, and Gerald R. Salancik. *The External Control of Organizations*. New York: HarperOne, 1978.
Phan, Peter. *Christianity with an Asian Face: Asian American Theology in the Making*. Maryknoll, NY: Orbis, 2003.
Phillips, Robert. *Stakeholder Theory and Organizational Ethics*. San Francisco: Berrett-Koehler, 2003.
Pitts, Jamie. "Baptism, Postliberal and Anabaptist Theologies, and the Ambiguity of Christian Practice." *Mennonite Quarterly Review* 90 (2016) 323–45.
Plantinga, Cornelius, Jr. *Engaging God's World*. Grand Rapids: Eerdmans, 2002.
Possamai, Adam. *The I-zation of Society, Religion, and Neoliberal Post-Secularism*. New York: Palgrave, 2018.
Potts, Matthew. *Cormac McCarthy and the Signs of the Sacrament*. New York: Bloomsbury, 2015.
Putnam, Robert. *Bowling Alone*. New York: Simon & Schuster, 2001.
Quatro, Scott. "Is Business as Mission (Bam) a Flawed Concept? A Reformed Christian Response to the Bam Movement." *Journal of Biblical Integration in Business* 15 (2012) 80–87.
Quine, W. V., and J. S. Ullian. *The Web of Belief*. New York: Random House, 1978.
Quinn, J. K., et al. "Honesty, Individualism, and Pragmatic Business Ethics: Implications for Corporate Hierarchy." *Journal of Business Ethics* 16 (1997) 1419–30.
Radler, Charlotte. "'In Love I Am More God': The Centrality of Love in Meister Eckhart's Mysticism." *Journal of Religion* 90 (2010) 171–98.
Railton, Peter. "Moral Realism." *Philosophical Review* 95 (1986) 168–75.
Ramm, Bernard. *The Evangelical Heritage: A Study in Historical Theology*. Grand Rapids: Baker, 1973.
Ramsey, Paul. *War and the Christian Conscience: How Shall Modern War Be Conducted Justly?* Durham: Duke University Press, 1961.
Rauschenbush, Water. *Christianity and the Social Crisis*. New York: Macmillan, 1907.
———. *The Righteousness of the Kingdom*. Nashville: Abingdon, 1968.
———. *A Theology for the Social Gospel*. New York: Macmillan, 1917.
Rawls, John. *Justice as Fairness: A Restatement*. Cambridge: Harvard University Press, 2001.
———. *A Theory of Justice*. Cambridge: Harvard University Press, 1978.
Ray, D. E., et al. "Refining Normative Stakeholder Theory: Insights from Judaism, Christianity, and Islam." *Journal of Management, Spirituality, and Religion* 11 (2014) 331–56.
Redekop, Benjamin W., and Calvin W. Redekop, eds. *Power, Authority, and the Anabaptist Tradition*. Baltimore: Johns Hopkins University Press, 2003.
Rees, W. E. "Globalization and Sustainability: Conflict or Convergence?" *Bulletin of Science, Technology, and Society* 22 (2002) 249–68.

Rempel, John. "Sacraments in the Radical Reformation." In *The Oxford Handbook of Sacramental Theology*, edited by Hans Boersma and Matthew Levering, 298–312. New York: Oxford University Press, 2015.

Richins, Marsha. "Valuing Things: The Public and Private Meanings of Possessions." *Journal of Consumer Research* 21 (1994) 504–23.

Richter, Don. "Religious Practices in Practical Theology." In *Opening the Field of Practical Theology: An Introduction*, edited by Kathleen A. Cahalan and Gordon S. Mikoski, 203–16. Lanham, MD: Rowman & Littlefield, 2014.

Riedemann, Peter. *Love Is Like Fire: The Confession of an Anabaptist Prisoner*. Translated and edited by the Hutterian Brethren. Farmington, PA: Plough, 2016.

Rieger, Joerg. *Globalizaton and Theology*. Nashville: Abingdon, 2010.

———. "Reconfiguring the Common Good and Religion in the Context of Capitalism: Abrhamic Alternatives." In *Common Goods: Economy, Ecology, and Political Theology*, edited by Catherine Keller, 149–68. Fordham: Fordham University Press, 2015.

Rinallo, Diego, et al. "Introduction: Unravelling Complexities at the Commercial/Spiritual Interface." In *Consumption and Spirituality*, edited by Diego Rinallo et al., 1–28. New York: Routledge, 2013.

Rittenhouse, Bruce P. *Shopping for Meaningful Lives: The Religious Motive of Consumerism*. Eugene, OR: Cascade, 2013.

Roberts, John. *The Modern Firm: Organizational Design for Performance and Growth*. Oxford: Oxford University Press, 2004.

Robins, R. G. *Pentecostalism in America*. Santa Barbara, CA: Praeger, 2014.

Robinson, Marilynne. *The Givenness of Things: Essays*. New York: Farrar, Straus & Giroux, 2015.

Robinson, William. *Global Capitalism and the Crisis of Humanity*. New York: Cambridge University Press, 2014.

Rogers-Vaughn, Bruce. *Caring for Souls in a Neoliberal Age*. New York: Palgrave Macmillan, 2016.

Root, Andrew. "Evangelical Practical Theology." In *Opening the Field of Practical Theology: An Introduction*, edited by Kathleen A. Cahalan and Gordon S. Mikoski, 79–96. Lanham, MD: Rowman & Littlefield, 2014.

Rorty, Richard. *Philosophy and the Mirror of Nature*. Princeton: Princeton University Press, 1981.

Rorty, Richard, and Gianni Vattimo. *The Future of Religion*. New York: Columbia University Press, 2007.

Ross, David. *The Right and the Good*. Indianapolis: Hackett, 1988.

Roth, Guenther, and Wolfgang Schluchter. *Max Weber's Vision of History: Ethics and Methods*. Berkeley: University of California Press, 1979.

Rundle, Steve. "Business as Mission Hybrids: A Review and Research Agenda." *Journal of Biblical Integration in Business* 15 (2012) 66–79.

Rupp, Gordon. "Andrew Karlstadt and Reformation Puritanism." *Journal of Theological Studies* 10 (1959) 308–26.

Ruthven, Malise. *The Divine Supermarket*. London: Chatto and Windus, 1988.

Rynes, Sara, et al. "Care and Compassion through an Organizational Lens: Opening Up New Possibilities." *Academy of Management Review* 37 (2012) 503–23.

Sachs, Jeffrey. *The End of Poverty*. New York: Penguin, 2006.

Saler, Benson. *Conceptualizing Religion*. New York: Berghahn, 1999.

Sanford, Jonathan. *Before Virtue: Assessing Contemporary Virtue Ethics*. Washington, DC: Catholic University of America Press, 2015.
Saul, John Ralston. *Voltaire's Bastards: The Dictatorship of Reason in the West*. New York: Vintage, 1993.
Schaeffer, Francis. *Escape from Reason*. Downers Grove, IL: InterVarsity, 2006.
———. *The God Who Is There*. Downers Grove, IL: InterVarsity, 1998.
———. *He Is There and He Is Not Silent*. New York: Tyndale, 2001.
Scharen, Christian, and Aana Marie Vigen, eds. *Ethnography as Christian Theology and Ethics*. New York: Continuum, 2011.
Schenk, Wilbert, ed. *Anabaptism and Mission*. Scottdale: Herald, 1984.
Schlabach, Gerald. "Ethics: *Ordo amoris*." In *Augustine Through the Ages: An Encyclopedia*, edited by Allan Fitzgerald, 322–24. Grand Rapids: Eerdmans, 1999.
Schleiermacher, Friedrich. *Brief Outline of Theology as a Field of Study*. Translated by Terrence N. Tice. 3rd ed. Louisville: Westminster John Knox, 2011.
"The Schleitheim Confession of Faith, 1527." Translated by J. C. Wenger. *Mennonite Quarterly Review* 49 (1945) 247–53.
Schmidt, Leigh Eric. *Restless Souls: The Making of American Spirituality*. San Francisco: HarperSanFrancisco, 2005.
Schmuck, Peter, and Kennon Marshall Sheldon. *Life Goals and Well-Being: Towards a Positive Psychology of Human Striving*. Kirkland, WA: Hogrefe & Huber, 2001.
Schneider, John. *The Good of Affluence*. Grand Rapids: Eerdmans, 2002.
Schockenhoff, Eberhard. "The Theological Virtue of Charity." In *The Ethics of Aquinas*, edited by Stephen Pope, 244–58. Washington, DC: Georgetown University Press, 2002.
Scholes, Jeffrey. *Vocation and the Politics of Work: Popular Theology and Consumer Culture*. Lanham, MD: Lexington, 2013.
Schon, Donald. *The Reflective Practitioner*. New York: Basic, 1983.
Schürmann, Reiner. "Heidegger and Meister Eckhart on Releasement." *Research in Phenomenology* 3 (1973) 95–120.
———. *Meister Eckhart: Mystic and Philosopher*. Bloomington: Indiana University Press, 1978.
Schweitzer, Friedrich. *The Postmodern Life Cycle: Challenges for Church and Theology*. St. Louis: Chalice, 2004.
Scruton, Roger. *An Intelligent Person's Guide to Modern Culture*. South Bend: St. Augustine, 2000.
Seddon, Philip. *Gospel and Sacrament: Reclaiming a Holistic Evangelical Spirituality*. Cambridge: Grove, 1962.
Segal, Charles, and David Stineback. *Puritans, Indians, and Manifest Destiny*. New York: Putnam, 1977.
Senge, Peter. *The Fifth Discipline*. New York: Doubleday, 1990.
Sennett, Richard. *The Culture of New Capitalism*. New Haven: Yale University Press, 2007.
Setzer, Claudia, and David A. Shefferman, eds. *The Bible and American Culture: A Sourcebook*. New York: Routledge, 2011.
Sherman, Amy. *Kingdom Calling: Vocational Stewardship for the Common Good*. Downers Grove, IL: InterVarsity, 2011.
Sider, Ronald. *Rich Christians in an Age of Hunger*. Downers Grove, IL: InterVarsity, 1978.

Siker, Louke. "Christ and Business: A Typology for Christian Business Ethics." *Journal of Business Ethics* 8 (1978) 883–88.
Simons, Menno. *The Complete Works of Menno Simons*. Scottdale: Herald, 1960.
Sire, James. *The Universe Next Door*. Downers Grove, IL: InterVarsity, 2009.
Sleeth, Ronald. "Schleiermacher: 'On Practical Theology'—a Summary and an Analysis." *The Princeton Seminary Bulletin* 68 (1976) 41–48.
Sludds, Kevin. *Emotions: Their Cognitive Base and Ontological Importance*. Bern: Peter Lang, 2008.
Smail, David. *Power, Interest, and Psychology*. Ross-on-Wye, UK: PCCS, 2008.
Smith, Adam. *The Wealth of Nations*. New York: Bantam, 2003.
Smith, Christian. *Evangelicalism: Embattled and Thriving*. Chicago: University of Chicago Press, 1998.
———. *Moral, Believing Animals: Human Personhood and Culture*. New York: Oxford University Press, 2003.
———. *To Flourish or Destruct: A Personalist Theory of Human Goods, Motivations, Failure, and Evil*. Chicago: Chicago University Press, 2016.
Smith, George. *The System of Liberty: Themes in the History of Classical Liberalism*. New York: Cambridge University Press, 2013.
Smith, James K. A. "Secular Liturgies and the Prospects for a 'Post-Secular' Sociology of Religion." In *The Post-Secular in Question*, edited by Philip S. Gorski et al., 159–84. New York: New York University Press, 2012.
———. *Who's Afraid of Relativism?* Grand Rapids: Baker Academic, 2014.
———. *You Are What You Love*. Grand Rapids: Brazos, 2016.
Smith, Jeffery, ed. *Normative Theory and Business Ethics*. Lanham, MD: Rowman & Littlefield, 2008.
Solomon, Robert. "Corporate Roles, Personal Virtues: An Aristotelean Approach to Business Ethics." In *Ethical Issues in Business*, edited by Thomas Donaldson et al., 71–82. Upper Saddle River, NJ: Prentice Hall, 2002.
———. *Ethics and Excellence: Cooperation and Integrity in Business*. New York: Oxford University Press, 2003.
———. "Victims of Circumstances? A Defense of Virtue Ethics in Business." *Business Ethics Quarterly* 13 (2003) 43–62.
Sorensen, Bent, et al. "Theology and Organization." *Organization* 19 (2012) 267–79.
Stackhouse, John G., Jr. "Evangelical Theology Should Be Evangelical." In *Evangelical Futures: A Conversation on Theological Method*, edited by John G. Stackhouse Jr., 6–19. Grand Rapids: Baker, 2010.
Stackhouse, Max. "Public Theology and Democracy's Future." *The Review of Faith & International Affairs* 7 (2010) 49–54.
———. *Public Theology and Political Economy: Christian Stewardship in Modern Society*. Grand Rapids: Eerdmans, 1991.
Stark, Rodney, and William Sims Bainbridge. *The Future of Religion: Secularization, Revival, and Cult Formation*. Berkeley: University of California Press, 1985.
———. "Towards a Theory of Religion: Religious Commitment." *Journal for the Scientific Study of Religion* 19 (1980) 114–28.
Stayer, James. "The Anabaptist Revolt and Political and Religious Power." In *Power, Authority, and the Anabaptist Tradition*, edited by Benjamin W. Redekop and Calvin W. Redekop, 50–72. Baltimore: Johns Hopkins University Press, 2001.

Sternberg, Meir. *The Poetics of Biblical Narrative: Ideological Literature and the Drama of Reading*. Bloomington: Indiana University Press, 1985.

Stoddart, Eric. *Advancing Practical Theology: Critical Discipleship for Disturbing Times*. London: SCM, 2014.

Stoddart, Eric, and Mark Johnson. "Retail Faith: Relationships of Theology, Economics, Need and Desire in the UK Christian bookstore." *Practical Theology* 1 (2008) 323–40.

Strathern, Marilyn. "From Improvement to Enhancement: An Anthropological Comment on the Audit Culture." *The Cambridge Journal of Anthropology* 19 (1997) 1–21.

Swinton, John. "Spirituality and Mental Health: A Perspective from the Research." In *Spirituality, Values, and Mental Health: Jewels for the Journey*, edited by Mary Ellen Coyte et al., 292–305. London: Jessica Kingsley, 2007.

Tanner, Kathryn. "Theological Reflection and Christian Practices." In *Practicing Theology: Beliefs and Practices in Christian Life*, edited by Miroslav Volf and Dorothy Bass, 228–42. Grand Rapids: Eerdsman, 2001.

Taylor, Bernard. "The Future Development of Corporate Strategy." *Journal of Business Policy* 2 (1971) 22–38.

Taylor, Charles. *The Malaise of Modernity*. Toronto: Anansi, 1998.

———. *A Secular Age*. Cambridge: Harvard University Press, 2018.

———. *Sources of the Self: The Making of the Modern Identity*. Cambridge: Cambridge University Press, 1992.

Taylor, Frederick. *The Principles of Scientific Management*. 1911. Reprint, Mineola, NY: Dover, 2012.

Thiem, Annika. "Schmittian Shadows and Contemporary Theological-Political Constellations." *Social Research* 80 (2013) 1–32.

Thiselton, Anthony. *The Two Horizons: New Testament Hermeneutics and Philosophical Description*. Grand Rapids: Eerdmans, 1980.

Thorsen, Don. *The Wesleyan Quadrilateral: Scripture, Tradition, Reason, and Experience as a Model of Evangelical Theology*. Lexington, KY: Emeth, 2005.

Tillich, Paul. *Love, Power, and Justice: Ontological Analyses and Ethical Applications*. Oxford: Oxford University Press, 1960.

Tracy, David. *The Analogical Imagination: Christian Theology and the Culture of Pluralism*. New York: Crossroad, 1981.

Treier, Daniel. "Scripture and Hermeneutics." In *The Cambridge Companion to Evangelical Theology*, edited by Timothy Larsen and Daniel Treier, 35–50. Cambridge: Cambridge University Press, 2007.

Troeltsch, Ernst. *The Social Teachings of the Christian Churches*. New York: Harper, 1960.

Tunehag, Mats, et al., eds. *Business as Mission*. Lausanne Occasional Paper 59. Pattaya, Thailand: Lausanne Committee for World Evangelization, 2004.

Turner, Bryan. "Post-Secular Society: Consumerism and the Democratization of Religion." In *The Post-Secular in Question*, edited by Philip S. Gorski et al., 135–58. New York: New York University Press, 2012.

Turner, Denys. *The Darkness of God: Negativity in Christian Mysticism*. Cambridge: Cambridge University Press, 1995.

Turner, Philip. *Christian Ethics and the Church*. Grand Rapids: Baker, 2015.

Turpin, Kathryn. *Branded: Adolescents Converting from Consumer Faith*. Cleveland: Pilgrim, 2006.
Urry, James. "Wealth and Poverty in the Mennonite Experience: Dilemmas and Challenges." *Journal of Mennonite Studies* 27 (2011) 11–41.
VanDrunen, David. *Biblical Case for Natural Law*. Grand Rapids: Acton Institute, 2012.
———. *Living in God's Two Kingdoms*. Wheaton: Crossway, 2010.
Vanhoozer, Kevin. "The Semantics of Biblical Literature: Truth and Scripture's Diverse Literary Forms." In *Hermeneutics, Authority, and Canon*, edited by D. A. Carson and John D. Woodbridge, 49–104. Grand Rapids: Baker, 1995.
———. "The Voice and the Actor." In *Evangelical Futures: A Conversation on Theological Method*, edited by John G. Stackhouse Jr., 61–106. Grand Rapids: Baker, 2000.
Veith, Gene. *God at Work*. Wheaton: Crossway, 2002.
Veling, Terry. "In the Name of Who? Levinas and the Other Side of Theology." *Pacifica* 12 (1999) 275–92.
Verschoor, Curtis. "Global Survey Measures Workplace Integrity." *Strategic Finance* 98 (2016) 19–20.
———. "New Survey of Workplace Ethics Shows Surprising Results." *Strategic Finance* 93 (2012) 13–15.
Viljoen, Francois. "The Double Love Commandment." *In die Skriflig* 49 (2015) 1–11.
Viswanathan, Gauri. "Secularism in the Framework of Heterodoxy." *PMLA* 123 (2008) 466–76.
Vries, Hent de. "Introduction: Why Still 'Religion'?" In *Religion: Beyond a Concept*, edited by Hent de Vries, 1–100. New York: Fordham University Press, 2008.
Wallis, Jim. *The Call to Conversion: Recovering the Gospel for These Times*. New York: Harper & Row, 1981.
Walsh, J. P. "Taking Stock of Stakeholder Management." *Academy of Management Review* 30 (2005) 426–38.
Walton, Heather. "Seeking Wisdom in Practical Theology." *Practical Theology* 7 (2014) 5–18.
Ward, Graham. *Christ and Culture*. Oxford: Blackwell, 2005.
Ward, Peter. *Introducing Practical Theology: Mission, Ministry, and the Life of the Church*. Grand Rapids: Baker, 2017.
Weaver, Darlene Fozard. *Self Love and Christian Ethics*. Cambridge: Cambridge University Press, 2002.
Weber, Max. *The Protestant Ethic and the Spirit of Capitalism*. New York: Scribner's, 1958.
Weick, Karl. *Sensemaking in Organizations*. Thousand Oaks, CA: Sage, 1995.
Weir, Stuart. *The Good Work of Non-Christians, Empowerment, and the New Creation*. Eugene, OR: Pickwick, 2016.
Welch, Sharon. *Sweet Dreams in America*. New York: Routledge, 1998.
Wenger, J. C. *The Doctrines of the Mennonites*. Scottdale, PA: Mennonite, 1950.
Werhane, Patricia H. *Moral Imagination and Management Decision-Making*. Oxford: Oxford University Press, 1999.
Wesley, John. *John Wesley's Sermons: An Anthology*. Edited by Albert C. Outler and Richard P. Heitzenrater. Nashville: Abingdon, 1991.
Westphal, Merold. "A Reader's Guide to Reformed Epistemology." *Perspectives* 7 (1992) 10–13.

White, Ronald C., Jr., and C. Howard Hopkins. *Social Gospel: Religion and Reform in Changing America*. Philadelphia: Temple University Press, 1976.

Wicks, Andrew C., et al. "A Feminist Reinterpretation of the Stakeholder Concept." *Business Ethics Quarterly* 4 (1994) 475–97.

Wilford, Justin. *Sacred Subdivisions*. New York: New York University Press, 2012.

Williams, D. H. *Spiritual and Anabaptist Writers*. Louisville: Westminster John Knox, 1996.

Williams, George. *The Radical Reformation*. Kirksville, MO: Sixteenth Century Journal, 2000.

Wilson-Hartgrove, Jonathan. *New Monasticism*. Grand Rapids: Brazos, 2008.

Wingren, Gustav. *The Christian's Calling: Luther on Vocation*. Edinburgh: Oliver & Boyd, 1958.

Wittgenstein, Ludwig. *Culture and Value*. Edited by G. H. von Wright and Heikki Nyman. Translated by Peter Winch. Chicago: University of Chicago Press, 1984.

———. *Philosophical Investigations*. Translated by G. E. M. Anscombe. New York: Macmillan, 1973.

Woggon, Frank. "Deliberate Activity as an Art for (Almost) Everyone: Friedrich Schleiermacher on Practical Theology." *Journal of Pastoral Care* 48 (1994) 3–13.

Wolfe, Alan. "The Evangelical MIND Revisited." *Change: The Magazine of Higher Learning* 38 (2006) 8–13.

Wolterstorff, Nicolas. *John Locke and the Ethics of Belief*. Cambridge: Cambridge University Press, 1996.

Woodward, Ian. *Understanding Material Culture*. Los Angeles: Sage, 2007.

Woodward, James, and Stephen Pattison. "An Introduction to Pastoral and Practical Theology." In *The Blackwell Reader in Pastoral and Practical Theology*, edited by James Woodward and Stephen Pattison, 300–310. Oxford: Blackwell, 2000.

Wright, J. B. "Adam Smith and Greed." *Journal of Private Enterprise* 21 (2005) 46–58.

Wright, N. T. *The New Testament and the People of God*. Minneapolis: Fortress, 2002.

———. *Surprised by Hope*. New York: HarperOne, 2008.

Wuthnow, Robert. *After Heaven: Spirituality in America since the 1950s*. Berkeley: University of California Press, 2003.

Zsolnai, Laszlo. "Extended Stakeholder Theory." *Society and Business Review* 1 (2006) 37–44.

www.ingramcontent.com/pod-product-compliance
Lightning Source LLC
Chambersburg PA
CBHW070323230426
43663CB00011B/2203